THE MAKING OF A
PHILOSOPHER-KING

THE MAKING *of a* PHILOSOPHER-KING

*A Selection From the Speeches of Omo
N'Oba Erediauwa, CFR., Oba of Benin*

Formerly

Chancellor of the University of Ibadan

Permanent Secretary, Federal Ministry of Health, Lagos

Permanent Secretary, Federal Ministry
of Mines and Power, Lagos

Commissioner for Finance, Bendel State

Chairman, Tate & Lyle (Nig.) Co. Ltd.

COMPILED & EDITED BY

IDU AKENZUA

NEWSOUTH BOOKS

Montgomery

NewSouth Books
105 S. Court Street
Montgomery, AL 36104

Copyright © 2021. All rights reserved under International and Pan-American
Copyright Conventions. Published in the United States by NewSouth Books, a
division of NewSouth, Inc., Montgomery, Alabama.
(Tel. 1-334-834-3556; www.newsouthbooks.com)

Publisher's Cataloging-in-Publication Data
Names: Akenzua, T. I., editor. | Erediauwa, Omo n'Oba, author.
Title: The making of a philosopher-king. | by T. I. Akenzua
Description: Montgomery : NewSouth [2021]
Identifiers: ISBN 978-1-58838-367-9 (trade paper) |
ISBN 978-1-58838-368-6 (ebook)
Subjects: Erediauwa, Omo n'Oba, 1923–2016. |
African—World—Political Science. | West—Africa—History. |
Public Speaking—Reference.
Design by Randall Williams
Printed in the United States of America

IIIIIIIIIIIIIIIIIIIIIIIIIIIIIIIIIIIIIIIIIIIIIIIIIII

Note to Readers about This Edition

Portions of this volume were privately published in a 2010 edition in Nigeria
by Idu Akenzua & Co. This is the first U.S. and World edition, produced for
the editor, the late T. I. Akenzua, through his U.S. publishing representative,
Muyideen Badru, an associate of NewSouth Books.

The original edition, and the speeches, papers, and documents which it
reproduced, used British standard spellings and punctuation. In the present
edition, these have been converted to American standard spellings and
punctuation.

The source documents quote liberally from Bible passages. Unless otherwise indicated, the version cited is the Revised Standard Version of the
Catholic Edition of the Holy Bible.

To the Blessed Memory of

Omo N'Oba N'Edo,

Uku Akpolokpolo, Oba Akenzua II, CMG

L.L.D. (Honoris Causa)

OBA OF BENIN

(1899–1978)

▲

Contents

A Short Biography

Oba Erediauwa, CFR., Uku Akpolokpolo, Oba of Benin, was born Prince Solomon Igbinoghodua Aisiokuoba Akenzua to Oba Akenzua II (of blessed memory) on June 22, 1923. He attended the Government School, Benin City, 1931–1937, for his primary school education, before going on to Edo College, Benin City, for two years. He completed his secondary school education at the Government College, Ibadan.

In 1946, Prince Solomon Akenzua (as he then was) went on government scholarship to Higher College, Yaba, to read Arts. From there he proceeded to England in 1947 and in 1948 enrolled to read Law at the King's College, Cambridge, where he graduated in 1951. Later he took a postgraduate Devonshire course for British administrative officers.

Armed with these academic tools, Prince Akenzua returned to Nigeria in 1952 and was appointed Assistant Administrative Officer in the Nigerian Civil Service. Even though regional administration was introduced by the British colonial government in 1954, he was retained in the Eastern Regional Administrative Service in Enugu, where he served in various ministries and rose to the post of Acting Permanent Secretary.

Prince Akenzua retired voluntarily from the Federal Public (Civil) Service in 1973. After retirement, he continued to render public service, serving briefly as Commissioner of Finance in the then-Bendel State in 1975, as a representative of Gulf Oil Company in Bendel State, and as chairman of Tate and Lyle (Nig) Co. Ltd., etc.

He was chairman of various boards, including Lagos University Teaching Hospital and University College Hospital, Ibadan. He was also chairman of the board of management of the National Electric Power Authority (NEPA) when he was permanent secretary, Federal Ministry of Mines and Power, Lagos.

On March 23, 1979, Prince S.I.A. Akenzua was crowned with the title of Oba Erediauwa, making him the thirty-ninth Oba of Benin in the Second Benin Dynasty, which began with the reign of Oba Oronmiyan about the twelfth century A.D. (approximately thirty-one Ogisos had reigned in the First (Ogiso) Dynasty). He succeeded his father, Oba Akenzua II, the thirty-eighth Oba of Benin in the Second Benin Dynasty, who had reigned for forty-five years.

As can be seen, the journey to the throne of His Royal Majesty, Omo N'Oba N'Edo, Uku Akpolokpolo, Oba Erediauwa, CFR., was not, in fact, easy. Like every other person, he had to burn the proverbial midnight candles to scale the highest citadels of learning.

His dedication to duty and effective practicality of what he learned saw him through the rigors of administration into a quiet retirement, and his interaction with people of other tribes and races and orientation equipped him with that ability to deal with all as one people that need understanding, tolerance, and love.

Omo N'Oba N'Edo, Uku Akpolokpolo, Oba Erediauwa, CFR., had won many national and international awards and honorary degrees, in addition to his well-earned degrees. He reigned for thirty-seven years on the ancient throne of Benin Kingdom before his death at age ninety-two in April 2016.

Oba Gha to, Okpere. Ise!

— IDU AKENZUA

Foreword

MATTHIAS IGBARUMAH

As schoolmates at higher school in Ilesha, Osun State, Tennent Idu Akenzua, or "Tenny" as he was popularly known then, was a walking historical encyclopaedia. There was the saying that if you wake up Tenny in mid-slumber and ask him to tell you about the Benin Kingdom or the Songhai empire he would readily give you the exact names and dates of the great rulers of these civilizations of yore without even opening his eyes. So profound was his knowledge of history that many thought he was going to end up as a professor of history in one of the country's universities. We thought his love for history was a product of his royal blood. Perhaps.

But Tenny proved us wrong then. He went to the United States to study mass communication and political science and later added a law degree to his academic feathers. He now runs a legal practice in Benin City. I had thought his interest in jurisprudence had ended his romance with history. But this work, of no mean importance, gave a lie to my expectations. We were right all along. Tenny, it seems, couldn't resist the pull of history. Hardly surprising.

Indeed by editing this book on selected speeches of his uncle, Omo N'Oba N'Edo, Uku Akpolokpolo, Oba Erediauwa, he has brought to bear his expert knowledge of history and his grasp of the historical importance of the Benin Monarch. He rightly describes his uncle as a philosopher-king, a man in whom the values of western education of which he is a glowing product blends perfectly well with traditional African culture and civilization of which he has become a custodian. The picture, as portrayed in the diversity of the issues treated in this book, is that of an Oba who has deep insight into the political, social and economic problems of this country: an

Oba who through deep reflection and inner meditation proffers original solutions to the myriad of social ills afflicting this country.

In view of the wide range of issues discussed in this book, I believe critics of the traditional institution should do well to read this book. I also recommend it to academics, administrators, journalists and indeed every Nigerian patriot who is genuinely interested in the resolution of our national problems and the development of this country.

The late Matthias Igbarumah was at different times a senior staff writer for Newswatch *magazine, Lagos, and a U.S. broadcast correspondent of Africa Independent Television, Lagos.*

Preface

IDU AKENZUA, ESQ.

Many well-wishers have urged me to use my journalistic training and legal education to put together for publication the speeches and addresses which my uncle, Omo N'Oba N'Edo, Uku Akpolokpolo, Oba Erediauwa, CFR., delivered over a number of years. Such well-wishers acknowledge the invaluable role the Omo N'Oba played in the socioeconomic, political, and cultural development of this great country.

In his palace, for instance, he handled volumes of cases daily, disposing them with speed and precision that baffled the keen observer. In his daily dispensation of justice, he brought his enormous wealth of education, training and natural selection as an Oba to bear on his judgments, which were often fine expositions of the law. And, although his judgments were usually not reduced to writing, as there was neither statutory nor customary duty on him to do so, the few of such judgments that went "on appeal," so to speak, were affirmed *in toto* by the Customary Courts, Magistrates' Courts, High Courts, Court of Appeal and the Supreme Court. See, for instance, the case of *Amaghizemwen v. Eguaemwense,* which went all the way to the Supreme Court.

He had long advocated that Nigeria should give the world her own brand of political system, rather than hinge hers on the British parliamentary or American presidential system (See Chapter 4); he had consistently espoused that Nigerian politicians should seek greater ideals and stop attacking themselves, families and relations—all in the name of politics—where and when they ought reasonably to be attacking issues; he had insisted, in short, that Nigerian politicians should eschew politics of bitterness (See Chapter 6).

The Omo N'Oba had long stressed good governance, prudent spending, sanity in public affairs, purposeful public administration, dynamic self-reliance, and respect for tradition and custom in *pari pasu* with modernity and western education (See Chapters 2, 3 & 7). He urged that the valiant, the best mind or learned person, was not he who mimics the symbols of his upbringing, religion, tradition, and custom or he who dogmatically pulled down his roots, tradition, and custom in the name of enlightenment (Chapter 2 & 3).

He spoke publicly and courageously against corruption and bared his mind unequivocally on such national issues as the relevance of the Land Use Act, 1978, the idea of peace, religious intolerance, students' demonstrations, politics, love, morals, morality, etc.

Even by Plato's standard, rigid as it were, the Omo N'Oba N'Edo was eminently a Philosopher-King, and he had perfected the Socratic injunctions that man should discover himself and should at one time or the other philosophize.

Here was a king who constantly philosophized and who, in spite of his preeminent position and tight schedule, still found time to ponder on and proffer solutions to man's most pressing needs, to the end that the world would be a better place for all.

For everything he said, every assertion he made, he provided facts and figures and cited authorities for his propositions. He speculated not only on the theoretical but also on the practical. He had, in the last four decades, supported all genuine efforts made by successive governments towards enhancing the development of this great country. His belief in God was unshaken and unparalleled (see his various speeches).

Surprisingly, however, some little minds, in the garb of western education, used unfortunate situations to lampoon him, demonstrating for the most part their glaring ignorance and acute cultural myopia.

Some hid under the façade of media publicity blitz to fire their salvos. A product of Western education, himself a Benin man, now dead, ironically once said that the Omo N'Oba was "vindictive." But those sufficiently close to the Omo N'Oba knew that nothing could be farther from the truth.

In yet another case, the editor of the *New Nigerian*, an erstwhile popular national daily, once asked the Omo N'Oba "to swear" that the traditional rulers had not abused land whose ownership was vested in them (Chapter 5), thereby challenging the monarch to do that which was not only silly and insulting but also incompatible with the status of a natural ruler, a philosopher-king.

In the face of all these slights, the Omo N'Oba kept his cool, always reminding the misguided and the youths of the potency of the sanctions of our traditional customs and the person of the Oba of Benin but never recklessly invoking it.

Quite naturally, the Omo N' Oba remained neither pompous nor arrogant, but all-serving and giving and ever grateful for any opportunity given to him to serve or address humanity (see his various speeches).

Truly, no prophet is acknowledged in his own country, and history is replete with instances where we have recklessly crucified our saviours (see the case of Jesus Christ), given them hemlock or poison to drink (in the matter of Socrates), and assassinated them (Re: Gen. Murtala Mohammed, Rev. Dr. Martin Luther King Jr., Malcolm X, Nkrumah, Lumumba, et al.).

In this book, meticulously put together, we present to the world and posterity the workings of a great mind, a great Philosopher-King who was called the Omo N'Oba N'Edo, Uku Akpolokpolo, Oba Erediauwa, CFR, LL.D. (*Honoris causa*), Oba of Benin.

The book represents a first comprehensive attempt to document the thinking and scholarly efforts of Oba Erediauwa. The publication will, it is hoped, enable his former critics to appraise more intelligently the great role the Omo N'Oba played over the years in the positive development of Nigeria and the World at large, as well as the consistent stands he took on issues of fundamental importance.

The student of theology will find the Omo N'Oba's address to the Benin Anglican Diocesan Synod (Chapter 1) challenging and inspiring; historians and students of government will find the Omo N'Oba's special lecture titled "The Roles of Traditional Rulers in Local Government" (Chapter 3) and his paper titled "The Problems of the Transition from Colonial Status to Independence with Special Emphasis on District Administration" (Chapter 7) exhilarating and academically well-researched. Students and masters of political science will find the paper on "A New Political Order" (Chapter

4) rewarding, as it is distinctively indigenous, imaginative and original. Practitioners and students of law will, no doubt, find the paper on the Land Use Act (Chapter 5) vexing but irresistible; and, of course, researchers, journalists, biographers, archaeologists, anthropologists, and sociologists will all find the various speeches invaluable as would any other person/ professional seeking knowledge.

The reader is advised to read the speeches and addresses very well, particularly his address to the opening sessions of the Benin Anglican Diocesan Synod (Chapter 1), his special lecture titled "The Roles of Traditional Rulers in Local Government" (Chapter 3), his memorandum submitted to the Political Bureau on a New Political Order (Chapter 4), the Paper on the Land Use Act (Chapter 5), his paper titled "The Problems of the Transition from Colonial Status to Independence with Special Emphasis on District Administration" (Chapter 7) and his address titled "Let there be peace," his addresses to congregation on the occasion of the 40th Foundation Ceremonies of the University of Ibadan, as well as the memorandum he submitted at a meeting of traditional rulers held in Owerri titled "Students' Unrest-Suggested causes and Solution" (all in Chapter 9), etc.

But, the caveat here is this: The reader who brings his predilections, prejudice and bias about this great King to bear on his reading of this work will find the book drab, but the person with a skeptical, objective, analytical mind who reads with a view to informing and educating himself or herself will find the work most illuminating and enjoying.

Acknowledgments

First, I remain grateful to the late Omo N'Oba for the invaluable support he gave to me all through my life and, second, for having made available through my late father the materials for this publication; to my father, Prince Ekpen Akenzua, the first Enogie of Oghbaghase (blessed be his name), for all he did for me while he was alive and for greatly inspiring this work; and to my mother, Pastor (Dr.) Mrs. F. S. Osahon (Nee Giwa-Osagie), for her inestimable love and support.

I also thank my late younger brother, Prince Uwagboe Virgo Akenzua, a social worker who lived in the United Kingdom, for his words of encouragement; and my good friend, Mr. Pat. Igbinogun, an educationist, for his useful suggestions. I am also grateful to the late Mr. Matthias Igbarumah, who was a senior staff writer with *Newswatch* magazine when he took time out of his tight schedule to write the foreword to this book.

I thank the Omo N'Oba's friend, Dr. Davidson Nicol, of the University of Cambridge, also of the United Nations. Dr. Nicol visited the Omo N'Oba some years ago, and the Oba gave him to take away a few of the addresses herein published. Dr. Nicol later wrote to the Omo N'Oba to suggest that the addresses could be put together by a good editor for publication. So, when my father mentioned to the Oba that I had already embarked on the mission, the Oba mentioned his friend's advice to my father and asked him to encourage me to carry on. Dr. Nicol, therefore, greatly inspired this work, for which I am immensely grateful.

I acknowledge with gratitude the cordial relationship and invaluable support of my cousins, H.R.H. Crown Prince Eheneden Erediauwa, the Ediaken of Uselu, Prince Aghatise Erediauwa, Princess (Mrs.) Theresa Ogiogwa (Nee Erediauwa) and Prince Omoregbe Erediauwa.

A special mention must be made of Major General Charles Ehigie

Airhiavbere, MBA, mni (Rtd.). The general was my classmate at Eghosa Anglican Grammar School, Benin City, where he spent one year with us and later joined the Nigeria Military School (NMS) Zaria, to complete his secondary education from 1969–1973 as a "boy soldier." We thereafter studied and lived apart at different institutions of higher learning and places, and never saw face to face or even communicated one way or the other with each other since 1969 until sometime in October 2011 when we eventually met after his retirement, a period of forty-two years. A divine reunion, you may say!

General Charles, as he is fondly called by his superiors, peers and subordinates, saw a printed sample copy, call it "dummy," if you like, of this book for the first time in my house in October 2011—it was a project that started in 1992—and immediately said he would sponsor its printing and publishing for as long as the book was on the Omo N'Oba, and he did. Mere words cannot express my appreciation to him for making this book possible.

I thank Mr. Tony Osarumen Uzzi, a contemporary, more or less, and until very recently a selfless Director of Security Services (DSS) in my Palace at Oghobaghase Dukedom, for enabling me to meet General Charles after forty-two years. I also thank my bosom friend and cousin Prince N'Ohiutete Obaseki, a graduate of mass communication and a one-time Director of Protocol (DOP) in my Palace at Oghobaghase, functions which he performed meritoriously without remuneration, for his very useful suggestions.

I remain indebted to my personal assistant, Mr. Kingsley Odaro-Ekhaguebor, a social work graduate and now a final-year student of law at the University of Benin, Benin City, Nigeria, for finding time to proofread the computer typing of the addresses and speeches, and to my cousin and very good friend, Mr. M. Ola Badru, retired Assistant Director of Forestry with the Federal Ministry of Environment, Abuja, who assisted me greatly in the computer typing and typesetting of the materials used in this book. The same goes for my secretary, Miss Precious O. Okungbowa, who did the computer work, as well as the printers and publishers.

Finally, I thank my wife Gladys and my children; namely, Ilerhunuwa, Udinyiwe, Ewemade, Aimionmwanvbekhomwan (Ekhoe, or Ekhomwan, for short) and Eronmwon for their uncommonly elegant love and understanding.

Responsibility for any shortcoming in the compilation and editing of this book is entirely mine.

Idu Akenzua, who died in 2020, was a journalist, political scientist, and a lawyer in Benin City. A barrister and solicitor of the Supreme Court of Nigeria and the Enogie (Duke) of Oghobaghase Dukedom in Benin Kingdom, Nigeria, he holds an English Language Certificate (Washington), B.A. (Alabama), LL.B. (Hons.) (Benin), and B.L. degrees.

The late Idu Akenzua,
Enogie (Duke) of Oghobaghase

Background Information
on the Benin Kingdom in Relation to Nigeria

MUYIDEEN OLA BADRU

The Benin Kingdom where the Philosopher King—Oba Erdiauwa, Uku 'Akpolokpolo—reigned is presently located in what is now called the Niger-Delta or South-South Region of Nigeria, but the kingdom had a rich, ancient history before the formation of Nigeria in 1914 by the British Colonial Power, represented by the Governor-General, Lord Frederick Lugard.

The Benin Kingdom flourished and was considered one of the most highly developed coastal city-states in the hinterland of West Africa from about 1180 until her fall in the nineteenth century. The capital, also known as Benin City, was the trading center of a network exclusively controlled by the King—Oba, in the Edo language. Benin had a thriving trade with Portuguese merchants who were in search of gold, ivory, and slaves. The heartland of the Kingdom was a forty-five mile radius circle around Benin City, ruled directly by the Oba. The outer territories or rural communities, or dukedoms, were governed by princes called Enigie in Edo. The princes coordinated local administrators, or Odionwere, who directed local affairs of villages on behalf of the Oba, while facilitating tributes offered by the people to the palace.

The Kingdom was formed by Edo-speaking people in the rain forest of West African regions under the rulership of the Ogisos—Kings of the Sky. The land was named Igodomigodo. The first ruler, Ogiso Igodo, was considered good and successful, unlike his eldest son Ere who succeeded him.

In the twelfth century, Ekaladeran, the heir apparent and son of the last

Ogiso, was ousted from the succession and condemned to death through a process akin to a coup d'état that had been orchestrated by the first queen, his stepmother. As fate would have it, Ekaladeran was spared and exiled from the Kingdom by the executioners at Ughoton some distance from Benin City.

The exiled Ekaladeran adopted the new name of Izoduwa, meaning I-have-chosen-the-course-of blessings. His search for a new abode led him to Ile-Ife in the present-day Osun state of Nigeria. He assumed leadership of his new community and was advanced in age by the time his father, the reigning Ogiso, died. The Benin elders, led by Chief Oliha, were able to trace the Benin prince to Ile-Ife. Izoduwa could not grant the elders' desire for his return to Benin to be crowned as the next King, or the new Ogiso. But Izoduwa approved his son, Oranmiyan, to serve as king in his place. The elders accepted Oranmiyan, though Ogiamen Irebor, the leader of the palace chiefs, put up a short-lived resistance.

Thus Oranmiyan settled at the new palace built for him at Usama by the elders. That palace now serves as the Coronation Center for new Obas. The new King married Erinmwinde, the beautiful daughter of the Duke, or Ogie-Egor, who gave birth to a son who was found to be deaf and dumb. But the son was healed after Oranmiyan sent the elders some mystic marble seeds, or ayo, to enable his son to play one of Africa's traditional relaxation games with assurance that he would talk in the process. While playing the game, the son struck his target and shouted Owomika (my hand overcame), which would become his royal name, pronounced as Eweka by the people of Edo. Meanwhile Oranmiyan decided to return to Ile-Ife after agreeing with the elders for his son to be made King in his place.

EWEKA BEGAN A NEW dynasty in the Benin Kingdom that produced several dynamic and successful Obas such as Ewuare, Ozolua, Esigie. Oba Ewuare in particular is recognized as a great warrior king who developed Benin City with fortified gateways and expanded the kingdom.

The Oba became the supreme political, judicial, economic, and religious or spiritual leader of the State. The Benin Kingdom at its greatest power controlled the coastal trade from the Western Niger Delta across Lagos to as far as Ghana, hence the coastline was called the Bight of Benin. The

Kingdom ruled over the tribes of the Niger Delta and acted as middlemen or traders between other kingdoms, facilitating exchange of goods such as gold, precious stones, textiles, and salt, using cowrie shells as currency long before contact with the Europeans. Tales of Benin's greatness and prosperity attracted Europeans traders to the city gates for many years after Oba Ewuare's era.

Early European contact with the Benin Kingdom started with Portuguese explorers and traders in the late fifteenth century, a commerce which developed quickly around the sale of ivory, pepper, natural rubber, and palm oil to the Portuguese in exchange for guns and gunpowder. The relationship led to exchange of ambassadors in the sixteenth century. The Oba sent an ambassador to Lisbon, Portugal, with hope of negotiating for arms, while the Portuguese king sent missionaries to Benin, possibly to avoid arming a potential enemy. Christianity thus came to Benin before colonial conquest. This made several other European nations such as France, Britain, Belgium, the Netherlands, and Germany interested in West Africa in the sixteenth century. Europeans found Benin to be an amazing place ruled by a powerful king. The people of Benin were strict, disciplined, and respected their culture or tradition.

A great trading relationship had developed between Benin and England by around 1553 but the result was a British determination to break the stronghold of the Oba of Benin on the growing coastal trade. The situation changed when the Oba realized the British colonial aspirations against his Kingdom and began to curtail contact.

In the late nineteenth century, the Oba, in his efforts to protect the kingdom, restricted trade to palm oil. Meanwhile the British were scheming to control trade in the entire area as well as to gain access into growing natural rubber resources as raw material for their tire industry.

In 1862, Richard Francis Burton, the British Consul in Fernando Po in Equatorial Guinea, began the first official visit in pursuit of British colonial interest in the area. This was followed by failed attempts of British officials Hewitt, Blair, and Annesley in 1884, 1885, and 1886 to establish a treaty between Benin and Britain. The Henry Galway Treaty of 1892, led by the British Consul of Oil Rivers Protectorate visit to Benin, was intended to open up trade and bring Benin Kingdom into the British Protectorate. But Oba Ovonramwen and his chiefs were reluctant to sign a treaty that gave the British legal justification to place more demands on the Kingdom, thereby setting the stage for the Benin massacre.

The treaty granted freedom of trade within Benin kingdom, but the Oba's insistence on payment of custom duties was seen as a hostile violation of terms which the British considered legal and binding. There were several failed attempts to enforce the Galway Treaty of 1892 between September 1895 and 1896 by British protectorate officials Major Copeland-Crawford, Vice-Consul of Benin District, followed by Mr. Locke, Vice-Consul Assistant, and lastly by Captain Arthur Making, the Commandant of the Niger Coast Protectorate Force detachment based in Sapele.

THE OBA'S INSISTENCE IN March 1896 on collection of required tributes or duties and failure of the middlemen to pay led to the imposition of a trade embargo on the Benin River region, bringing commercial activities to a halt to the displeasure of the British traders.

To continue the lucrative trade, British investors appealed to their home government to open up the Benin territories and remove the Oba. Without yet having approval from London, in December 1896 General James Philip, the Acting Consul, undertook a military expedition with officers from the Niger Coast Protectorate Force, requesting the Oba to grant unlawful permission into the territory for a Trade and Peace Mission, not knowing that Itsekiri traders had tipped the Oba that the British actually were coming for war.

Against the Oba's counsel to allow the British mission to come into the territory, the Iyase or Prime Minister in January 4, 1897, ordered Benin army commander Ologbosere to lead his troops to destroy the invaders at Ughoton, a seaport. Only two British officers survived what became known as the Benin Massacre. Philip, in his request to the colonial office, had asserted that he would replace the Oba and pay for the expedition with ivory and other treasures he believed he would find in the king's palace.

The subsequent British invasion in pursuit of economic gains would terribly interrupt Benin's succession of Obas.

On January 12, 1897, the British appointed Rear Admiral Harry Rawson to lead an operation called the Benin Punitive Expedition. After bitter fighting, on February 9, 1897, the Oba surrendered to British Consul Ralph Moor to avert further bloodshed. The British auctioned the Benin royal arts to cover the cost of their Punitive Expedition.

The British Empire forcefully annexed Benin Kingdom as part of the new protectorate it formed to create the present-day Nigeria. The dethroned Oba Ovonramwen was banished to Calabar in southeastern Nigeria, where he lived until his death in 1914.

BENIN THUS DECLINED DURING the 18th century as the kingdom was racked by civil wars and was ultimately conquered by the British in 1897. Today Benin Kingdom is perhaps best known for its impressive and classical artworks in wood and brass sculptures, often depicting rulers and their families or important events in the Kingdom such as festivals or ceremonies. Benin art ranks among the best collections in the world.

The son of Oba Ovonramwen, Prince Aiguobasimwin Ovonramwen, was crowned Oba Eweka II. He was birthed by Queen Eghaghe of the Egbede family from the Uvbe community in the Orhionmwon Local Government Area of Edo State. Oba Eweka II was bold and courageous during a difficult period when he had to rebuild his kingdom under a condition of internal intrigue and division created by the British Occupation Force of 1897.

The crowning of Oba Eweka II on July 24, 1914, was a great victory for the Edo people who cherished their tradition of hereditary succession even if the Oba had to swear allegiance to another king, the British Imperial Monarch. This situation was the first of its kind at the time, and it was strange.

Oba Eweka built the present palace after the 1897 destruction by the British forces. The Oba was skillful in wood and ivory carving and as well was a master brass smith and agriculturalist, all of which he had engaged in before his coronation. His enemies were unsuccessful in their efforts to set the colonial government against him. After a successful reign, Oba Eweka joined his ancestors in 1933.

Prince Edokpa Aiguobasimwin Eweka, son of Oba Eweka II, was born on April 5, 1899, at Irhirhi near Benin. He was crowned the Oba Akenzua

II of Benin on April 5, 1933, after the death of his father. The new Oba was educated at Kings College, Lagos, and in other administrative training programs. He held positions under the colonial administration before assuming the throne.

Oba Akenzua's reign was considered a period of great development in the Benin kingdom and the nation. He played a great role before and after the independence of Nigeria in 1960. His contribution towards the creation of Mid-West and Bendel helped to make these efforts fruitful at that time in the history of Nigeria. There was peace and harmony in his domain while he was on the throne. The reign of Oba Akenzua II came to an end when he joined his ancestors in 1978.

The first son of Oba Akenzua II, Prince Solomon Igbinoghodua Aiseokuoba, succeeded his father and was crowned on March 23, 1979, with the title of Omo N' Oba Erediauwa, Oba of Benin. He was born June 22,1923, and was named by his grandfather, Oba Eweka II. He was educated at Government College, Ibadan, in 1939, Yaba College in 1945, and proceeded to King's College, Cambridge, to study law and administration. In 1957, he served in the Eastern Nigeria Civil Service before transferring to the Federal Civil Service of Nigeria, where he retired as Permanent Secretary.

Following his coronation, he used his wealth of experience and influence to promote the interest of his people within the Nigerian space, as chronicled in the pages of this book. Omo N' Oba Erediauwa joined his ancestors in 2016.

Oba Erediauwa was succeeded by his first son, Crown Prince Eheneden Erediauwa, who was crowned on October 20, 2016, as Oba Ewuare II, Oba of Benin. He was born October 20, 1953. He was educated at Immaculate Conception College, Benin City, University of Wales, Cardiff, United Kingdom, where he obtained his bachelor's degree in economics in 1977 and completed his graduate degree in public administration (MPA) at Rutgers University in the United States in 1981.

Prior to his ascension to the throne, Oba Ewuare served in the Nigerian Diplomatic Corps as an ambassador to countries such as Italy, Sweden, Denmark, and Angola, among others.

Oba Ewuare II's rich experience in handling difficult situations has

*His Royal Majesty Omo N' Oba N' Edo Uku Akpolokpolo
Ewuare II, Oba of Benin*

brought progress to his kingdom, Edo State, and the nation at large. The
people of Benin expect he will bring new tonic to traditional administration in the kingdom.

THE BRITISH COLONIAL GOVERNMENT headed by Lord Frederick Lugard
amalgamated in 1914 the Northern and Southern Protectorates to form the
Federal Republic of Nigeria consisting of numerous ethnic nationalities that

had existed independently before they fell under British control.

Lord Lugard administered the new nation through the system of indirect rule by employing the existing local administrative system in governance through the traditional rulers or Chiefs as titular heads in a way to gain local support for the colonial Administration. This system continued until the commencement of the process for self-rule and eventually independence on October 1, 1960.

The Benin Kingdom was incorporated into the new country of Nigeria, consisting of ethnic nationalities such as the Edo, Yoruba, Igbo, Hausa, Ijaw, Kanuri, Nupe, Tiv, Igala, Idoma, Urthobo, and Fulani, among others.

Nigeria was considered the largest economy in Africa in 2013 but has been shrinking since the historic election of 2015. Nigeria has 201 million people, occupying a landmass of 923,000 square kilometers. She is rich in biological diversity and has a great endowment in mineral resources awaiting full and efficient utilization.

The Federal Republic of Nigeria is bordered in the north by the Niger and Chad republics, Cameroon to the east, and the Republic of Benin in the west, while the Gulf of Guinea is to the south. Nigeria at independence in 1960 had three regions: Northern, Eastern, and Western. Midwest was created in 1965 after a plebiscite. Nigeria presently consists of thirty-six states and a federal capital territory, Abuja, which has served as the seat of government after the capital was moved from Lagos. The states are administered by governors and state legislatures as well as the judiciary.

At the national level are the president and National Assembly (legislature or congress) and the judiciary. Among Nigeria's many ethnic groups, the most numerous in terms of population are Yoruba in the South-West, Igbo in the South-East, and Hausa in the North. The official language in Nigeria is English.

Nigeria's diverse ethnicity gives the country her strength and uniquely rich cultural and religious heritage.

THE MAKING OF A
PHILOSOPHER-KING

Chapter 1

On Christians, Christianity, African Traditional Religionists, and the Divinity and Dignity of Labour

The Christian has retorted that the laws of the realm are made, more often than not, by non-Christians who themselves do not conform to the Christian standard, hence the Christian objection. If this argument is tenable, then it renders Romans Chapter 13, Verses 1–3 a nullity. But, of course, that is an impossibility, for as we have seen: "There is no authority, except from God, and God instituted those that exist . . . for rulers are not a terror to good conduct but to bad."
     — Omo N'Oba Erediauwa, June 3, 1980

In my view, the reason for the confused state of the world is that man has turned away from his maker through total disregard for all injunctions that were meant to make every man his brother's keeper, and make the world a good place for all, irrespective of race, religion or class.
     — Omo N'Oba Erediauwa, September 9, 1986

||||||||||||||||||||||||||||||||||||||||||||||

An Address Delivered at the Opening Session of the Benin Anglican Diocesan Synod on Tuesday, 3rd June, 1980

Lord Spiritual and Temporal, Church Dignitaries, Ladies and Gentlemen:
 It is a rare opportunity and unique privilege for me to be invited to address this galaxy of church dignitaries. The opportunity is rare and the

privilege unique because, I believe, this is the first time that an Oba of Benin has addressed a Synod.

As you must be aware by now, I am a Traditional Ruler who believes very much in tradition. I have read a bit, but I cannot claim to be a Theologian or an Evangelist; I cannot claim to be a Christian, though I believe in God Almighty. I think I am right in saying that African traditional religionists and Christians do not always agree with one another. In my view, it is not that African tradition does not want to be a friend, but, I think, the Christian (as distinct from Christian teaching) has not thought much of the former.

I must, therefore, plead with you at the onset to make allowance for what I may say here should it fall out of line with your practice. You will immediately notice that I have drawn a distinction between Christian practice and Christian teaching. It is a real distinction for as I will show later, the conflict between traditional religion and Christian religion is not supported by scriptural teaching. When I ask you, therefore, to make allowance for what I will say I do not mean that you should brush it off with a wave of hand and say: "Oh well, he's a traditionalist, what do you expect." The allowance I am asking you to make is that when I have had my say, rather than brushing aside what is not in line with your practice, please spend a few minutes of your spare time to reflect on the points that I have made. I may seem to be critical; but, I believe that is the whole purpose of choosing the subject for the Synod: to examine to what extent, if at all, Christians have fallen below standard. Even Paul was known to have been very critical of fellow Christians and sometimes even of himself—not with a view to condemning but to exciting reappraisal and making amends, if need be.

I propose to speak on the very theme of the Synod. It is a very wide subject, and to do justice to it, I must ask you to bear with me with your patience.

The theme is: "Christian Standard of Service to God and Man, especially in the Presidential System of Government." This is a very interesting subject and very appropriate, I think, in the present time of our national history and in view of the goings-on within the Church itself.

The subject is really in two parts: one, service to God and two, service to man. With due deference to those who chose the subject, I would like to observe that it is not necessary to be particular about the presidential system of government, for, in my view, Christian standard is, or should be, the same whether the Christian lives in a presidential system or parliamentary system or any other form of government.

If this standard varies or a Christian deviates from the standard in order to fit in with the change in government, then something is seriously wrong somewhere. I propose, therefore, instead, to discuss the subject in three parts:

(a) Christian standard of service to God;

(b) Christian standard of service to man; and

(c) Christian standard of service to government.

In doing this, I must first of all attempt to identify what the standards are as given us by the Christian's one and only authority, the Holy Bible. Thereafter, I will attempt to examine to what extent Christians have lived or taught men to live up to these standards.

What is the Christian standard of service to God? For an answer, my mind immediately goes back to the catechism we were taught many years ago in school which goes thus:

"Who made you?"

"God made me."

"Why did God make you?"

"God made me to know Him, to love Him and to serve him."

As we become more advanced in Christian teaching, we are referred to Exodus, Chapter 20, popularly known as the Ten Commandments. As is well known, the first four of these Commandments clearly tell us how our Creator expects us to regard Him.

He is even more forthright elsewhere: in Ecclesiasticus (not Ecclesiastes) Chapter 25, Verse 1, He tells us the three things that are most pleasing to Him: "My soul takes pleasure in three things, and they are beautiful in the sight of the Lord and men: Agreement between brothers; friendship between neighbors and a wife and husband who live in harmony."

I believe the reason for the introduction of marriage here must be obvious to you Christians. And in Verse 2 of the same chapter, He tells us of the three kinds of men that He hates: *"My soul hates three kinds of men, and I am greatly offended at their life: a beggar who is proud; a rich man who is a liar, and an adulterous old man who lacks good sense."*

Of course, you know that a "beggar" in the context does not refer to the hungry poor man on the roadside. The Master came and summed up all the foregoing in Matthew, Chapter 22, Verses 36 and 37, when, in answering a question, He said: *"Thou shall love thy God with all thy heart and with all thy soul and with all thy mind."*

We cannot go through all, but I think enough has been said for us to know what standard of service He expects us to render to Him.

NEXT IS SERVICE TO man. What are the standards? I have already referred to the Ten Commandments. While the first four Commandments relate to service to God the remaining six set for us the standard of behavior to our fellow men. Again, the Master came and summed it up in Matthew, Chapter 22, Verse 39, when He said: *"Thou shall love thy neighbor as thyself."*

After giving the injunction, He went on in Matthew, Chapter 25, Verses 34 to 40 to illustrate what He meant: the verses where He thanked those who fed Him when He was hungry, gave Him water when He was thirsty, etc., and drew for us the moral of what He was saying that *"in as much as ye have done it unto one of the least of these my brethren ye have done it unto Me."*

Enough, I think, as regards the standard of service to man.

WE NOW CONSIDER THE standard of service to government. It is a well-known historical fact that from the beginning Christians (as distinct from Christianity) have been at daggers-drawn with the authority. Yet, we are told in Romans, Chapter 13, Verses 1 to 3 how every person should behave to the governing authorities and why. The relevant verses go thus:

> Let every soul be subject unto the higher powers. For there is no power but of God: the powers that be are ordained of God. Whosoever therefore resisteth the power, resisteth the ordinance of God: and they that resist shall

receive to themselves damnation. For rulers are not a terror to good, but to evil. Wilt thou then not be afraid of the power? Do that which is good, and thou shall have praise of the same.

The injunction is repeated in First Peter, Chapter 2, Verses 13 to 17, which I shall refer to later. In this connection, and perhaps for the avoidance of doubt, the Master went on in Titus. Chapter 3 to give six qualifications which make a Christian a good citizen. These may be summarized thus:

1. He must be duly subject to those who are in power and authority and obey their commands;
2. He should be ready to perform any type of work provided it is good;
3. He must speak evil of no man;
4. He must be tolerant, although not servile;
5. He should be kind and show the love of God towards his fellow man; and
6. He must be gentle with complete control of his temper.

Here, again, I cannot go through all. But, I think enough has been said for us to know what standard of behavior is expected of us towards our government.

HAVING, I HOPE, IDENTIFIED the standards required of Christians, the next question is: to what extent have Christians lived up to these standards or have taught men to recognize them? In answering these questions, I know I must tread warily so as not to appear to criticize in a gathering such as this, but I hope I would be able to throw out a few salient points to form food for thought in your deliberations.

As I had earlier done, I will begin by considering the question in relation to service to God. We have already referred to Matthew, Chapter 25, Verses 34 to 40 and also the first four of the Ten Commandments. It is, however, difficult, if not impossible, indeed presumptuous, for any person to judge whether or not another person is living up to the standard, because the relationship is purely a personal matter between a man and his Maker, and everyone has to search his conscience in relation to the injunctions in the Holy Book. What seems clear to me, however, is that our service to

God is nothing other than our service to our fellow man. Therefore, I will not elaborate further on this aspect of the subject but will examine it from the other angle.

As regards service to Man, to what extent are Christians living up to the standard? When, in the words of the Catechism, we were told that God made us to serve him, what did He mean? Again, Matthew, Chapter 25, Verses 34 to 40 immediately come to mind. In this world in which the rich want to see the poor poorer; in this world in which money (instead of manner) maketh a man (a big man!), no matter how the wealth was acquired; in this world in which even Christians themselves use all manner of means to vie for position in and outside the Church; in this world in which people render services only with the hope of reward, where do we go from there? Of course, you will say those who so behave are not Christians. All right, what has the Church done to make such people know and accept the standard? I will pose the question later whether the Church is gaining or losing ground.

The Master tells us that His Father prefers to deal with a straightforward and honest person: we hear it in Revelations, Chapter 3, Verse 15 and 16 in this form: *"I know your works: you are neither cold nor hot, I would that you were cold or hot. So because you are lukewarm, and neither cold nor hot, I will spew you out of my mouth."*

Today, even people in highly-placed positions, because of the love for material wealth, are neither cold nor hot. These are people who are evasive or dubious and have not the courage to speak the truth, or to even tell a lie. So, one does not know which way to go with such people: they just sit on the fence, watching which way the good fortune blows and then jump for it.

The sum total of Christian standard of service to Man is, I submit, inherent in the practice of Brotherhood, for the Master tells us in Matthew, Chapter 23, Verse 8: *"But be not ye called Rabbi: For One is your Master, Christ; And all ye are brethren."*

Those of you Evangelists and Theologians will know that in some texts this word *"One"* is spelt as I have done with capital *"O"* and is indivisible. This is what the Master meant when He went further to say in First Peter, Chapter 2, Verse 17: *"Honor all men. Love the Brotherhood, Fear God, Honor the king"*

And of course the well-known injunction "Do unto others as you would like them to do to you." In Brotherhood, we are all one, whether Christian, Moslem, agnostic, pagans and even sinners. It is not the business of anyone of us to condemn the other person. We have a Bini adage: *Osa oren "nogae"* meaning *"God knows his worshippers."* Which is the Edo man's way of saying what God Himself said: *"Vengeance is mine sayeth the Lord."*

Now, what about Christian standard of service of government? Are Christians living up to the standard? I was almost tempted to answer *"No"* outright. As we have already observed, Christians and Government have been at loggerheads from the beginning, and many Christians followed Christ in paying the supreme penalty. Christians have defied the ordinances of the Government, just as in our own life time we have heard of some Christian sects who refused to vote at elections or sing their country's National Anthem. And, yet, the injunction is quite clear in Romans, Chapter 13, Verses 1 to 3, which we had earlier on quoted. And, also, in First Peter, Chapter 2, Verses 13 to 16, we are taught:

> Submit yourselves to every ordinance of man for the Lord's sake: whether it be to the king, as supreme.
>
> Or unto governors, as unto them that are sent by him for the punishment of evildoers, and for the praise of them that do well.
>
> For so is the will of God, that with well doing ye may put to silence the ignorance of foolish men.
>
> As free, and not using your liberty for a cloak of maliciousness, but as the servants of God."

The Christian had retorted that the laws of the realm are made, more often than not, by non-Christians who themselves do not conform to the Christian standard, hence the Christian objection. If this argument is tenable, then it renders Romans, Chapter 13, Verses 1 to 3 a nullity. But, of course, that is an impossibility, for as we have seen: "there is no authority, except from God, and those that exist have been instituted by God . . . for rulers are not a terror to good conduct but to bad." But even where the ruler is a terror, there is still an injunction to guide the Christian, for we are told in

First Timothy, Chapter 6, Verses 1 and 2, thus:

> Let all who are under the yoke of slavery regard their masters as worthy of all honor, so that the name of God and the teaching may not be defamed.
>
> Those who have believing master must not be disrespectful on the ground that they are brethren; rather they must serve all the better, since those who benefit by their service are believers and beloved.

So much for service to government.

I CRAVE THE INDULGENCE of the church dignitaries here present, but I cannot speak on this subject without saying a few words about the position of the traditional ruler and traditional institutions in the context of what I have been talking about. It is another aspect of service to God and man. I have heard sermons delivered from the pulpits of some churches around us condemning in very strong terms traditional customs and institutions, particularly the worth of the so-called native doctors and herbalists. Personally, I have found such sermons in very bad taste and most distressing, and I have wondered whether those doing the condemnation from the pulpits know their Scriptures.

I believe the position of the King (or, in our own terminology, traditional ruler) is covered by the references so far quoted. But, specifically, to mention it again, First Peter, Chapter 2, Verse 17, which says *"Honor the king"* is relevant. I have no doubt in my mind that Christians seriously observe this injunction, and give due respect to traditional rulers, but it is also a fact, from practical experience, that some, if not all the Christians, watch traditional rulers, particularly those who believe in traditional worship, with the corner of their eyes, since by the very nature of our position, we attend to what Christians describe as idols and shrines all over the place. But must Christian religion condemn and push out the traditional? Must traditional worship and Christian worship not be seen as complementary? Or what is meant in Mark, Chapter 12, Verse 17, which says: *". . . Render to Caesar the things that are Caesar's, and to God the things that are God's"*?

The most controversial, however, is the Christian attitude to the activities of the so-called native doctors and herbalists. Christians condemn these outright. Since I believe the reason for this condemnation is ignorance, you will permit me to dwell on it a little bit. I think all concerned should know one fact: it is that the so-called native doctor or herbalist never does anything without first praying to God Almighty, for he knows, even before the advent of Christian teaching, that all powers derive from God. African Traditional Religion has been condemned as being idol worshipping, but, I tell you, even when the worshipper kneels before his shrine, he first calls on God the Father to shower His blessings on him; he knows that it is not the wooden staff (or what we call "ukhurhe" or other images on the shrine) that he is worshipping. No. The native man knows God, but he also knows that his departed ancestor is over there to intercede for him before God. After all, the injunction is "Thou shall have no other gods before me." It does not forbid us to have other gods at all, but these must be subordinate to God the Father, and not be allowed to take pride of place in our thought and belief. In other words, we must put God the Father first in whatever we do. With all due deference to the Roman Catholic, I recall spending nearly a whole day visiting the nooks and crannies of the Vatican and the St. Peter's Cathedral in Rome. St. Peter's Cathedral in Rome is, of course, the Rock. I was most impressed by the number of idols and images of all kinds that I saw (the civilized people will call them statues).

I saw, for example, the replica of the fishing net said to have been used by the fisherman, Peter; there were images of Jesus Christ in various experience, wearing the crown of thorns; there were those of the Virgin Mary; there was the image of the saint with the arrows by which he died piecing his body; and of course, at the very entrance, is the pot of holy water that adherents sprinkle on their head and body. All these were most impressive, looked at against the background of the magnificent architecture of the great Cathedral. But to the African like myself, I was also astonished when I saw the fervor and reverence with which the adherents knelt down before every one of these images, kissed it or touched it with his or her head as he or she prayed.

I have described this visit to St. Peter's Cathedral, Rome, not with any intention to ridicule the Roman Catholic; I have referred to it only to support my contention that the commandment does not forbid us to have other gods at all (like I saw in Rome), but rather we should not make these substitute for God the Father. I believe my interpretation is correct; were it not so, how then does one explain the many objects in St. Peter's that adherents bow to, kiss and touch their heads with as they pray in the Rock of the Church in Christendom? In the Westminster Abbey in England, the coronation chair, the sacred chair on which the English Monarchs are crowned, sits on a piece of stone centuries old, known as the coronation stone. When this stone was stolen all the British investigating machinery did not rest until the stone was found and restored to its proper place. Among us here, the stone would be called "juju."

Our native doctors and herbalists are ridiculed from every Christian pulpit, but are they really doing something that is not ordained by God? Look at Ezekiel, Chapter 47, verse 12, which says:

> And by the river upon the ban thereof on this side and on that side, shall grow all trees for meat, whose leaf shall not fade, neither shall the fruit thereof be consumed: It shall bring forth new fruit according to its months, because their waters they issued out of the sanctuary: and the fruit thereof shall be for meat, and the leaf thereof for medicine.

I understand the word "medicine." So why all the quarrel with herbalists or native doctors? The problem of Christianity in relation to God is whom do you know to help you reach your father who art in heaven: Christ, Buddha, Mohammed or departed ancestors? I think one can illustrate this relationship by reference to the position of the Oba in the community. The normal channel by which the ordinary citizens reach the Oba is Chiefs: but other people sometimes find it easier to make their approach to the Oba through the Oba's child or wife or brother or sister or mother. It is all a question of which line one is more familiar with or finds easier to reach.

Agnostics, that is, those who do not believe in the existence of God, have been known, when in agony on their death bed, to cry out directly to God. Does God not answer them? The Master advised us: *"Ask and it shall be given, knock and it shall be opened,"* and our Father Himself had said in Jeremiah, Chapter 29, Verses 12 and 13: *". . . you will find me when you pray with your heart."* Note that He said with all your heart and not through any particular intermediary.

I think, distinguished Ladies and Gentlemen, enough has been said on this subject. I hope I have sufficiently identified the Christian standard of service to God, to man and to government. I believe also I have been able to demonstrate whether or not these standards have been attained by Christians.

I will now, by the way of conclusion, pose the question: Is the Church gathering or losing more flock? As I ask this question, my mind goes to a television program I watched in Lagos a few years ago. It was a program for youths, some time in December of that year, and there was quite a large number of youth participants. In the course of it, being Christmas season, the Moderator invited the participants to say what Christmas meant to them. Everyone of them had something to say, ranging from picnicking at the Bar Beach, buying new dresses, attending parties or visiting friends, anything that came to their fancy. Surprisingly, there was not a single one who said anything about Jesus Christ or His Birthday; the Moderator had to ask: "Is that all you can tell the viewers about Christmas? Why is it called Christmas?" It was then one of the chaps said the birthday of Christ. I did not know why it struck me, but I reflected on it and wondered who was to blame for this lapse; the youth or the Church? Perhaps, we can say that the Church is not losing grounds, but is it gaining or has it gained anything more than what has been handed down? This is a question for you church dignitaries. But one may dare to say that there is still schism in the Church today as there was in the days of Luther.

I think the time has come for the Church Assembly to call to order some leaders of certain Christian denominations who engage in outright condemnation of non-Christians. For as long as these non-Christians are condemned in the practice of what they believe in, so will they hold their ground and keep away. Nobody will go with you if all you do is to prevail upon him to forget his ancestors, whom he knows, and follow the Master who is a total stranger to him. I think we know from the experience of human nature that we do not win by condemning, but by letting the other see your point of view. I venture to suggest that the Church is letting too many things slide; the teaching is no longer permeating the barrier; and people, including Christians themselves, are beginning to take the Church for granted. The important thing to them is go to Church on Sunday; what happens on return from Church is anybody's guess! The world of today ought to be a better place, but alas, is it? I have no doubt in my mind that it is the lack of the knowledge about God in our young generation that has contributed in no small measure to the present day rise in juvenile delinquency. Our school children now know only "R.K." or "B.K." (as they term scripture teaching) only in so far as it leads to passing their examinations; it does not help them to know God. It is the failure of society to remember God that is leading today to chaos, confusion and vice in modern society. I call on Church leaders to think on these things, and examine how far the Church is holding its own against other religions. Finally, in the words of Ecclesiastes, Chapter 12, Verse 13: *"Let us hear the conclusion of the whole matter; Fear God, and keep His Commandments, For this is the whole duty of man."*

I pray that God may shower His blessings on the deliberations of the Synod.

Thank you, and may God bless you all.

|||||||||||||||||||||||||||||||||||||||||||||

An Address Titled, "The Church in the Life of the Nation," Delivered to the 1984 Benin Anglican Diocesan Synod on Monday, 4th June, 1984

It gives me very great pleasure to be with you again today, and I like to express my appreciation to the Diocese for always inviting me to participate in your synod. It was a pity that I was not able to personally attend the last couple of meetings especially the synod that was held outside Benin City in Sabongida-Ora. That would have afforded me a fine opportunity to see at first hand the Anglican Church following outside the state capital.

The theme for this year's synod is "The church in the life of the Nation." Since my first address to the synod in 1980, I have found everyone of your subjects most topical and thought-provoking, not only for those within the church but also those outside. I wish, therefore, to commend those who exercise their minds to select the topic for each synod. On each occasion that I have been opportuned to address your synod, one thought has always occupied my mind. I have often wondered what the synod and church leaders think of my words to them and I sometimes ask myself whether they ever discuss me afterwards. I often wished I had a means of monitoring your thoughts. Be that as it may, it will always give me pleasure to have the opportunity to pass my thoughts to a synod audience such as this.

When the topic says "the church in the life of the nation," what does that synod committee expect to hear? There are several questions rolled up in the theme: what is the church doing to redeem the nation; or which is more powerful, the church or the nation; or what must the church do to be saved from the secular world. It is obvious, and I trust you will appreciate, that a discourse on a subject of this nature must of necessity involve a "self-examination" by the church. I trust that any criticism that will be made in the course of this address will be taken in good faith.

Let us then begin by going back into the history of the church to try find out first of all what "the church" in fact is. The popular conception (or misconception) of "the church" today lies in its dictionary meaning: i.e. a building set aside for Christian worship. Young and old Christians (and I dare say some church leaders themselves!) have this meaning of the church. And since it is ordained that they shall rest on the Sabbath day, those who claim to believe troop themselves in gorgeous dresses to that special building on Sundays (or on Saturdays if they are Adventists).

We will try first to examine this question as a back-ground to the topic itself. My research for this talk tells me that as seen by the prophets of the Bible (and those were truly prophets!) "the church" means something deeper to mankind than the present day dictionary meaning. You are all conversant with the scriptures. Therefore, of these prophets and their prophesies 1 will only refer you to the books of Isaiah, Daniel, Zechariah, to mention a few. I will, however, quote Isaiah 2:2–3:

It shall come to pass in the latter days that the mountain of the house of the LORD shall be established as the highest of the mountains, and shall be raised above the hills; and all the nations shall flow to it, and many peoples shall come, and say:

"Come, let us go up to the mountain of the LORD, to the house of the God of Jacob; that he may teach us his ways and that we may walk in his paths."

For out of Zion shall go forth the law, and the word of the LORD from Jerusalem.

This and similar scriptures demonstrate, to my understanding, that the church had always been in the purpose of God for mankind. Of course, Isaiah and the other prophets did not explicitly mention the word "church," but one will recognize in the Isaiah quoted such expressions as "mountain of the house of the Lord" and "all nations shall flow into it." Thus we hear Christ Himself saying in Luke 24:44: *"These are my words which I spoke to you, while I was still with you, that everything written about me in the law of Moses and the prophets and the psalms must be fulfilled."*

Note that He said *"everything written about me . . ."* must be fulfilled. In Matthew 16:18, He promised to build His "church." Here we find the word "church" from the Master Himself as something for the future—"I will."

Were these prophesies and promises fulfilled? We have evidence of their fulfillment in the Acts of the Apostles, in particular Acts 2, which I commend to your reading. This is where we learn of the Pentecost after the resurrection. We must now turn to the "letter of Paul to the Ephesians" Chapter 3:9–12, where Paul speaks also of the "church"; Verses 9–12 say:

And to make all men see what is the plan of the mystery hidden for ages in God who created all things; that through the church the manifold wisdom of God might now be made known to the principalities and powers in the heavenly places. This was according to the eternal purpose which has realized in Christ Jesus our Lord, in whom we have boldness and confidence of access through our faith in him.

When all these scriptures are read together, one is able to draw the following conclusions:

(i) It was God's purpose to establish a focal point, for all those who believe to gather and hear him.

(ii) This focal point, as foretold by the prophets of old (Isaiah and others) was to be God's kingdom and this kingdom was to be *in* Jesus the Christ.

(iii) So in Matt. 16:18 the promise to build a "church" was made

(iv) This was eventually fulfilled at the Pentecost after the resurrection as we see in Acts 2 which Paul described to the Ephesians.

In my view, the church, therefore, is an embodiment of the whole teachings and the exemplary life of Christ which He commanded His disciples to go forth and preach to the whole world. (Mark 16:15). I wonder how many of you will disagree with these conclusions?

If you have doubt let us examine two questions that have been asked in popular conversation and which seem to bother mankind:

(a) If Jesus Christ died about 2000 years ago to wash away the sin of mankind, how can mankind about 2000 years after benefit from that grace?

(b) Jesus Christ, the same yesterday, today and forever: how was he alive yesterday, is alive today and will be alive tomorrow or day after?

I submit that these two declarations (viz: dying to wash away sin, and being the same yesterday and today) refer to the "church" as personified in Jesus the Christ. Hence Paul was able to say after establishing the "church" in Corinth: *"I have laid the foundation. . . And other foundation can no man lay than that is laid, which is Jesus Christ"* (1 Cor. 3:10–11) and Peter also said: *"the word of the Lord abides forever. That word is the good news which was preached to you."* (1 Peter 1:25) Jesus Christ which is the church as ordained by God liveth forever, being the Alpha and Omega (Rev. 1:8).

Having said all that about the church, the question now arises: is the church today fulfilling its role as intended by God in Jesus Christ? My answer is No! or, I think I ought to say not so in many cases. One only needs to listen to sermons, especially those we hear these days on the T. V. screens, or hear the claims in court cases among church leaders, to see that sermons, and activities in many churches today reflect nothing but materialism and personal advertisement, or at best playing to the gallery. More disgusting are the innumerable adjectives used today to describe Jesus Christ, all in the desire of some individuals to lead rather than humble themselves to follow as Christ demonstrated in washing of the disciples' feet: "a servant is not greater than his master," He said. In many churches today, he who tried unsuccessfully to be at the head goes off to found a new church (and empire) for himself and give some ridiculous advertising name to Jesus the Christ. And yet Paul and Peter tell us clearly in 1st Corinthians and lst Peter respectively that the Lord is the foundation that must be laid and that in order to carry the church from place to place gospel preachers must preach the original gospel of Christ as did Paul and Peter. I am myself not a regular Sunday churchgoer; but if you listen to what is put across on the television pulpit every week, one cannot but agree that sermons are deviating from what Peter an Paul termed the "original gospel.'

What then is expected of the church in the life of the nation? In my address to your synod in 1980, I discussed, as that year's theme demanded, what I considered to be Christian standard of service to man and to the Government. Those are the principal elements in the life of a nation. May I, therefore, advise those who have copies to read that my address again where we dealt with man and Government. I think, in the present context, Psalm 24 should be a good pointer for me. We are told, *"The earth is the Lord's and the fullness thereof . . . etc."* Then the Psalmist asked *"who shall ascend the hill of the Lords?"* and we are given the very interesting answer in Psalm 24:4 thus: *"He who has clean hands and a pure heart; who does not lift up his soul to what is false."* The "original gospel" means that the church was the fulfillment of Jesus Christ in that (as we have said) the church was planted by God and executed in Jesus Christ. The church became the body of Christ as we are told in Ephesians 1:22–23 that *"he has put all things under his feet and has made him the head over all things for the church, which is his body, the fullness of him who fills all in all."*

In spite of the "original gospel," the world is full of problems—international war; civil war; coup d'etat, internal violence of varying degrees. Not long ago 1 read an interesting article by an experienced university don in which he posed two very serious questions to his fellow Nigerians. The two questions were: "what exactly is wrong with Nigeria?" and "what is it in our system that produces the kind of leadership we have had?" These are very searching questions when we recall (as I am sure many of you do) that since the country attained independence this our nation has never known peace and stability; and yet we have had great leaders. Since independence the country has been blessed (in the words of the populace who coined the phrase) with "God-fearing leaders — Muslims as well as Christians — who have steered the ship of this state. Name them: Balewa, Zik, Gowon (a staunch Christian military leader) Murtala (who at war front had time to pray five times a day) Obasanjo (who from account in his book was a gallant and honest soldier); then Shagari, another Muslim leader. What then is in our system that produces the kind of leadership we have had which seem unable to keep the country stable, and prevent the military from ousting civilian or military kicking out the military. Not in Nigeria alone is this happening, but in many countries of the world. What exactly is wrong with Nigeria, with the world? Did God forsake our leaders who feared and believed in him? If so, what went wrong with them? The reverse of this question, "if not,' does not arise for it is written that the fault is not in our stars but in ourselves.

Our nation, indeed the whole world, is in a state of turmoil. Military weapons have failed to engender peace and stability. There are said to be four estates of the Realm; they are the lords spiritual (the church), the Lords temporal (judiciary), the commons (parliament) and the press (News Media), in that order. From our own experience of events in this our great country, Nigeria, and from what one reads of other countries, one must be bold enough to admit that the last three estates have failed the nation. Here in our country we have seen judgments of competent courts openly rejected and defied because those on trial were able to "see through' their lordships; or the law has been seen to be a respecter of some persons; our parliament (or House of Assembly) became forum for fighting with chairs and the mace in members' bid to scramble for the "goodies': the press (whose pen is said to be mightier than the sword) has become "his master's voice." As regards the press one recalls the message to the 17th World Communication Day in 1983, when His Holiness, Pope John Paul 11, sent their charge, among others, to the participants: that social communications can promote peace "through the establishment on the institutional plane of an order of communication that guarantees a correct, just and constructive use of information, free from oppressions, abuses and discriminations based on political, economic or ideological power." One only has to read any of our newspapers or listen to discussions from our different Television studios to discern that the hand does not belong to the voice behind it.

What has the first estate of the realm (the Lords spiritual, the church), mankind's only hope through Christ, got to offer the nation, nay the world, to save it from this terrible confusion? Alas, one bows down one's head in shame to say there is not much. When we were privileged to host the Archbishop of Canterbury in our palace in 1982, I seized the opportunity to draw attention to the unhappy situation in our country and in the world, and I ventured to suggest that he, in conjunction with his Roman catholic counterpart, as heads of the Christendom, should galvanise the church into action and rekindle it to play the role that Christ set out for it for the betterment of mankind.

Our great country Nigeria is in such disarray in its body politic and the entire world is full of such disturbances, all of which are man-made, that I personally begin to feel that the church is loosing grip of the situation or else the much talked about Armageddon is drawing near. Why do I think that the church is loosing grip? First, the church, and therefore, Jesus Christ Himself, is never taken seriously anymore. It loses its value. That the church is now taken for granted is evident from the mushroom break-away factions and by the different names by which each such faction arrogate the holy name of Jesus Christ to itself. I could cite examples here, but I refrain from so doing in order not to disclose the identity of and embarrass the factions that use expressions that I regard as the advertiser's sales names to describe our Lord the Christ, in a manner that I am sure Christ Himself did not bargain for. Secondly, those whom the church is supposed to lead or win can see for themselves that the desire to break into another faction is motivated not so much by the desire to spread the gospel but more by the materialistic gain from such leadership. Third, when we were at school, our European Headmaster used to instill fear in us by preaching to us daily that "example is the support for your authority.' Can one say that today of the church when laymen see church leaders vying, and sometime actually fighting, for material wealth in and outside the church? One reads these accounts in the newspapers of in-fighting in this or that church or of members dragging themselves to courts or of aspirants to church position "lobbying' for such position, whatever meaning we place on the word "lobby' in the Nigerian context. One does not have to be in the church to see these things, for very often when the issue has boiled for a long time, those in it explode and the controversy becomes one for public consumption. I am sure those of you here know the kind of cases I am alluding to.

The church has weakened itself through proliferation and fragmentation and both Rome and Canterbury must do something to save the situation. A close study of these factions discloses two phenomena. First, leaders or founders are seeking after materialism and they now justify this by saying their God is not a poor God; so, why should they not amass wealth? Note that they never say their Jesus Christ for they know what Christ said, that it is easier for the head of a camel to pass through the eye of a needle than for a rich man to enter the kingdom of God. This is further amplified when He commissioned the Twelve to go out and preach the gospel, and He said in Luke 9:3 *"take nothing for your journey, no staff, nor bag, nor bread, nor money; and do not have two tunics . . ."*

Of course, this is not to say that the lord condemns riches and the rich man, for in Sirach 13:21–24 we are told of the virtues of riches like *"when the rich man speaks all are silent; when a poor man speaks, they say "who is this fellow?'* and the warning that *"riches are good if they are free from sin."* Secondly, these leaders take undue advantage of gullibility of the multitude of innocent or ignorant people who are striving earnestly to know Christ and be saved.

So one finds that in many cases today the Christian preaching (not Christian teaching for there is hardly any now) is almost like selling Christ's name, commercializing on it as it were. Such is bound to derogate from the stature of the master and dilute His teaching.

I have already referred to what I said to you in 1980 as regards Christian service to man and the Government. Suffice it to say at this juncture that my "Encyclopedia of Bible" tells me that the Bible does not put forward any one form of government as the right way to organize society. From the beginning, it says, the nation of Israel was meant to be a "theocracy' i.e. a nation with God as its King. But because men and women became sinful it became clear that society needed its human rulers to make laws and enforce them.

Hence the injunction in Romans 13:1–7 *"Let every person be subject to the governing authorities, for there is no authority except from God, and those that exist have been instituted by God . . ."* At the same time, God expects rulers to uphold justice, not to pervert it: *"And when governments oppress their subjects, the people of God must stand up fearlessly and condemn them. If it comes to a straight choice between what the Government says and doing God's will. Christians must obey God."*

Note that it is a "must"; then see Daniel 3, and Acts 5:29. Can the church today honestly boast of men who can stand up to their conviction? On the other hand, the world is confused by the multiplicity of religious bodies which claim to be "churches," each describing Christ and preaching in their own way. The leaders seems oblivious of the fact that the average person, the so-called man in the street, sees the conflicting denominations and he is in a quandary, wondering whether it is all worth pursuing. So you are confronted with the so-called "free-thinker,' which simply means he does not know which way to go or he cannot make up his mind in the multitude of organizations.

We have been rather critical of the church leaders. In spite of all that has been said, all is not lost. There is hope. It is important that Christian must re-dedicate themselves. The church must return to God to be able to carry society back to God. It is said that if nations perished in their sins the leprosy took off from the church. What terrible prospect! I believe church leaders have three areas in our nation today through which to bring the church (and therefore the society) back to God. First, let the church leaders refrain from attempting to remove the mote in another's eye when he has not removed the beam in his own. What right has a Christian preacher to condemn what another person believes in? Christ did not, and he had come not to destroy the existing law but to fulfill them, by which he meant to improve on them. When he performed a miracle of healing He did it quietly out of public view and left the healed to go out to proclaim God's grace. Secondly, the field of education was one area in which the church rendered the greatest service to the nation through establishing their mission schools and teaching of the scriptures and Christian morals to young persons. But, unfortunately, the church leaders abdicated their responsibility in this area. I say "abdicated" because they resigned themselves to the fact, as some have openly admitted, that "it is a government decision." I plead with the church leaders to speak with one strong united voice on this issue and prevail on the governments to give opportunity for Christian religious teaching in schools. By this I do not mean *"R.K."* or *"B.K."* that our children learn by rote for passing their examination. Thirdly, the latest development in our society now is *WAI* (War Against Indiscipline). The churches have been preaching it from their pulpits since it was launched as if they were not aware of the indiscipline in society. But this they do only on Sundays. The church must devise ways and means of making their flock feel the impact; first, by those who profess to be Christians setting the example in their daily public appearances. What use is it to preach WAI on a Sunday morning only for a church member to see his leader sneaking around to lobby for lucrative secular office or engaging in personal land dispute. Since the primary function of the church is to teach the will of Jesus Christ, it is imperative that Christians apply the teachings of Christ to their daily lives for lay men to emulate. This is the only way they can bring significant changes to the strife-torn world.

I trust that my criticism of the church will be excused; but self-examination is sometimes salutary. My criticism stems from my concern that with so much confusion and conflict around, the church, the only hope for mankind, seem helpless. I appeal to the church to arrest the incident of mushroom denominations and churches, and the ridiculous advertising catchphrases that are now being used by the commercial organizations that call themselves churches to describe Christ. These are the pitfalls that have caused the church to be taken for granted and to be ineffective. I urge the church to pray constantly so its leaders may always remember the lord's words in Luke 22:27, "I am among you as one who serves." So indeed is a king among his subjects.

Thank you for your attention and God bless you all.

III

An Address Delivered at the 95th Annual Conference of the First African Church Mission (Inc.) of Nigeria and the Republic of Benin in Benin City on September 9, 1986.

I am glad to have been invited to participate at this 95th Annual Conference of the first African Church Mission of Nigeria and the Republic of Benin. I understand that this is the fifth in the series of such conferences. We, in Bendel State, and in Benin City in particular, are glad to be hosting this conference. We commend the Benin-Ondo Zone of the Mission for making itself worthy to be host. I hereby welcome all those who have come from outside Benin City to attend the conference.

The history of the origin of the African Church, or First African Church, is very well known to many of us. Dating back to about 1891 or 1897, depending on where you want to start, it came into being as a Christian body whose objective was to relate Christian teaching, as brought to us by expatriate from Europe through Sierra Leone, to truly African way of life. Specifically, many of us know how the UNA Church (United Native African Church) came to Benin City in about 1929. The introduction caught on very well with the Benin people who believed in Christ but wanted to worship God as near as possible to the African way. I recall that the first pastor in charge of the Church in Oza Lane was the son of a hereditary traditional chieftaincy titleholder and a ritual title at that. He declined to succeed to his father's title in order to be able to devote full time to the service of Christ. I like also to recall the few occasions that, as a child, I accompanied my father from Uselu to this very Church. It is, therefore, a matter of personal joy that this conference, first in Benin City, is taking place in my reign.

I understand that the theme of this year's conference is "The Divinity and Dignity of Service." Although, the letter of invitation to me suggested that I could speak on any subject of my choice, I have decided to say a few words on the theme chosen by the conference. I think it is an interesting subject and very appropriate at this time in our country's life when many Nigerians (including, I regret to say, some of those in the Church) have become self-seekers and render service only because of the personal reward to be gained from such service. We shall try to examine it. The Bible text from which the theme is derived is taken from Luke 22:23 where Jesus said thus: *"I am amongst you as he that serveth."*

Imagine Christ Himself, with His immense power, saying that to his disciples! And this immediately recalls to my mind a famous saying by that great statesman/politician, Sir Winston Churchill, as he was addressing a mammoth gathering of his party when he said: I am your leader, and that's why I follow you." We, Edo people, also have a saying that reflects the divinity and dignity of service. We say *"evbayoboru erakha vbase erinmwin."* And to my mind, it is this same thought that the theologians expanded saying something to the effect that on "the day of reckoning" God will not ask your race or religion but simply what you have to show for your service during your sojourn on earth.

I understand "the divinity of service" to mean service to God, while "the dignity of service" relates to service to our fellow man. In this connection, if my understanding is correct within the Christian context, then I will refer myself to what I said about the "Ten Commandments" when I addressed the Benin Anglican Diocesan Synod in June 1980. The theme for that Synod was "Christian standard of service to God and man, . . ." permit me to observe that, when analyzed, there is very close similarity between that 1980 Anglican Synod and the theme for this year's conference. In my address to the Anglican Synod, I observed that the first four of the Ten Commandments instruct us on how to deal with our fellowman.

To me, that is the whole essence of the divinity and dignity of service. And there are many episodes in the Holy Book to illustrate this. The Lord said: *"Verily I say unto you, in as much as ye have done it unto one of the least of these my brethren, ye have done it unto me."*

And He invited those concerned to come and inherit the Kingdom prepared for them. In Revelation 22:11–12; He said: *"I am coming soon, bringing my recompense, to repay every one what he has done."*

In fact, the whole life of Christ thirty-three years up to the Cross was a life of divine service coupled with a demonstration of the joy derivable from service to one's fellowman, and at the end of it all, He said, *"it is finished."* Was it not St. Paul, too, who said that he (St. Paul) had run the race and fought the fight, and what remained for him was the crown of glory?

Having said all that, it is useful to examine the subject in the context of the traditional setting before I proceed to relate the whole idea to the society we live in. I think we will find that there is not much of a difference between the Christian teaching and the Edo traditional beliefs, as far as the theme of the conference is concerned, and I believe this assertion is very well exemplified in the origin of your Church that I shall speak about. *I* have often said that one difference between you, the Christians, and us the traditionalists, is that whereas we traditionalists believe that, as children of God, we can call on our Father directly, the Christians say "go through His Son." But like the Christians, the traditionalists believe in the divinity and dignity of service. An examination of the Ten Commandments, in comparison with the Edo customary beliefs and rules, will show clearly what I mean: *ghe diyi Osa; ghe rha; ghe kpanu gie vbibo,* etc. I have already quoted an Edo adage, which translates into English to mean, "It is one's handiwork on earth that one presents to one's Maker in Heaven." Edo People believe that *"erhan edin ikhinmwin, orisa ere orodion"* (no tree is older than "ikhinmwin" which is a kind of sacred tree among the Edo people). The traditionalists believe that whatever one does on earth will be rewarded in like manner by the supreme God; a good turn or a bad turn to your fellowman will be rewarded in like manner. Hence the Edo adage; *"enofie kho ogha vba ekhuen"* (implying what some mystics would term the law of Karma). The traditionalists entreat our Maker in these words: *Osamwen, izede gaa, ughuriede me niya ruogho mwen no damwen.* " (my God I have devoted days to your service, I beseech you give me some time for myself to do that which is dear to my heart)—thus admitting that we are all here by the grace of God.

IN SHORT, LADIES AND Gentlemen, the whole essence of Christ's life and teaching on earth was entirely a demonstration of the divinity and dignity of service. So, where does all this lead us to? If God made us to know Him, love Him and serve Him, if God enjoins you to do unto others as you would wish them do unto you (all of which, in my view, is implicit in the theme of the conference) why then is the world in a state of turmoil? Look around the whole world and tell me which part is free of violence or disturbance?

Everywhere, there is evidence of man's inhumanity to man; the strong oppressing the weak; there is the danger of the super-power causing a world holocaust just to demonstrate who is more technologically advanced. Here at home in Nigeria, suspicion and mistrust of one another is rife; the love of material wealth (money) has taken over control of men's mind. In my view, the reason for the confused state of the world is that man has turned away from his Maker through total disregard for all injunctions that were meant to make every man his brother's keeper, and make the world a good place for all, irrespective of race, religion or class.

The question then, is, why all these human failings the world over in the midst of the multitude of Christian denominations, sects and evangelical groups?

Are their teaching simply falling on deaf ears? I can do no better in answering this question to you than to refer myself again to my address to another Synod of the Benin Anglican Diocese held in June 1984. I observed on that occasion that Christian teaching appeared to be gradually becoming meaningless to mankind, and that the Church was losing grip of the situation. I gave reasons for reaching that conclusion which was taken for granted because of the mushroom breakaway factions and the different names (some sounding downright commercial) by which each faction arrogates the holy name of Jesus Christ to itself. Secondly, those whom the Church is supposed to lead or win over can now see for themselves that the desire of some factions to breakaway is not in every case motivated by the desire to spread the gospel but moved by the materialistic gains desirable therefore. Thirdly, laymen now see Church leaders vying, sometimes actually fighting, for material wealth inside and outside the Church. Who would have thought that Church leaders would ever resort to the law courts to resolve their Episcopal differences? With all these patently obvious shortcomings, it is easy to see why there are oppression, disturbances, even wars, in different parts of the world, including our country, Nigeria and yet the Church seems helpless and unable to intervene effectively.

The lessons in the story of the "Good Samaritan," the admonition that "in so far as you do it to anyone of these brethren you do it to me," or be thy brother's keeper all these moral teaching are what, I believe, is implied in the "divinity and dignity of service" to uplift man; and yet all seem now to have been jettisoned.

The situation seems to have been aggravated by the open antagonism that some sections of the church of Christians have created for themselves through attacks on and utter disregard for other religions, especially in this country. No Christian has the right to castigate and condemn another person's religions (more so in the unprintable expressions as some use), no matter how much the Church may disagree with their practice, for your Master Himself said he had come not to destroy but to improve and further advised His followers to give to Caesar that which is Caesar's. As I said on another occasion "Osarenogae" (God knows who serves Him). I believe it is this unsavory attitude of the Church to other religions that is partly responsible for more and more people (who would otherwise have liked to follow Christ) having to find a medium that can accommodate their own beliefs, but still with the fear of God in them. This is more so in the case of the traditional religion whose followership is really the target of attack of some Christian evangelists.

I THINK, AT THIS point, it is appropriate to pay tribute to the African Church. The African Church was born out of the desire of indigenous Nigerians who have accepted Christ to reconcile the African way of life and mode of worship of God with the newly-found imported Christian religion but without deviating from the path of righteousness as decreed by Christ. You will please find time to come to the Palace to correct me if I have stated the philosophy of your Founding Father incorrectly. If I am correct (and I think I am) then there is a lot to commend your church. This is not the place to discuss the scriptures as understood and interpreted by the African Church vis-à-vis the other Churches in Christendom. Suffice it to illustrate by brief reference only to some of the actions and pronouncements of the Founding Fathers of your Church that take after my heart as a traditional ruler. For instance, it is said that the educated Africans had established the Native Pastorate (the forerunner of the African Church), "the (CMS) Prayer Book was edited and prayers for the Queen (of England) were replaced by prayers for the native kings." Secondly, the proposed African Church "would incorporate some parts of indigenous religion which bore resemblance to Christianity, adopt the vernacular languages, have its own hymns and liturgy." Thirdly, it is said that "in order to render Christianity indigenous to Africa it must be watered by native hands, pruned with the native hatchets and tended with native earth . . ." Furthermore, your Founding Fathers enjoined the converts to the new Christian religion to appreciate "self-government . . . retention of native names, native dress, healthful native customs and habits, and the use of the native language in worship." All these happened long before our politicians ever dreamt of political independence.

I have brought in here the philosophy behind the founding of the African Church because it is my belief that "service" in the context of the theme of this conference, must be seen in the context of a people's culture. And I like to appeal to the Church to do more of its evangelical work in teaching us Nigerians not to turn away from our African traditional values. In the rural communities, for example, not yet split by modernity, everybody is still "his brother's keeper," people still render "selfless service," a good turn for the love of doing it without hope of reward. I am, of course, not urging the Church to fraternize with traditional worship. All I am urging the Church to do is to refrain from condemning the traditional religion for therein lies our traditional values which, as I have already observed, are not different from those enshrined in the Ten Commandments and which our illiterate people understand and appreciate.

The sum total of all that I have been saying amounts to this. When the Christian teaching is examined we find that the "divinity and dignity of service" are manifest in the following: Benevolence; Justice; Gratitude; Charity; and Sincerity.

I believe that values need no elaboration. I have no doubt in my mind at all that the world would be a much better place today if men respected these values. But alas, the world had spurned the dignity of service and thereby missed the divinity of service, which is the ultimate reward. "Thy kingdom come. . ." but rather allowing God's Kingdom on earth (wherein lies peace and harmony) men are creating their individual kingdoms (of greed and materialism) and have thereby thrown the world into utter chaos, for "the love of money is the root of evil." More often than not, because of political power and the material gains therefrom, it is now "man's will" rather than God's will be done!

For the stability of the world, and our dear country, Nigeria, therefore, man must let God's Kingdom reign supreme on earth. And this would come to be only if man recognized and practised the five values earlier on listed. Happily, the world is not devoid of good persons. There are still good persons around willing, if given the opportunity, to render selfless service. But such persons have withdrawn. There is so much sin and corruption around that good people would rather keep to themselves and their honest occupation than to have their good name soiled by being counted among the ungodly.

The church must, therefore, intensify its prayers for such men of honor to come out to lead by their example of selfless service, and for the ungodly to follow the example, for it is written: *"My son, perform your tasks in meekness: then you will be loved by those whom God accepts."* (Sirach 3:17)

Finally, I like once again to thank the First African Church Mission for having invited me to address this August gathering of your church leaders and distinguished ladies and gentlemen. I do not, of course, expect the Church to agree with or accept what I have said. I will be satisfied to know that you found something in it to give you food for thought.

Now, Ladies and Gentlemen, let me end by leaving with you this wonderful prayer. It is a bit lengthy, so, I will skip some parts of it:

> Just and Holy Lord,
> You have commanded us to do right,
> And to see that right is done,
> Free my heart and my hands from
> All dishonesty and wrong-doing.
> Let me never let you down
> By living dishonestly.
> But let me behave in this world with
> Simplicity and godly sincerity;
> Not looking to amass wealth—
> Preferring only to have enough and
> Behave justly rather than to be a

Millionaire and dishonest.
So let me behave before God—
Innocently, truthfully—
That I may have peace at last
With Him through Jesus Christ our Lord.

I wish your Conference God's Guidance for successful deliberations.
Thank you.

Chapter 2

On Tradition, Custom, Culture, Youth and Western Education

It is . . . not true that the traditional society is culturally and politically simplistic and incapable of sustaining the hazards associating with modernity. African history and politics have recorded nations and empires that were enormous in size and complex in administration. The great states of the Egyptians, Abyssinians, Asantes and Zulus as well as those of the Hausa—Fulani, Yorubas and Edos . . . remain potent examples of the traditional societies established on complex foundation and possessing sophisticated governmental structures . . .

— Omo N'Oba Erediauwa, October 15, 1989

God, grant us the serenity to accept the things we cannot change; the courage to change the things we can; and the wisdom to know the difference.

— Francis of Assissi, cited per Omo N'Oba Erediauwa, March 23, 1979

llllllllllllllllllllllllllllllllllllllllll

"The Role of Tradition, Language and Culture in the Promotion of Societal Values," a Paper Presented During the Family Day Seminar Held at the National Assembly Complex, Tafawa Balewa Square, Lagos, on October 15, 1989

I thank the Honorable Minister, Federal Ministry of Youth, Sports and

Social Development, Mr. Tonye Graham Douglas, for inviting me to this seminar to present a paper on the "Role of Tradition, Language and Culture in the Promotion of Societal Values."

In a paper of this nature, there is always the temptation to attempt a definition of each of the component parts of the subject matter in order to lay an effective foundation for the analytical process. This is so particularly when each of these component parts can form a subject of meaningful analysis in its own right when considered separately and is also capable of arousing serious debate if considered together with the others. I also consider some definitions desirable to ensure that the speaker and the audience are, as much as possible, on the same wave length. Let me explain what I mean.

For the meaning of *culture*, I will go by the definition in the Federal Government's "Cultural Policy for Nigeria" wherein culture is defined as "the totality of the way of life evolved by a people in their attempts to meet the challenge of living in their environment, which gives order and meaning to their social, political, economic, aesthetic and religious norms and modes of organization thus distinguishing a people from their neighbors." Since culture contains material, institutional, philosophical and creative aspects, it is an embodiment of the attitude of people to the future of their traditional values confronted with the demands of modernity which is an essential ingredient for development and progress.

The vehicle for the expression and transmission of these cultural values is the *language*. By language we mean, accepting W. H. Goodenough's definition, "a body of standards for speech behavior, a body of organizing principles for giving order to such behavior." The point, therefore, is that language is part of culture in that it is a medium through which culture is expressed and sustained. Culture is unlikely to withstand the test of time if it is not propelled by language, and language, on the other hand, cannot be sustained if it is not passed from generation to generation, through the cultural process. This implies that both concepts are inseparable and constitute the foundation of tradition. *Tradition* comprises the beliefs, opinions and customs of a people also handed down from generation to generation and since beliefs, opinions and customs form part of the way of life and therefore the culture of a people, tradition constitutes a formidable foundation stone of the cultural structure of the community.

There is a statement by the great Sir Winston Churchill from which I always draw inspiration whenever I have occasion to speak on tradition. He said:

> I must confess myself to be a great admirer of tradition. The longer you can look back, the farther you can look forward. This is not a philosophical or political argument-any occultist will tell you this is true. The wider the span, the longer the continuity, the greater is the sense of duty in individual men and women . . .

And we often hear the expression "in the true British tradition," or something "just isn't done." All this implies that there are certain social values derived from tradition that one simply cannot trample underfoot if a stable society is to be maintained. The assertion therefore is that tradition, language and culture are closely interwoven; language is part of a people's culture as it is part of their tradition, while tradition is part of culture as culture is part of tradition, so long as it is the sum total of the beliefs, opinions and customs handed down from one generation to another. What then is the role of this interwoven concept in the promotion of societal values? In any case, what do we understand by societal value? Perhaps the easiest way out is to describe societal values as the value system of a given community. But even then that raises the question of the content of societal values or value system. The content of value system does vary from society to society although the sum total is expected to reflect the direction of preferences of the given community. It is not the intention of this paper to debate the semantics of value system or delve into the various problems associated with the value judgment of our heterogeneous communities. It is, however, obvious that our communities abound with sound societal values derived from tradition that seem to be struggling for survival against unhealthy craze for material wealth, which is a product of modernity.

At this point, let me remind you of the theme of this seminar, which is "A Disciplined Family—Foundation for Nation Building," and quickly tie up the topic of this paper to it. When we talk of societal values, we mean the values or value judgment of the people that constitute the society made up of father, mother and child(ren). It is the children who grow to become the men, women, father and mother through whom societal values are expressed, mirrored and measured. It is therefore imperative that in order to enhance the quality of societal values children must be given guidance and direction by helping them to develop a positive, creative mind, which is of far greater value and importance than all the wealth he might inherit. Children, they say, have plastic minds. They constanly record and tend to perpetuate every thought or suggestion to which they are exposed. "Recognizing this fact," said Dr. Bremer, "thoughtful parents should exercise extreme care in the mind molding of their children by permitting only uplifting good, kind, helpful, positive, constructive, loving thoughts to enter their little plastic minds." During childhood, the plastic minds can easily be shaped and formed. *In my opinion, the failure of many parents to pay attention to these details of upbringing, due to commitments of modern living, has contributed to the high rate of juvenile delinquency in this country.*

There are several areas where tradition and culture help to promote decent values in a community. Because it is often said that charity begins at home, let me begin with my own people. And because we are here under the umbrella of the Family Week celebration, I shall begin by looking at the contributions that the family, being the smallest unit of society, makes or can make to the promotion of societal values. The Bible says:

> Children, obey your parents in the Lord, for this is right. Honor thy father and mother; which is the first commandment with promise (Ephesians 6:1–2).

My English translation of the Quran has this to say on the same subject:

> Thy Lord hath decreed, that ye worship none but Him, and that ye be kind to parents. Whether one or both of them attain old age in thy life, say not to them a word of contempt, nor repel them, but address them in terms of honor" (Quran, Chapter 17:23)

The Edo people of Bendel State owe a lot of their societal values to their age-long traditions. Let us begin by a brief examination of the upbringing of children. Because of what I am, by the grace of God, I will draw a distinction between the children of the Royal Family and other children. In Benin Kingdom, as I believe it is in other parts of Nigeria with similar institution, the upbringing of children of the royal family follows certain laid down customary norms. For example, although they mixed with other children, especially in the modern age of schooling, certain types of abusive languages were forbidden to be used on them. There are "do's" and "don'ts" too many to enumerate here. From the point of view of "education," in the sense of good upbringing, children of the royal family (and they have this in common with other children) are taught first and foremost, respect for elders, and this begins with learning to give the family morning salutation.

Whether royal or otherwise, religion was very important. As soon as children were old enough to appreciate things, usually from about the age of six, they were taught about "Osanobuwa" (God, the Supreme Being), "aro Erha" (ancestral shrine) and such other deity. Not only were they encouraged to attend traditional festivals, they were taught the rudiments of the powers of these "Beings" in respect of children's pranks like telling a lie, stealing, and of course, desecrating the shrine. The fear of the supernatural punishment for evil doing was so indelibly imprinted in the young mind that the child found it virtually impossible to contemplate evil as he grows up.

Needless to say that a child who was tutored in this manner and in these matters at the tender age was bound to grow up into a well-behaved adult with not only the fear of God in him, but the realization that the good name of his family must be held sacrosanct. Can we now say that a child still has the benefit of such training when through modern living a 5-year-old child would say casually "good morning or hello daddy" or "don't be silly daddy"?

The strong belief of the Edo people in life after death and the relative powers of the spirits of the dead, and also the strong belief that God the Supreme Being has ultimate power to punish evil and reward good, to a large extent, do assist in regulating the possible excesses in the value judgment of the average Edo person. The respect for the dead is encouraged by the traditional conviction that the spirit of the living, particularly those of the existing family line, to protect and prosper the good and to punish those who misbehave. And hence Edo person will tell another: "God is seeing you"! There is the need to mention that this belief is entertained amongst the generality of the Edo people including the western educated, although there has been the tendency for it to be more prevalent amongst the traditional religionists and rural population than the new (imported) religions and rural dwellers.

This accounts for the high standard of morality and discipline in the rural community. Thus, for instance, in the truly traditional rural area even today, when an article is lost or misplaced and is picked up by someone, the finder goes to leave it in the village square or by a nearby shrub on the bush path where the owner will see and retrieve it. Because of the fear of the traditional sanction believed to derive from God and the village deity, the finder will not make away with the lost article. For the same reason the truly traditional rural society, yet unspoilt by modernity, knows nothing about bribery and corruption. Truth is sacred in the traditional society. If there is an argument or a statement is made by one person and the other person retorts by exclaiming the word "togha" and the maker of the statement replies "Ise" the latter is virtually confirming the veracity of his assertion on oath. This form of establishing veracity is stronger than the other form of simply asking: "tell the truth."

Another aspect of the Edo tradition that helps to regulate our societal behavior and value system is our traditional morning salutation. Every truly Edo family has a family salutation by which that family is identified. For instance, if someone greets "Lamogun," he or she is immediately identified as belonging to the Benin royal family. Similarly, if the salutation is "Lavbieze" it immediately identifies the family of the Iyase of Benin. It is an accepted fact that any Benin person who does not have any of the recognized family salutations is not an original Benin person: He would be said to have been "brought into Benin." It simply implies that he came in as a slave or non-indigene settler. Furthermore, persons who belong to such recognized families spoke what one may term "court language"; in other words, they are never associated with vulgar language. It is therefore customary in Edo land to strive to protect the image of one's family and deliberate efforts are made by the respective members of such family to present a good account of themselves in order to sustain the respect with which they are regarded.

This invariably imposes upon the average Edo family a measure of self-discipline that in turn helps to promote some responsible societal value judgments, firstly, within the given family; secondly, amongst the society at large. I do believe that this tradition is also prevalent amongst the other ethnic groups in the country. We know, for example, that if we meet a man who answers Mallam Dodo Tafawa Balewa or Zulu Kontagora or Aliu Mongonu, you will immediately identify him with the original founder of the village that goes by the name Tafawa Balewa (in present day Bauchi State) or Kontagora (in Niger State) or Mongonu (in Borno State). Since their parentage or place of origin is so well known, it hehoves those who answer the family name or village name to comport themselves with decorum. If the names I have used as examples fit any living persons, I ask them to excuse it and regard the reference as a worthy compliment.

Perhaps the most obvious areas where tradition and culture have assisted in the promotion of societal values is the pre-colonial governmental system. The Empires of Benin and Oyo and the great states of the Hausa-Fulani and Borno evolved a rather sophisticated administrative machinery, the bulk of which has survived till date. These Empires, like those of Dahomey, Asante and Mende, to mention a few in West Africa, welded together by tradition, language and culture, were endowed with societal values from which the modern state has benefited immensely. A case in point is the inter and intra communal self-help tradition which, though had gone through some modifications, remains to a large extent the basis of co-operation, progress and development of the modern rural community. That modern governments have learned from this age-old tradition is evidenced in their encouragement of self-help efforts amongst both urban and rural populations.

Let me mention that the value judgments of the contemporary rural community are in many ways identical to those of today's urban community. These values tend to revolve around class-consciousness with all the attending evils and paraphernalia. A notable difference, however, is the fact that while the drive for urban societal values seems to be governed by unrestricted ruthlessness, the approach of the rural population to their values is still regulated to a reasonable extent by the respect, if not fear, of tradition and culture. This in turn helps to moderate the excesses of the rural communities, create a spirit of mutual understanding amongst the inhabitants and restrict the gap between the privileged and the under-privileged in the rural set-up; much unlike the situation prevailing in urban polity which is heavily characterized by communal avarice. As Edward Shils has observed:

> In almost every aspect of their social structures the societies in which the new states are based are characterized by a gap . . . between the few rich and the mass of the poor, between modern and the traditional, between the rulers and the ruled.

At this point, I must ask for your permission to deviate slightly from the question at hand. By this, I am not suggesting that the areas mentioned above are the only areas where tradition and culture have contributed to promoting or regulating our values system. Rather, I am suggesting that our *contemporary societies have not gained enough from our traditions, not because our traditions have not much to offer, but because there has been in recent times the tendency for tradition to be underrated by modernity.* I know that my line of thinking would raise many an eye brow; so, let me explain.

Fears have been expressed about the supposed incompatibility of tradition and modernity. The advocates of modernity believe that for modernity to thrive, tradition has to be trampled upon or completely eliminated. Let me quickly explain that tradition is not against modernity and that the advocates of traditionalism are not anti-modernity. *All that the traditionalists advocate is the blending of traditional values with modernity such that modernity is afforded a solid base and structural framework as its foundation and support. It is the absence of such a foundation that has facilitated the fragility of African polity. By all means, I am not unmindful of the need for modernity. But I do also believe that for modernity to be meaningful, it must be made relevant to the culture of the community it serves. My objective is not to condemn modernity, because I believe in the co-existence of both, being personally a full-fledged product of both.* Rather, the idea is to examine the erroneous concept that tradition is inimical to modernity and that the two systems are incompatible with each other. The goal is to underline areas of mutual cooperation of both concepts to the advantage of the developmental process of the community.

In the first place, it has often been assumed that tradition is static and that the traditional society is hardly susceptible to change; secondly, that the traditional society is culturally and politically simplistic and comprise homogeneous social structure incapable of withstanding the stresses and strains associating with modernity; thirdly, that tradition and modernity pursue different objectives (namely, conservatism and radical progress) in the course of which they always conflict; and finally, that tradition weakens or at least slows down modernity and threatens the developmental process of the community.

Let me take the point one by one. Firstly, it is not true that tradition and the traditional society are static. The traditional community as it is today is itself a product of change. You will agree with me that the British culture made great impact on the Nigeria society. The same can be said of the impact of the French on her ex-colonial territories. Even then, as noted by J.R. Gusfield, "tradition has been open to change before its present encounters with the West and with purposeful, planned change." Secondly, *it is also not true that the traditional society is culturally and politically simplistic and incapable of sustaining the hazards associating with modernity. African history and politics have recorded nations and empires that were enormous in size and complex in administration. The great states of the Egyptians, Abyssinians, Asantes and Zulus as well as those of the Housa-Fulani, Yorubas and Edos, as said earlier, remain potent examples of the traditional societies established on complex foundations and possessing sophisticated governmental structures. None of those states can be said to be culturally or socially homogenous. Neither can it be said that their administration was any less complex or efficient.*

Thirdly, I also do not believe that tradition and modernity are incompatible. There exist great opportunities for the old and new cultures to co-exist and mutually adapt themselves to the processes of social changes without the old being trampled upon or thrown overboard by the new. After all, traditional religion, Islam and Christianity have successfully co-existed, just as both magic and medicine have lived side by side, patronized alternatively by the same people. "We have been increasingly aware," observed Gusfiled, "that the outcome of modernizing processes and traditional forms is often an admixture in which each derives a degree of support from the other rather than a clash of opposites." Japan provides an example of an admixture of the old and new. Japanese "monarchical feudalism" has fused with bourgeois modernity to facilitate the rapid economic growth and industrial development of that country. In Japan today, traditional structures have been successfully harnessed to produce cheap skilled manpower, while traditional norms and values have successfully legitimized societal relationships to the advantageous realization of new goals and processes. So says Robert Scalapino. Nigeria can learn from the Japanese example.

Finally, it is not true that tradition and modernity pursue different aims and objectives or that they are mutually exclusive systems. Instead, *tradition and modernity can co-exist and do co-exist not only side by side but also mutually reinforcing each other rather than being systems in perpetual conflict.* Going by our traditional norms and values which we all know, tradition can only encourage mutual trust and obligation in our inter personal relationships. Indeed, as Finkle and Gable have also noted, "the role of traditional values in the form of segmental loyalties and principles of legitimate authority are of great importance in understanding the possibilities for the occurrence of unified and stable politics at a national level."

This raises another important argument. What role can our traditional values play in ensuring a unified and stable politics at the national level? *Tradition can form the foundation for the ideological development of a nation. Tradition can provide the base for the projection of the spirit of national unification. Tradition can constitute the focal point for the effective growth of national nationalism.* Let us consider the points one by one.

Tradition can become an ideology when aspects of the past are relied upon as a tradition in grounding our present actions in some legitimating principle, and when it becomes a program of action in which it functions as justificatory base. Tradition can become the source of national unification if and when it is successfully utilized as a base for the preservation and development of culture. An example of this can be found in French speaking West Africa where the revival of indigenous traditions as a phase of nationalistic and independence movements eventually metamorphosed into the ideological development of Negritude. Finally, tradition can form the source of national nationalism if and when it is geared towards evolving a national heritage in the form of a set of continuing traditions aimed at coping with the wide gap that separate elite and mass, city and village and if it is developed into a common culture that cuts across the segmental and primordial loyalties towards national identity and consensus. Indeed, national nationalism devoid of solid cultural foundation obviously lacks the base for legitimating central authority.

From all indications, therefore, both tradition and modernity, far from being outright opposites, actually work for the same objectives of national unity and consciousness. Modernity stands for national ideology, unity and national nationalism, the same position as tradition. Thus, since we cannot easily separate tradition from modernity and vice verse, it is only appropriate that the desire to be modern and the desire to preserve tradition should be synchronized to operate jointly in the developmental process of the community. As I have mentioned in another address, these desires functioning as ideologies are not always in conflict; that the quest for modernity depends upon and often finds support in the ideological upsurge of traditionalism. That being the case, the issue is not so much that of overcoming tradition, but of finding ways of synthesizing and blending tradition and modernity. India provides a good example of this.

It is obvious that the greater population of Nigeria, for instance, reside in the rural or sub-urban environments and practise societal relationships based principally on our traditional values. The communal co-existence of our rural population also derives largely from the age-old polity of mutual assistance traceable to functional governance by example. Today, our spirit of mutual personal and communal relationship has given way to individualism, and greed has taken over from the spirit of mutual exchange. For us to recover at least some part of our lost traditional values, there is the need to re-evaluate our value system.

The undermining of our cultural heritage and value system has led to an erosion of the foundation of mutual co-operation for which the African society was well known. The point I am making is that the problems of Nigeria are indeed pivoted on the abuse of our traditional values. I am not arguing that our traditional society never experienced some of the vices that have crippled our contemporary societies. All I am postulating is that while our traditional systems successfully shunned, isolated and invariably suppressed those vices, our modern governments seem overwhelmed by the very vices created by their own value system. And since the majority of the Nigerian population still live under traditional set-up, it is only appropriate that a measure of traditional values is infused into our modern governmental process in order to give it at least part of the human face it once possessed. That is why I was thrilled to read the 4th section of the preamble to the Cultural Policy for Nigeria, which states thus:

"When therefore we talk of self-reliance, self-sufficiency and a national identity as the core of our national development objectives, we are referring to culture as the fountain spring of all policies, whether educational, social, political or economical. The strategies of national development would thus depend on the understanding of the culture, the adaptation of its elements for political, educational and economic development, as well as its strengths for social integration and development."

There is no doubt that tradition, language and culture have made note-worthy contributions to our societal values, either through promoting or regulating them. Traditional beliefs and cultural values do help to moderate the value judgments of the society. We have given an example, for instance, with the traditional belief in life after death and in the powers of the dead to influence the destiny of the living and how this belief regulates the behavioral pattern of the traditional community. The influence of tradition, language and culture on societal values seems to be more prominent in the rural set-up than in the urban centers most probably because rural environments are more traditionally and culturally homogenous than the cities. What is important, in any case, is that tradition, language and culture together constitute a resource from which our societal values draw their strength.

Having said all that, we come to what I fear must be regarded as sensitive aspect of this subject. Can we discuss tradition and culture in this context without mentioning, if only briefly, the role of religion (as part of culture) in the promotion of societal values? I would think not. The Christian Bible and the Muslim Quran are replete with the teachings of the masters relevant to societal values. The traditional religion also has some principles in this regard. The whole of the Ten Commandments in the Christian Bible come readily to mind. My English translation of the Quran has something similar, thus:

> Come, I will rehearse
> What God hath (really)
> Prohibited you from: join not
> anything as equal with Him;
> Be good to your parents;
> Kill not your children
> On a plea of want—we
> Provide sustenance for you
> and for them;—come not
> Nigh to shameful deeds
> Whether open or secret
> Take not life, which God
> Hath made sacred . . . (Quran, Chapter 6: 151)

The traditional religion simply says that God or the deity of the community will deal with the person who commits this or that abomination (or sin as I believe the Christians would term it). In view of the special position that the religious bodies, especially the Christian and Muslim religions, hold in the society, one must urge the adherents to tighten their belt and join hands with the government to promote societal values by propagating more purposefully the teaching of their founders, rather than rocking the state boat every time in head-on collision. "Our religion, whether it be Jewish, Christian, Moslem, Animist, Buddhist, Confucianist, Taoist, Hindus, Shintoist, or others, is nothing more than a label unless we utilize its teachings of goodness for the attainment of the ideal life in self," said Dr. Newton Bremer. "if men are so wicked with religion what would they be without it"? Asked Benjamin Franklin.

Conclusion

A paper of this nature on a topic like this does not actually desire a conclusion because almost all the postulations are in themselves some conclusions. All the same, we must conclude. I apologize I could not be more brief. Tradition, language and culture are closely intertwined and they together represent the sum total of the way of life of a people. They together constitute not only the foundation of our societal values, but also the vehicle for transporting such values from generation to generation. Like tradition and culture, societal values are subject to change and in the case of Nigeria, there had been in recent times a rising tendency for such values to be devoid of human face in the name of modernity. For our societal value to represent the aspirations of the majority of Nigerians, there is the need to infuse a measure of our tradition and culture into our governmental system.

Rather than accept the growing norm that tradition and modernity are parallel concepts, areas of possible joint utilization of both in the interest of promoting our societal values should be exploited. Here, the traditional institution can be made to play a role. And the religious bodies (Christianity, Islam and the traditional) should join hands with government in this task by intensifying and spreading the teachings of their Founders.

I now end by leaving with you, if I may, for your reflection, some words of the other Master regarding the Social Duties of Man which, I suggest, should be taught to children in every home. First is BENEVOLENCE. The master teaches that if we reflect on all the good things the Creator has bestowed on us, then it becomes the duty of everyone to be a friend to mankind as it is also in our own interest that man should be friendly to us. Secondly, we must remember that the peace of society depends on JUSTICE and the happiness of the individual depends on the safe enjoyment of all the possessions. Thirdly, it is written that happy is the man who has sown in his breast the seeds of benevolence, the product of which are CHARITY and LOVE. Then there is GRATITUDE, and we are told that a grateful person acknowledges his obligation with cheerfulness, and looks on his benefactor with love and esteem. Lastly, is SINCERITY. It is written that the tongue of the sincere is rooted in his heart, and hypocrisy and deceit have no place in his words. He is confident with himself.

Ladies and Gentlemen, may I, at this point, thank you for lending me your attention and may God bless you all.

||||||||||||||||||||||||||||||||||||||||||||||

Excerpts from an Address Delivered on the Occasion of His Coronation as the 38th OBA of Benin on March 23rd, 1979

. . . We are entering the beginning of a new era. We are a great believer in tradition, and it is our intention to re-establish the tradition of our land. If we may quote Churchill again, (for the benefit of those who have acquired European education) even Churchill, with all his stature, saw nothing but good in tradition. For he once admitted: "I must confess myself to be a great admirer of tradition. The longer you can look back the farther you can look forward. This is not a philosophical or political argument; any occultist will tell you this is true. The wider the span, the longer the continuity, the greater is the sense of duty in individual men and women . . ."

Coming home to our domestic matters we like to say it with some emphasis that we are essentially traditionalist, and we shall do everything in our power, including even invoking the assistance of our ancestors, to uphold our custom and tradition. We, therefore, like to make this strong appeal to all Edo land to cooperate by respecting our customs and traditions. We realize, of course, that we now live in a modern world; many of our people, young and old, have acquired western education and have traveled far and wide. This ancient city is now a state government capital and has, therefore, become a cosmopolitan city. It is, therefore, obvious that we cannot really always insist on the observance of all our customs and traditions; this would be unwise in our contemporary world. For that reason, if and when circumstances so dictate, we will have due regard always for the law made by the government. You all should, therefore, join us in a short prayer that we cherish very much; it is that God may *grant us the serenity to accept the things we cannot change; the courage to change the things we can; and the wisdom to know the difference, Amen.*

Let us hasten at this point to draw attention to one matter of custom that is very dear to our heart and has been causing us concern. This is the impunity with which our sacred land areas and ancient shrines have been desecrated by the unscrupulous money-hunter. In the course of preparations for the present ceremonies we discovered, for the first time, how many of such sacred place have been built upon. We have had difficulty in gaining access to some of them that are required for these ceremonies. We intend to take inventory of such parcels of land and request the state government to assist us to protect them.

We must say a few words to our youths. There is the saying that old men see vision and young men dream dreams. A great many of our old men have left us, and we have all around us young men with their dreams. So much has been said and seen about juvenile delinquency, about anti-social activities, and about all forms of vices generally. We belong to the school of thought, however small it may be, which believes that all the anti-social activities we are witnessing today stem from the fact that the so-called western education has led our society to throw over-board our customs and traditions and the sanctions that go with them. In the name of western education, children nowadays no longer have respect for their fathers and elders; they hardly have time or remember to even give the customary morning salutation which in Edo has always been a constant reminder of one's birth and ancestry; in the good old days, young persons kept away from mischief or violation of the customs of the land because they feared that the gods would be angry or that the customary sanction would be imposed by the elders. Young men nowadays believe that these are now things of the past and that they have no effect on the so-called educated persons.

Let it be borne in mind, in the interest of all concerned, that customary sanctions are still there and very much alive and active. The Edo adage "Ota ihen khe Ole," which is another way of describing the law of retribution, is worth remembering constantly by our young persons. So, we appeal to all parents, particularly the educated ones, to acquaint themselves with Edo customs and pass the knowledge to their children. This can be done without prejudice to Christian or Muslim teaching and without the fear of exposing oneself as uneducated. In fact, we would venture to say that it is no education at all if all that it does is to make a man forsake or ignore his own culture, which in effect is what custom and tradition amount to.

Chapter 3

On Traditional Rulership
and the Roles of Traditional Rulers

What I advocate is that traditional rulers be given protection in the Constitution so that they can perform their traditional functions according to the dictates of the community's customs. The kind of constitutional protection I have in mind is the type given to the members of the Judiciary and Auditors-General. The Constitution does not allow them to be pushed around.

— Omo N'Oba Erediauwa, April 25, 1983

We firmly believe that in any society the monarchy or traditional ruler is the hub that holds up the wheel, the tap root of the system. You may modify the role of the traditional institution but its total abolition cannot but have serious repercussions.

— Omo N'Oba Erediauwa, March 23, 1979

‖‖‖‖‖‖‖‖‖‖‖‖‖‖‖‖‖‖‖‖‖‖‖‖‖‖‖‖‖‖‖‖‖‖

"The Evolution of Traditional Rulership in Nigeria," a Lecture Delivered at the Conference on the Role of Traditional Rulers in the Governance of Nigeria, Held under the Auspices of the University of Ibadan Institute of African Studies, 11 September, 1984

It gives me great pleasure to have the opportunity to participate at this your conference which is to examine the position of traditional Rulers in the governance of Nigeria. There have been similar seminars/conferences in recent times in which this same subject had been discussed but I consider the one opening today of particular significance, coming on just when the Federal Government committee on the Review of Local Government is at work. The work of that committee will be of special interest to traditional rulers because of the inclusion in its terms of reference an examination of the position of traditional rulers. With this conference discussing the same subject from a different angle, it is to be hoped that the Local Government Review Committee will wish to read the conclusions of the present conference.

I must plead for your perseverance to hear me out. I tried ever so hard to keep within the usual 60 minutes, but I found I will not be doing justice to myself nor to those who invited me here if I unduly compressed myself. I must in the circumstance ask you to give me the better part of your two hours for me to say my piece.

I will speak on the subject, "The Evolution of Traditional Rulership in Nigeria." I have spoken, and written, so much on various topics relating to Traditional Rulership in Nigeria in the recent past that I begin to wonder if I will not be boring some of you on this occasion with those facts or views which you must have heard from me or read from some of my papers. If any of you belong to this group, I ask you to accept my apology for the inevitable situation in which I have found myself. You will agree with me that unless I have come about new facts that disprove what I said or wrote in the past I am bound to repeat myself if I have to speak on the same or similar subject. For instance, I delivered a lecture titled "The Role of Traditional Rulers in Local Government" at the University of Ife under the auspices of that University's Department of Public Administration on the 25th of April, 1983. In that talk, I gave my views on the definition of "traditional ruler" and traced his roles before, during and after the colonial period. I submitted a memorandum in 1983 on the same subject to a Conference of Traditional Rulers drawn from all the States of the Federation. There was also the talk I delivered in 1982 in the University of Benin, titled "Tradition in the Service of Modern Society in the Nigerian Context," in which I dealt with some aspects of the roles of Traditional Rulers in Government. In those papers, I said a number of things which I cannot avoid repeating here. I propose to treat my topic for today under the following headings:

(a) Who is a traditional ruler?

(b) Origin of the traditional ruler.

(c) The role of the traditional ruler in the Community and in government.

(d) The future of the institution.

DEFINITION OF TRADITIONAL RULER

4. In order to put my talk in the proper perspective, I shall begin by describing the person I will refer to as a Traditional Ruler. In one of the papers I presented to the National Conference of Traditional Rulers that took place in Kaduna in November, 1983, I defined a Traditional Ruler as follows:

> Traditional Ruler means the traditional head of an ethnic Community whose stool conferred the highest traditional authority on the incumbent since the time before the beginning of British rule.

Before British rule, Traditional Rulers were known by various indigenous titles which when translated to English aggregated to the word "King" in many cases, "President" in some and "Chief Priest" in others. In Benin, and all over Yoruba land, he was and is still known as Oba; in the Northern parts of Nigeria he was and is still referred to as Sultan, Emir, Shehu, Etsu, etc. Elsewhere in Bendel State, he was an Obi, Ovie, Onojie or Okpala Uku. Anyone who was not a Traditional head when the British rule was established ought not now to claim to be one in the true sense of the word. He would be a British creation, a British agent for the fulfillment of British administrative policy. He would not be truly serving the needs of his people's culture and tradition. But because a place has been carved out for him by the British, and his people have got used to his headship position, a tradition has developed through the years which could bring such a person to the fold of Traditional Ruler.

5. These were some of the factors that weighed on the minds of the traditional rulers at the 1983 Kaduna Conference that led us to formulate a definition that was unanimously adopted as follows:

> A Traditional Ruler is the person who by virtue of his ancestry occupies

the throne or stool of an area and who has been appointed to it in accordance with the customs and traditions of the area and whose throne has been in existence before the advent of the British in Nigeria. The area over which he and his forebears before him have ruled or reigned must have at least a Native Authority created for it in 1910 or the date of the introduction of Native Authority to the area concerned provided that in the case of the former Eastern Region of Nigeria, traditional stools established according to the custom and tradition of the people and recognized by the Governments in those areas and occupied at the date of this resolution will not by virtue of this definition be disqualified; provided also that in respect of other parts of the Federation of Nigeria, traditional stools similarly established prior to the 1st of October, 1979, will not by virtue of this definition be disqualified.

This, then, shall be our definition of the Traditional Ruler. A little reflection will, I believe, indicate the varied situations that this definition tried to accommodate.

ORIGIN OF TRADITIONAL RULERSHIP

6. To deal with this subject, which is wide and varied in the context of Nigeria, one has to start from somewhere. I have, therefore, decided to start from the Benin Kingdom where I come from, which I know best, and work from there outwards. Traditional Rulership in Nigeria has no common origin; it is as diversified as the Country's resources! Each title has its own origin which is different from the other. To be able to treat the subject successfully one would need to compile the list of all the traditional ruler titles in Nigeria and trace the origin of each. (Bendel State alone has as many as 185 of them!) Even if one had the time and means to do this, it would still be an impossible task because the origins of the oldest titles are shrouded in myths and legends, some of which are sometimes contentious. Take, for instance, the following account of the origin of Kingship in Benin Kingdom which is narrated almost by rote by most Benin adults:

According to our traditional history that evolved out of our ritualistic beliefs, this land of Edo is the origin of the world. It was founded by the first Oba of Benin who was the youngest son of the Supreme God. When the Supreme God decided to send his children to the world, He gave an option to each of them to choose what to take away. At this time (as the Holy Book came to confirm at a much later age) the universe was all water and no land. One of the children chose the sign for wealth; the other one took wisdom (or knowledge), another one chose medicine (mystical knowledge).

When it came to the turn of the youngest child, there was apparently nothing left for him to choose; but after looking around the whole place, he saw a snail shell which his senior brothers had overlooked because it was very dirty. He took that, broke it open only to find that it contained ordinary sand. The Father commended him for his intuition and told him that on getting to the world he should empty the shell in any place of his choice and the place would be his. He emptied it in the area that is now Edo (Benin) and the whole place became land. His other brother who had been hovering around for somewhere to rest then came round to request for a portion of land to settle on. These other brothers represent the three shades of "ebo" or "white men"—as we call them—who occupy the rest of the world. That is why one of the attributes of the Oba of Benin is that he owns land up to "evbo—ebo," meaning European country. And this is also why the earth features so prominently as part of our "coronation rituals." (note—the words in parenthesis are mine).

7. Although some contemporary historians claim that the Benin (Edo) people migrated from the Sudan, the truth is that no scientific historical explanation has been found to account for how the ethnic group known as the Edo (Benin) people came to be where they are today. This is an area I personally would like to see some more work done.

8. Generally speaking, Traditional Rulership is as old as the community to which it relates. Although, as earlier observed, the origin may differ from community to community, there seems to be one feature common to all, and one can use the feature in the Benin Kingdom to illustrate. What came to be known as the Benin Kingdom did not begin its existence as a kingdom in the sense of its being headed by a King or a Traditional Ruler as is known

today. It began as a conglomeration of villages, each of which was headed by the oldest man in the community which we refer to as Odionwere or village head. But, even then, the village did not begin with the village head but with a cluster of family compounds each of which was headed by the householder or head of the family. I believe this is the pattern of origin of Traditional Rulership in many parts of the country. As time went on, several of the villages joined together for purposes of security against external aggression and for commerce, and the most powerful of the old people automatically became the head of the group. This was what happened in Benin, and the first to emerge as such a leader, almost immediately assumed the position of a King, for by the wisdom he was supposed to have exhibited in adjudicating on matters he was described as being like a king in heaven or a king from heaven (Oyevbogie Noriso). This is the origin of the title "Ogiso" which came to be the title of the earliest Benin Kings, before the advent of Oranmiyan.

9. Another important Traditional Ruler whose origin deserves examination is the Oduduwa of Ife whose origin is also shrouded in myths or legend. He is believed to be the father of the principal rulers of the Yorubaland, the father of Oranmiyan who was the father of Eweka I of Benin, and who was also the founder and the first Alaafin of Oyo Kingdom. Ife traditional history says Oduduwa descended from heaven (in a like manner to the Edo account). Some modern historians say that the great Oduduwa was a fugitive from the Moslems of the Middle East and that he came to settle in what is present-day Ile-Ife. We in Benin believe, and there are historical landmarks for such belief, that the person whom the Yorubas call Oduduwa was the fugitive Prince Ekaladerhan, son of the last Ogiso of Benin by name Ogiso Owodo; he found his way to what is now Ile-Ife after gaining freedom from his executioners and wandering for years through the forests. It was after the demise of his father and when, in the interregnum, Evian, and later his son, Ogiamien, tried to assume the kingship that those who knew that Ekaladerhan was alive organized a search party to fetch him. It was this search party that emerged at Ile-Ife and discovered Ekaladerhan, known then to the people of Ile-Ife as Oduduwa and already enjoying the status of a king. After failing to persuade him

to return with them to Benin, they succeeded in getting him to send his son Oranmiyan to rule in Benin.

10. This leads us immediately to the origin of kingship of Oyo Kingdom. Oranmiyan's stay in Benin was brief. Our own account is that he returned to his father in Ife. His father then told him that since he had been a king in his own right, it was improper for both of them to live in Ife. He then sent him to rule over Oyo where he became the first Alaafin from where he ruled over Ife after the demise of Oduduwa. I am aware of another account which says that Orianmiyan's emergence in Oyo was the failure of his attempt to march a punitive expedition to the Middle East to avenge the expulsion of his father. This other account, of course, we in Benin do not accept, and I doubt whether it is acceptable to Oyo people.

11. We have so far discussed the origin of Kingship in Benin, Ife and Oyo and indicated the link between these kingdoms. Let us now look at Lagos which also has an age-long kingship and which also had historical link with us in Benin.

OBA OF LAGOS

12. There is a lot of traditional history at both the Benin and Lagos ends relating to the origin of what is now Lagos, its ruler and its connection with Benin. But, perhaps to avoid inadequacies and controversy which the academics claim surround traditional history, we may like to hear what some modern historians have to say on this subject. Robert S. Smith, in his book *Kingdoms of the Yoruba*, after examining the early history of some principal Yoruba towns, especially in and around Oyo, and the westward expansion in the 17th century of Benin Kingdom with its number of subject towns on or near to the coast, which included Lagos, went on to say this about Lagos in particular:

> Its name reflects its past: to the Yoruba it is Eko, deriving probably from the farm (oko) of the earliest settlers, though alternatively—or additionally—it may be the Benin word (eko) for a war-camp . . .

We say "Eko" is a Benin word that means "camp."

13. After describing the activities of the armies of Benin under Oba Orhogbua, culminating in his arrival at what is now Lagos, Smith went on to add:

> Some time later the Oba appointed a ruler for Lagos to represent the interest of Benin and to forward tribute there. The man chosen is named in both Lagos and Benin tradition as Ashipa.

Smith says that by Lagos account this Ashipa was an Isheri Chief, while the Benin account says Ashikpa was a grandson of the Oba of Benin. We shall come to this later. Smith was, however, satisfied that Benin has established its ascendancy in Lagos and had founded a dynasty there at some period before 1700. The dynasty's dependence on Benin, Smith found, was emphasized by the appointment of another chief, the Eletu Odibo, who alone had the right to crown the Oba and who in early times probably maintained close connection with Benin. (Eletu Odibo is a corruption of the Edo equivalent Olotu Odibo).

14. G. T. Stride and C. Ifeka, in their book *Peoples and Empires of West Africa* have this to say on the same subject:

> Oba Orhogbua was clearly a strong warrior for he enforced tribute payments from all parts of the empire and in the mid-1550's conquered all the coastal lands up to Lagos where he left a permanent garrison. Traditional history in Lagos says that their first Oba, the Eleko of Eko, was a son of Oba Orhogbua of Benin.

15. It will be seen, therefore, that even if we were to disregard traditional history, there is enough material from modern historians to confirm the fact that what is now Lagos was founded by an Oba of Benin who also gave it its first ruler. But we really cannot disregard traditional history. In Benin tradition, and we believe the same of Yoruba and other ethnic groups in this court, one way to establish that an event in traditional history did occur is by the type of anecdote or adage that evolves from that event. Thus, for instance, we the Edo people say that "Orhogbua gb'Olague, ona y'ukpe

abekpen z'umwen rie Edo," meaning that Oba Orhogbua defeated Olague and used the sword to bring his salt to Benin. This is in allusion to the exploits of Oba Orhogbua defeated Olague and used the sword to bring his salt to Benin. This is in allusion to the exploits of Oba Orhogbua while in his camp (eko) from where he overran the place known as Mahin with its ruler whom the Benin people nicknamed Olague. There Orhogbua discovered the common rock salt and brought it to Benin who thereby tasted it for the first time.

16. Now the name "Ashipa" has featured quite prominently (and rightly too) in the history of Lagos. After the Oba Orhogbua returned to Benin from his "eko," he appointed a commander or an administrator, who was called "Aisikpa" to look after the skeleton troop left in the camp (eko) until he returned again from Benin. He could no longer return having seen the situation at home. The name "Aisikpa" was specially chosen for the administrator to commemorate the Oba's many years sojourn at Eko and it is simply a contraction of a Benin phrase, "Aisikpa—hienvborre" which means "people do not desert their homeland." This is how Aisikpa, whom the Yoruba now call Ashipa, came into Lagos (Eko) history. "Eko" is still there as the traditional Benin name for Lagos; Ashipa has been retained as a senior traditional chieftaincy title while his descendants now retain the modern name of "Oba of Lagos."

17. We have taken examples of the origins of kingship from Bendel State and the Yoruba areas, pointing out how they are shrouded in myths or legends or uncertainty. I like us now to take a look at the Northern parts of the country and examine some of the Emirates. We have extensive accounts in Michael Crowder's *The Story of Nigeria* and *Studies in the History of the Sokoto Caliphate*, edited by Y. B. Usman, both of which I believe many of you have devoured! Of the Kanem-Borno Empire, Crowder says "The future empire of Kanem-Borno began to emerge some time in the 9th or 10th centuries A.D. . . . The origins of Kanem are very shadowy. Arabs writings in the 9th century . . . refer to their inhabitants as Zaghawa . . ." The zaghawa to whom early Arab writing refer seem to have imposed themselves on the inhabitants of Kanem and established a number of small states. One of these was eventually to dominate the whole of Kanem. In

the 10th century the Arab writer al–Muhallabi records that the Zaghawa consisted of many tribes ruled by a "divine" king who was worshipped by his people and regarded as the giver of life and death. He was also thought to exist without food. He imposed taxes on the peasantry and was entitled to their goods and animals for use as he wished. The ruler was the "King of Kanem." Kanem-Borno was later to expand and be transformed into the new kingdom (and empire) of Borno.

18. West of this kingdom, in the parts that are commonly referred to as Hausaland, we have another example of the legendary origin of kingship. Those of you who have been to Daura (as I have done) will no doubt recollect the traditional history of the famous well. Crowder narrates the story thus:

> Legend has it that Bayajidda, son of Abdullahi, King of Baghda, having quarreled with his father, left home and journeyed into Borno and thence to Daura. There he killed a dreaded snake which prevented the people from using their only well for water except on Fridays. The Queen of Daura in gratitude married Bayajidda, and their son, called Bawo, succeeded his father and had six sons who became kings of Daura, Kano, Zaria, Gobir, Katsina and Rano.

Crowder was quick to point out though that there were other versions of this legend and origin of all of them still remains obscure. They nevertheless explain how kingship arose in those parts of Hausaland. What is significant, however, in the context of this talk as regards family unit I referred to earlier is what Crowder went further to say about these new States:

> Prior to the rise of States, it seems that most of the peoples in Hausaland and the plain of Borno lived in small hamlets and villages, some of which were walled for defensive purpose. The family was the most important element in these communities. But leadership emerged where work that could not be organized by one family alone had to be undertaken. Thus where large-scale farming activities had to be arranged, a Sarkin noma, king of farmers, would be responsible. Likewise there was "father of hunting."

Reading from the papers on the "History of the Sokoto Caliphate," one

finds that before the advent of Shehu Uthman Dan Fodio and the establishment of the caliphate, the areas known as Hausaland had "rulers" of a
sort, most of whom were "pagans." The success of the caliphate, or Uthman
Dan Fodio's mission, depended on the one hand on the Shehu's program of
conversion of the pagan rulers to Islam, and, on the other hand, the support that the Hausa peasantry gave to a movement that attacked what was
regarded as an arbitrary feudal system and imposition of excessive taxes.

19. If we go to the Eastern parts of Nigeria, one's mind immediately goes
to the great Jaja of Opobo, and the Obong of Calabar. These are examples
of kingship that have evolved from powerful family heads as chief priest of
a cult or powerful and successful trader. Elsewhere in the former Eastern
Region, especially in what came to be known as the Igbo heartland, where
the institution of traditional rulership was virtually nonexistent, the British
Administration introduced a class that came to be known as "warrant chiefs"
to function in much the same way as the Obas and the Emirs.

20. In many other cases, Traditional Rulership is the natural consequence
of the desire of a trusted and reliable person for their protection against
enemies, preservation of their customs and traditions and the progress of
the community. Some rulers emerge as a popular choice of their people
because of some qualities which distinguish them from others within
their community, as we have found in the case of the Ogiso. Some have
mystical powers on which the community depends for their general well-
being and progress. The great Oduduwa falls into this category. His was
the case of the fugitive Prince whom the Benin people called Ekaladerhan
and Ife people called Oduduwa, for it is known that his great mystical
powers brought him on the ascendancy over the community. There are
cases where a settlement was started by a family and the head of the family
plays the role of a ruler. His children or brothers could disperse to found
other settlements. The head of each group takes the role of their ruler. The
Community begins and grows with the ruler. Some settlements founded
by brothers are ruled in turn by the brothers according to their ages and in
such a case, succession has remained by rotation among the descendants of
the brothers up to date. Examples of this abound in Yorubaland. In some
cases, rulership rotates among the quarters or villages that form a clan. It

could be the oldest person in the community that rules and the age could either be natural age or age determined by date of performing age group ceremony. There are many examples of this in Bendel State. In some other places, rulership emanates from conquest. The captain of the conquering troops stayed to rule the conquered place or the conquering ruler leaves someone to rule and collect tributes for him. Examples of this abound in the Northern Emirates. When you examine all the traditional rulership titles. In Nigeria today, you will find that each has its origin from one or more of the circumstances described above.

THE ROLE OF TRADITIONAL RULERS

21. Having described in general terms the origin of traditional rulership in Nigeria and specifically the rulership in Benin and the associated places—Oyo, Ife, Lagos, and some Northern Emirates—I shall proceed to examine the roles of Traditional Rulers in our society. I will examine these as they were before the colonization of Nigeria by Britain, during British rule, and since Independence under civil rule and Military rule. I will also consider what roles Traditional Rulers can and should play in future.

PRE-COLONIAL PERIOD.

22. On this subject, I prefer, on this occasion, to quote verbatim from the "Report of an Investigation into the Role of Chiefs in the Midwestern State" conducted by the Administrative Research and Support Division of the Military Governor's Office from 1968–1974. The report is popularly referred to as the Partridge Report after Mr. D. B. Partridge, C.B.E. who was the Director of the Research work. Paragraphs 46–49 of the Report run thus:

"46. The traditional functions of Traditional Rulers can be classified into five broad categories, namely, Kingly or Presidential, Religious, Legislative, Administrative, and Judicial. The emphasis between these broad groupings varies, to some extent, according to the type of headship held i.e. whether it is monarchical, gerontocratic, etc. in nature, but in most cases functions falling within all these categories can be seen. Indeed, traditionally, there was little or no division between the various branches of government, and all were performed by the Traditional Ruler with the assistance, to a lesser or greater degree, of a traditional council comprising elders, subordinate title or office holders, or Clan functionaries, etc.

47. The Kingly or Presidential functions are most evident in headships which are more monarchical than segmentary (or gerontocratic) in nature. One example is the personal bestowal of subordinate chieftaincy titles which occurs, for instance, in the traditional systems of Benin, Ika, Itsekiri and Ishan. No matter the type, however, a primary function of all Traditional Rulers is to provide a living expression of the identity of their people and an embodiment of their common interests. One aspect of this function is what is described as being "the father" of all their people. Other functions which fall within this category include presiding at traditional council meetings, acting as the chief representative of their people and, as previously mentioned, bestowing subordinate titles in a monarchical system or, in other system, giving final approval of subordinate office or title holders.

48. The **Religious or Priestly** functions constitute a vital part of the traditional role of most traditional rulers and are closely connected with the "kingly" function and are, indeed, in many cases, indistinguishable from them. It is, in fact, their ability to control or call upon divine or supernatural forces which, in the past, has been the major mainstay of most headships and the most important source of their power and authority. This religious content of most headships seems to be expressed in one or two ways, either the actual person of the title holder is sacred or divine, or he is the chief priest or propitiator of one of the major deities in his area of authority. The basic concept, in either case, is the belief that either the actual person or the ruler is equated with the good or bad fortunes of his people, or that, as the Chief Priest of the most important deity in his area, he has a vital role to play in ensuring their general well-being. These religious duties include the fixing of dates for the various festivals which form an important part of the life of the people, e.g. the new yam and new year festivals.

49. The **Legislative** functions include the making of new laws and regulations, normally with the advice and consent of a traditional council. Under the **Administrative** and **Executive** headings fall such duties as the general maintenance of law and order, acting as the chief custodian of communal lands

and natural resources, e.g. forest produce, the reception and entertainment of distinguished visitors, and acting, in general, as the Clan's chief representative both internally and externally. Finally, the **Judicial** functions, which, traditionally, were a major part of the duties of headship, involved acting as the final judicial authority and the chief arbitrator in minor disputes."

I consider these findings to be applicable to most Traditional Rulers in the country before the Colonial period.

23. Two other researchers, Stride and Igbafe in their work "People and Empires of West Africa" have the following to say on the same subject regarding the Old Benin Empire:

The empire was governed on the three levels. The Oba, who became an increasingly secluded and sacred figure during the seventeenth century, was at the top of the hierarchy. On the second level, there were the chiefs who formed the State Council in Benin City. The third level of government consisted of tribute units. A tribute unit corresponded roughly, but not exactly, to a village or petty chiefdom. Each unit was headed by an overlord who represented the interests of his people to the Oba, and told the people what the Oba's wishes were. However, the overlord did not live in his tribute unit but, instead, was represented there by a faithful servant. Overlords received deputations at the capital. Each overlord was appointed by the Oba. The Queen Mother, the Oba's first son and chiefs in Benin were usually heads of tribute units. The Oba had the right to re-distribute tribute units to prevent any chief from becoming too rich and influential, and to reward any trusty supporters. It was an overlord's duty to transmit appeals from the people in his unit to the Oba's court. He also had to organize the yearly or twice-yearly collection of tribute of yams, palm oil, meat livestock and other foodstuffs to the Oba.

The same researchers found a similar pattern in respect of the old Oyo Empire. I also learnt in the course of my tour of the Northern parts of Nigeria and from discussions during the Traditional Rulers Conference in Kaduna in November, 1983 that the same pattern was existing in varying degrees in the Hausa area of the North before the advent of the British rule.

24. So you see that in pre-colonial times the traditional ruler of the caliber we are discussing was already at the head of a well-organized system of government. In that position he was the sole authority: he was the executive, the legislative and the judiciary. He had the power of life and death. It is a well-known fact that the pattern I have just described was obtainable in many parts of this country before 1914 and this was the pattern that Sir Frederick Lugard polished into his "Indirect Rule System."

THE COLONIAL ERA (1900–1954)

25. And so we move to the Colonial era. During this period, traditional rulers functioned in Government principally at the local level. Between 1900 and 1914, the organs of local government in the area now known as Bendel State were the Native Courts which combined executive with judicial functions. In both membership and area of authority, the British did not, in all cases, follow strictly the existing traditional pattern of government although they preferred, where it existed, to appoint the true traditional authorities to these courts. With the amalgamation of the Southern and Northern Provinces of Nigeria in 1914, the enactment of the Native Court Ordinance of 1914, and the Native Authority Ordinance of 1916, the Indirect Rule System was introduced. Many of you know that the essence of the Lugard (Indirect Rule) system was what the phrase implied; the British Administrators administered the community indirectly through the recognized (or paramount) head of the community. Thus, all the organs, as I had earlier described in the case of Benin, were allowed to remain but the Oba's sole authority immediately became curtailed (but only slightly): because he was now made responsible and accountable to the British Resident Administrator. But the situation was not intolerable at all for, as we shall see, the traditional ruler enjoyed far greater respect and recognition then than he came to do in the hands of his own people after Independence.

26. With the introduction of indirect rule by colonial administrations, the traditional ruler still held on to all his pre-colonial roles except that he lost his sovereignty to the British Monarch and operated under the guidance (or as the masters put it, the advice) of the British officials. Although the Oba had lost the power of life and death he wielded over his subjects,

he still exercised a greater measure of his executive, judicial and legislative powers, in all aspects of local administration, particularly in matters of customs and traditions which the British Administrators recognized could not be wiped off outright. Many of you will recollect that in judicial matters the Oba (or Traditional Ruler) was both a court of first instance as well as Court of Appeal, and appeal lay from Oba's Court to the Resident. The new situation did not affect his legislative powers, for custom was custom and the Oba's role here was to ensure its observance. His executive powers were affected only to the extent that he did nothing in conflict with the British Colonial Government policy. It was the "Sole Authority" that gave way to the Native Authority which subsequently gave way to our modern form of local Government.

PERIOD OF TRANSITION TO INDEPENDENCE (1954–1960)

27. That then was the position of Traditional Rulers up to the eve of attainment of Independence in 1960. But we must remember that Independence started creeping in from about 1956; the Native Authority was gradually fading away until the British type of Local Government was imported for us to absorb hook line and sinker. In the then Western Nigeria, the principal effect of the law was to replace the Native Authority, which was basically the traditional ruler-in-council, with the British type representative local government. This law changed, drastically, the role of the traditional ruler and his chiefs in Local Government for it provided, inter alia, that members who must be holders of recognized chieftaincy titles.

28. The then Western Region Chiefs Law made no distinction between traditional rulers and chiefs appointed by them; they were grouped together and classified as "recognized" or "minor" chiefs. The provisions in the Local Government Law for a recognized chief to be appointed as President or as a Traditional Member of a Council could therefore not be said to have created any specific roles for the traditional ruler as such roles could also be assigned to his chief, if recognized by Government. Even in those cases, they were mere ceremonial Presidents as they could not participate in the deliberations of the Councils unless they were invited by their Councils to preside over the particular meetings at which they were present. (Vide Section 39 (2) of

the Local Government Law, Cap. 68 of the Laws of Western Region.) As if to ensure that Traditional Rulers were excluded from active participation in local administration, the Local Government Law was amended by Western Region Legal Notice 40 of 1959 by the addition of sub-section (6) to Section 29 thereof under which no traditional ruler (or any other recognized chief) appointed as President of the Council could be appointed Chairman of the Council whereas any other person appointed as President under sub-section (2) of Section 17 of the same law, could be appointed.

29. Apart from presiding over council meeting when invited to do so by resolution of Council, the other roles left for the Traditional Ruler as President of the Council were the issuing of the letter of appointment of the Chairman within 24 hours after his election by the Council and power to summon a meeting of the Council. (Vide Section 30(h) and 33(1) of Cap. 68 of the Law of Western Nigeria.) These changes which were introduced during the period of decolonization (between 1952 and 1960) were the outcome of the pressures mounted by our politicians for more representative and democratic government. In addition to these minor roles, mention must also be made of the part he had to play as a member of the chieftaincy committee of the Local Government Council constituted under Section 5 of the Western Region Chiefs Law, 1957, Cap. 19 of the Laws of Western Region to make declarations under Section 4 of the same law "stating the customary law which regulates the selection of a person to be the holder of a recognized chieftaincy." The chieftaincy committee was composed of the President, if any, and all the traditional members of the Council." Under that law, power to determine the qualification and method of selection of a person for a recognized chieftaincy was vested in the Local Government Council although the declaration made by the Local Government Council subject to approval by the State Government.

30. It is pertinent to note that during this period the Northern and Eastern Regions largely retained the Native Authority system as in the earlier colonial period. Thus in the Northern parts the traditional rulers still functioned as the sole authority performing Legislative, Executive and Judicial functions while in the Eastern Region the "warrant chiefs" performed mainly judicial functions in the Native Courts.

AFTER INDEPENDENCE AND BEFORE FIRST
MILITARY INTERVENTION (1960–66)

31. We cannot really say that at this stage in the development of Local Government the traditional ruler had any role to play beyond that of being a ceremonial President. On the attainment of Independence, and throughout the period before the Military intervention of January, 1966, the position remained basically the same as described for the decolonization period except that the 1963 Constitution of the Federal Republic of Nigeria made provisions in the Constitution of each State for a House of Chiefs as a second chamber or upper house to the House of Assembly with which it shared the legislative power of the State. Here again, because of the grouping of Traditional Rulers with Chiefs, it was possible and, in fact, it did happen in some cases, that a chief was appointed to the House of Chiefs while his traditional ruler was left out.

PERIOD OF FIRST MILITARY RULE (1966–1979)

32. I think we may conveniently jump the first ten years of this period because there was nothing outstanding in the functions of traditional rulers in the administration of that period. However, towards the end of the Military era, local government was re-activated, and a completely new role was fashioned out for traditional rulers. This was when, in 1976, the Federal Military Government issued guidelines for the formation of local government councils and traditional councils in the country. These guidelines gave rise to the promulgation of the Local Government Edict, 1976 and the Traditional Rulers and Chiefs Edict, 1979 in Bendel State. Similar Edicts, with appropriate modifications where necessary, were promulgated in other parts of the country. In Bendel State, the 1976 Edict, like its predecessor the Local Government Law of 1955, made provision for a President of the Council where the instrument so provided but unlike the 1955 Law it restricted the Presidency to Traditional Rulers, so it was no longer possible for a chief or any other person to hold such office. But the 1976 Edict, like its predecessor, still made the President a ceremonial President with no specific role to play. The function which he had to perform regarding the appointment of the elected Chairman was

removed and vested in the Military Governor by Section 27 of the Local Government Edit, 1976.

33. Under the new arrangement, the important functions to be performed by the Traditional Ruler in Local administration are *principally* as a member of a Traditional Council and they are spelt out in the Bendel State Traditional Rulers and Chiefs Edict, 1979. To save time I will not enumerate them here again as I did that in my University of Ife lecture already referred to. We have some copies of that lecture here for those who may be interested. Notwithstanding these provisions, the traditional ruler has been effectively excluded from involvement in local government since the enactment of the relevant laws, mainly because of the council of Traditional Rulers comprising the Presidents of all the local government traditional councils. This Council also has no specific functions other than to advise the State Executive Council or the Commissioner for Local Government on matters referred to it.

34. Since the Military Administration's 1976 guidelines were of country-wide application, the new pattern of local government was expected to be the same throughout the whole country, no doubt with slight modifications here and there to suit local conditions in different States in the country. These Councils of Traditional Rulers do not exercise any executive, legislative or judicial functions. This was the situation up to the commencement of the civilian regime in 1979.

CIVILIAN REGIME, 1979–1983.

35. During this period there was no significant development in the role of Traditional Rulers in Local Government. Although the Local Government Edict, 1976 was replaced by the Bendel State Local Government Law, 1980, the provisions relating to the roles of Traditional Rulers as provided for in the 1979 Traditional Rulers and chiefs Edict remained unaltered.

36. However, the makers of our 1979 constitution did not altogether shut their eyes against Traditional rulers. As you know, traditional rulers were provided for in two places and in these places, they were referred to (derogatorily) as "chiefs." One place is section 3 of part 11 of the Third schedule to the constitution which provides for a state council of chiefs.

Here again, this council, like the local Government Traditional council is purely advisory. The second place is section 1 of part 1 of the Third schedule which included Traditional Rulers in the membership of the National Council of State.

37. Outside what the various legislations provide, it is worthy of note that Traditional Rulers now have significant role to play in the administration of institutions of higher learning through being appointed as chancellors and pro-chancellors of such institutions. I am sure all traditional rulers welcome this trend.

38. From what has been described, I leave you to compare the position of the Traditional Rulers before and after independence. It can be said without any fear of contradiction that since independence, traditional rulers no longer have any roles whatever to play in local administration except what the community's customs and traditions enjoin them to do. In effect, since independence, traditional rulers gradually got relegated to the background and became "under-utilized," to use a phrase that a newspaper attributed to a legislator in the now defunct civilian administration.

REAPPRAISAL OF THE POSITION OF TRADITIONAL RULERS

39. So let us examine their position again and re-assess it in the present scheme of things. I have said often that I do not subscribe to the suggestion that roles be found for traditional rulers in the constitution. Our roles are already clearly laid down for us in our community's customs and traditions, and traditional rulers must strive to perform them without fear of favor, and as fathers of their people. But alas, the Executive order of suspension or deposition hangs over every traditional ruler like the sword of Damocles. What I advocate is that traditional rulers be given adequate protection in the Constitution of the country so that they can perform their traditional functions according to the dictates of the community's customs. The kind of constitutional protection I have in mind is the type given to the members of the Judiciary and the Auditors-General: the Constitution does not allow them to be easily pushed around. If this was done, traditional ruler would have his hands full in the daily affairs of his people. There were instances known where an individual had a misunderstanding with his traditional

ruler; that individual by chance got into a political office or circle, and the first thing he sought to do was how to depose that his traditional ruler! As many of you know, the political office holder often won. May God save us from that kind of partisan politics again! The traditional ruler must, therefore, be constitutionally protected against this and other kinds of abuse of political power.

THE FUTURE OF TRADITIONAL INSTITUTIONS

40. Distinguished Ladies and Gentlemen, we have so far traced the evolution of the institution of Traditional Rulership in Nigeria. I have attempted to define who is a Traditional Ruler, traced the origin of Traditional Rulership in some parts of Nigeria, identified some of the different roles Traditional Rulers played in Nigeria before the Colonial era, during the Colonial era, in the transition period before Independence, during the first Republic, in the first Military interregnum, during the second Republic and now. It is clear that Traditional Rulers have fulfilled important functions in the spiritual and social lives of their communities. As I mentioned at the beginning of this talk this Conference is most timely as it coincides with the Local Government Review Committee set up by the Federal Military Government. It is our hope, therefore, that the outcome of the Committee's work and this Seminar will give brighter future to the position of Traditional Rulers in Nigeria. I consider it opportune, therefore, to end this discussion by leaving with you some of my thoughts on what should be the continued role of Traditional Rulers in the Governance of Nigeria. In doing this I would like to consider the future functions of Traditional Rulers at four levels, namely, Community level, Local Government level, State level and National level.

Community Level.

41. At Community level, I do not consider it necessary for this Conference to attempt to devise roles for Traditional Rulers to perform. As earlier stated, their functions have already been clearly laid down in the Community's customs and traditions. As these vary from community to community, it will not be possible to spell them out in this talk. In this

regard, one would like to recall with pleasure the very timely suggestion by Brigadier Ike Nwachukwu, Military Governor of Imo State, to the effect that the Traditional Rulers' Conference should consider setting up a Committee to collate and reduce to writing the customs of our people for the guidance of all. What is probably needed immediately is how to remove the constraints which are usually placed in the way of Traditional Rulers by political decisions. I would, therefore, like to focus attention on the judicial functions of the Traditional Ruler and his role in the communal land usage as areas in which such constraints could be eliminated:

(1) **Judicial Function:** It is my view that the role of Traditional Rulers in adjudicating over traditional and customary matters should be restored. To this end:

(a) Traditional Rulers should be empowered to hear and determine matters relating to customs and traditions as Courts of first instance and decisions by them on such matters should be final.

(b) Traditional Rulers should be given the opportunity to nominate some of the members of customary courts.

(c) Traditional Rulers should be empowered to hear, on appeal, decisions of Customary Courts on matters relating to customs and traditions.

As custodians of their people's customs and traditions Traditional Rulers and their Chiefs are more reliable interpreters of their people's cultural values and customary laws. By virtue of the position they hold they are often more knowledgeable in their people's customs and traditions and are, therefore, better placed than anyone else to constitute Customary courts. Furthermore, it is believed that partisan politicians wanted to keep the responsibility for appointing customary court members to themselves in order to use the courts in furthering their political interests and for oppressing their opponents. On the other hand, the common man in the community knows the value of traditional institutions and does not hesitate to turn there for help whenever he cannot find a solution elsewhere. Besides, when the poor are oppressed by the rich, the oppressed man, who had no means of taking his case to court, readily turns to his Traditional Ruler where as a rule he is charged no fees. This is why these people prefer to bring their cases before Traditional Rulers for settlement.

(2) **Communal Land Usage.** It is my view that in the allocation of community land, Traditional Rulers, as original custodians of their communal land, should be given a major role. They should, be therefore, be the approving authority in respect of land allocation in the rural areas, but in respect of urban areas they should be involved in the appointment of members of the Allocation Committee. Experience has shown that the objectives of the Land Use Decree, which were to make it easier for the Federal and State Governments to acquire land for development in any part of the country and the common man to acquire land for development in any part of the country and the common man to acquire land either for farming or for residential building, cannot be achieved because it has become more difficult for the ordinary citizen or industry to obtain Certificate of Occupancy while (in the now defunct civilian regime) some States used the decree to frustrate the Federal or other State Governments in their development projects. It is well known that Traditional Rulers, as custodians of community land, as it was in Benin, usually has no partisan political consideration for delaying or refusing to grant land to the Federal or State Government or anybody else for development purposes as the traditional ruler's primary aim is the development of his territory.

Local Government Level

42. At Local Government level Traditional Rulers should continue to perform their functions as Presidents of Local Government Councils and as members of Local Government Traditional Councils. In addition to the functions assigned to the Traditional Councils. In addition to the functions assigned to the Traditional Councils at present such Councils should be able to initiate proposals for development of their respective areas. It is, therefore, suggested that the Estimates of Local Government Councils should be cleared with the Traditional Councils before the Estimates are submitted to the Ministry of Local Government which should not entertain such submission unless there is a certificate to the effect that such Estimates were cleared by the respective Traditional Councils. It should also be possible for the President or any member of the Traditional Council to refer any matter to the Local Government Council for consideration and for him to

be present at the Council meeting whenever the matter is to be discussed.

State Level

43. At the State level the State Council of Traditional Rulers should be retained, but the Constitution of the country should be amended for its name "Traditional Rulers" to be used, for that is what, in fact, it is. The word "chief" should be left for use in relation to those on whom chieftaincy titles are conferred by Traditional Rulers. Moreover, the Council should continue to have power to make recommendations to Government on any matter which it considers to be in the interest of the State.

National Level

44. At the National level I had advocated the establishment of the National Council of Traditional Rulers as an advisory body to the Federal Government. Now that there is no partisan politics the Federal Military Government will no doubt find such a body invaluable in feeling the pulse of the people at the grassroots which is essential for the stability of Government, as any advice tendered will be the unanimous consideration of all traditional rulers.

WAVE OF ATTACKS ON TRADITIONAL RULERS

45. Finally, I would be missing an almost God-sent opportunity if I failed to use the occasion of this Conference to draw attention to a matter that is causing me considerable concern. It is the wave of attacks, actual insults and abuses, that some of the so-called educated elites in our society are pouring on Traditional Rulers. There is hardly any newspaper that one picks up these days that does not contain virulent attacks emanating from the pens of those members of our society who claim to be educated and yet they cannot draw distinction between a machinery and the operators of that machinery. If you bought a piece of equipment and it is badly operated by the technician you put on it, you do not discredit the equipment as useless but you will blame the operator. You do not do away with any organization of men simply because you disapprove of some of the office holders; nor would you throw away a whole basket of eggs simply because

you found some bad ones in it. By this, I mean that our so-called educated elites are in fact demonstrating their ignorance by the manner they attack the traditional institution as distinct from the holder of the position. So much attack has been leveled on Traditional Rulers in recent times that I am seizing this opportunity to acquaint this august gathering of what I have said in the past on the issue.

46. In my coronation address to the public on the 23rd of March, 1979, I had this to say on the position of Traditional Rulers:

> Things and times are changing fast and Traditional Rulers cannot afford to be left behind. Gradually by political evolution and a series of legislations traditional powers have been whittled down; first the legislative, then the judicial and finally the administrative. In more recent times it has become fashionable for some people to preach and advocate the abolition of the institution of the traditional ruler. Some of these people even went to the extent of describing traditional rulers as "a dying race" while some want to follow the example of India: all this in utter disregard of the Federal Military Government's constant pronouncement of its intention to up-hold the dignity of traditional rulers and enhance their status! We think that traditional rulers must begin now to read the handwriting on the wall. We pray earnestly to Almighty God and to our ancestors to create a change of heart in these people and show them the light so they can see for themselves that in the countries where traditional institutions have been abolished nothing but anarchy has followed, as we all see today. On the other hand, one can also point to a country that abolished monarchy and passed through a long period of anarchy but is now settling down to peace following the restoration of the monarchy by the people. We would therefore like to plead with the Federal and State Governments to live up to their public pronouncements as regards the status of traditional rulers and give these servants of the people (for truly they are servants of the people) their due place of honor in the scheme of things, and so put to shame those who advocate abolition of the institution.

47. In my lecture delivered at the University of Benin in 1982 titled "Tradition in the Service of Modern Society in the Nigerian Context" I also

made my views on this subject known. There is a statement of Sir Winston Churchill on tradition that I love very much and which I always quote when an opportunity presents itself. Sir Winston Churchill said in one of his books, "I must confess myself to be a great admirer of tradition. The longer you can look back, the farther you can look forward. This is not a philosophical or political argument—any oculist will tell you this is true. The wider the span, the longer the continuity, the greater is the same of duty in the individual men and women. . . ." I always believe no greater person or intellectual could have paid a more fitting tribute to tradition than a man of the stature of Sir Winston Churchill in those words and I always like to quote them for the benefit of our own so-called educated persons. In the rest of the relevant portions in that lecture. I referred my audience to the Holy Book, First Peter Chap. 2 Verse 17, which enjoins mankind to: "Fear God; Honor the King."

I also referred the Muslims in our society to what the Holy Qur'an says on the same point. You will find this in the Qur'an Chapter 2, Verse 247, the English translation of which says, inter alia,

> Their Prophet said to them: "God hath appointed Talut as King over you: God hath chosen him above you, and hath gifted him abundantly with knowledge And bodily prowess: God Granteth his authority to whom He pleaseth. God Careth For all, and He knoweth All things."

It is, therefore, a matter for regret that, with these Christian and Islamic teachings, the so-called educated in our society take it upon themselves to desecrate the institution. What education! What modernity!

48. I went further in that my lecture, and said the following:

> Those of our people who have had the benefit of Western (or European) education tend to look down on our customs and tradition. I wonder how many people know how much the British, for example, uphold and respect their own tradition. To give just two illustrations: if you watched the ceremony connected with the investiture of the Order of the Garter you would not fail to appreciate the authority and beauty of tradition. Two, the British Monarch

cannot just enter the City of London without going through what is known as the ceremony of the "Surrender of the Sword," during which the Lord Mayor waits at the boundary of the City, surrenders the City sword to the Monarch, thereby signifying the Monarch's omnipotence in the City, and surrendering the Mayor's own authority within the City to the Sovereign Majesty. The interesting feature in the ceremony is that after the Mayor has surrendered the sword, the Monarch returns it to the Mayor who then carries it to escort the Monarch. The ceremony is said to be some six centuries old and it is still observed to this day. If those who brought us education, who civilized us, still do that in the present century, what education have we Nigerians got that makes us look down on our own tradition?

49. Even the present Military Administration has not been spared the spate of attacks by those who do not see any wisdom in the right hand of fellowship that the present Administration has stretched to traditional rulers. Previous Administrations, military as well as civilian, made promises to and lauded the Traditional Rulers by word of mouth but the Buhari Administration is practicalizing it by actually consulting the Traditional Rulers either as individuals or though the State Council of Traditional Rulers. In the nine months of the Administration, Bendel State Military Governor has met with us three times at his own initiative something that has not happened in years.

50. I am, therefore, appealing through this Conference to all those very industrious feature writers and editorial boards in some of our newspapers to desist from their insults and abuses on Traditional Rulers; they should forget the individual incumbents and look at the institution. There is a world of difference between criticisms and downright insults and abuses as the traditional institution has been exposed to on the pages of some of our newspapers. When the Traditional Rulers from all over the country met in Kaduna in November last year, our first task was a self-examination of our position before we directed our mind to what we could do to safeguard it. I like to appeal to all our critics that instead of advocating the abolition of traditional rulership, such critics could offer useful suggestions that would help to stabilise the traditional institution or check what may seem as our

excesses. It is my hope that such critics, whose writings I have had the un-pleasantness to read on the pages of the newspapers, will offer suggestions to this Conference, for that is what the Conference is out to examine.

51. Ladies and Gentlemen, I believe I have given you something to think about in your Conference. I thank you for the attention and for the opportunity you have given me to be with you and to participate. I wish you fruitful deliberations, and God bless you all.

〰〰〰〰〰〰〰〰〰〰〰〰〰〰〰

"The Roles of Traditional Rulers in Local Government," a Special Lecture Presented at a National Conference Held Under the Auspices of the Department of Public Administration, University of IFE, ILE-IFE, April 25, 1983

INTRODUCTION

There are two special reasons why any one participating at this Confer-ence must feel honored by the opportunity for such participation.

First, the Department of Public administration of this University that mounted the Conference has become, not only nationally, but also inter-nationally, known in its contribution to the development of manpower and expertise in the field of Public Administration. Through the high standard the Department has set, especially in the post-graduate training, and respect that its graduates have earned for themselves outside, the Department of Public Administration of the University of Ife is now "the place" to go! A conference organized by such Department on any subject must be of the highest order, not to be taken lightly, and whose conference conclusions cannot be brushed aside.

The second reason why one should be glad at the opportunity to par-ticipate is the very topic of the Conference: "The Roles of Traditional Rul-ers in Local government." This should be a most important topic to every Nigerian who has or can trace his root. It is a fact that cannot be rebutted that the personalities, now somewhat loosely referred to as traditional rulers, are the embodiment and custodians of the community's customs/traditions (i.e. culture); and tradition is the bedrock of society and on which any kind of modern development (or civilization) is built. To create a forum at which to discuss the roles of the custodians of these customs/traditions in the field of local government is not only timely but also very farsighted of the Department of Public Administration of this University. This is more so because many of those in power (and sadly enough the drafters of our Constitution) do not seem to know what to do with these personalities or what name even to call them. It is particularly opportune at this time of partisan campaigns because this is the time traditional rulers are usually remembered-or fired!

Ladies and Gentlemen, for the two reasons I have adduced, I am happy and feel honored to have been invited to participate and given the opportunity to say a few words. Since I myself belong to the group whose position we wish to discuss, I would naturally be tempted to be subjective, sometimes, perhaps selfish in my approach. But by the time I finish I trust you yourselves will be able to discern my attempt to resist that temptation and to demonstrate some measure of impartial objectivity.

WHO IS A TRADITIONAL RULER?

The topic is "The roles of Traditional Rulers in Local Government." I think our starting point must be an attempt at some definition. This is important because, as I earlier hinted, people do not seem to know what even to call us. In the pre-colonial days we went by various titles which, in the aggregate, could be translated to English as "King." But the Colonial Masters could not tolerate such translation that would have detracted from the position of the British monarchy; so, they settled for the nearest dictionary word "Chief" which by my own dictionary means "Leader or Ruler." The Colonial Masters were nevertheless magnanimous enough not to tamper with our traditional titles and our traditional roles. They recognized some of us as "First class Chiefs" by the presentation of the appropriate staff of office. Records show that in the 1917 Official gazette and the Gazette supplement of 1933 and 1934, the Oba of Benin, Alafin of Oyo, Ooni of Ife, Alake of Abeokuta and the Awujale of Ijebu were accorded recognition as First Class

Chiefs in the Western Provinces. In the early years of our Independence, we were at various times referred to as "natural rulers" (which, to me, is only natural) and "traditional rulers" which became the most current, until the 1979 Constitution reduced us again to Chiefs," without giving us a word for those on whom traditional rulers confer chieftaincy titles. And we must not forget "Warrant chiefs" as they were called in those parts of the country which, by their custom, did not have the status we now term traditional rulers. To further compound the whole institution, it has now become fashionable to "promote" a traditional ruler from one level to another! So who then is the "traditional ruler"?

I have always felt that the expression does not currently reflect the status we wish to discuss, i.e., those whom the Colonial Masters properly (in my view) identified "Paramount Rulers": the Oba of Benin, Alafin of Oyo, Ooni of Ife, Alake of Egba, Eleko of Eko, Shehu of Borno, Emir of Zaria, Etsu Nupe, Obi of Onitsha, Obong of Calabar, just to mention a few for illustration. The inadequacy of this phrase "traditional ruler" is brought to focus when you see the different categories referred to these days as "His Highness" or when you consider the controversy as to who is or is not entitled to wear the beaded crown! This is why I have always stressed that I, for my part, want to be called and address by my customary title and style: "Omo N'Oba N'Edo, Uku Akpolokpolo." I have always believed that every truly traditional ruler, who has any historical antecedent, must have a traditional title and style used by his ancestors that predate the colonial era.

DEFINITION OF TRADITIONAL RULER

For the purpose of my discussion, I propose to refer to the definition of traditional ruler in Bendel State Traditional Rulers and Chiefs Law, 1979 and my suggested definition in a paper I recently circulated to my brother traditional rulers. Further, I will draw extensively on examples from my own domain, Benin, the pattern of which is more or less the same for every first-class Traditional Ruler or Paramount Ruler, and, of course, because of its age in history. The Bendel Law defines "Traditional Ruler" thus:

"Traditional Ruler" means the Traditional Head of an ethnic unit or clan who is for the time being the holder of the highest traditional authority within the ethnic unit or clan and whose title is recognized as a traditional ruler title by the government of the state.

The same Law defines "Clan" to mean "a town or village or a number of towns and villages the majority of the indigenes of which are believed to have a common ancestry and which are approved by the Executive Council to constitute a Clan." This is the best the drafters could do in the peculiar circumstance of Bendel State where over the years (and up to last month in at least two states) new village head springs up or a protégé is brought and gets transformed by politicians to the status of "Traditional Ruler" (or His Highness!)

The definition in Bendel State law is, however, in my opinion, an improvement on that in the old Western Region Law. The old Western Region law, Cap 19 of the Laws of Western Region of Nigeria, 1959, makes no distinction between a "Traditional Ruler" and a "Chief" appointed by him. They were all grouped together as Chiefs, and a "Chief" was defined as a person whose chieftaincy title is associated with a native community and include a "minor" and "Recognized Chief."

The law defined a "minor chief" as "a chief other than a recognized chief and a "recognized chief" as "a person appointed to a recognized chieftaincy to which the provisions of Part II of the Law were applicable." To appreciate the inadequacy of the foregoing definition, let us hear what one of your researchers has to say about the socio-political organization of Benin and the position of its traditional ruler (the Oba) in pre-colonial era. As I am speaking in a University campus I hesitate to quote from traditional history which, no matter how authentic, academicians are wont to take with a grain of salt, if they do not completely discountenance it! The researcher, Professor P. A. Igbafe, of the University of Benin, in his work *Benin under British Administration* (Ibadan History Series) has this to say in his opening paragraph:

The socio-political organization of Benin during the pre-colonial years of its history was dominated by the special position occupied by the Oba, who was the pivot around which everything revolved, the supreme religious as well as the civil authority in the land. This special position of the Oba found expression in the physical separation of his settlement or palace (eguae Oba) and those dependent on him or connected to him by special ties from the rest of the town and people. The Oba was by tradition the fount of honor and the giver of titles, his position being surrounded by an aura of sacrosanctity on account of his priestly function and as a representative of the long line of ancestors who had held the reins of power over the land before him.

We must reinforce Igbafe by what the Bible and the Quran teach us regarding the position of the King in society. I will not spend time on the quotations but will merely refer you, if you are interested, to First Peter, Chapter 2 Verse 17, and to Quran, Chapter 2, verse 247 (in English translation). Both these teachings tell us that the traditional ruler or king is not man-made but that who answers to that position is God-anointed and therefore not to be brushed aside or relegated or disrespected.

Needless to say that this was the position Sir Frederick (later Lord) Lugard found to be ideal for the construction of his now famous "Indirect Rule" system. It is the holder of this position that formed the cornerstone of the Colonial Masters' "Indirect Rule." He was appointed as "Sole Authority" for the administration of his area. It is this position that our own people, since attaining independence, are gradually relegating or making pawns of on the political chess board.

The definition in the law is not water-tight enough. In any case, because of the immense power given to the Governor-in-Council in this matter, proliferation of traditional rulers has been on the increase. Experience has shown that a community can present a "traditional ruler" where there was none "from time immemorial," as the phrase goes, and such new-comer would be accorded government recognition by the premier (of old) and the Governor of today, in order to score a political point in that community. As I have already observed, it is now possible, without any custom to support, to "create" a traditional ruler for a section of an already existing domain of a traditional ruler or "promote" a traditional ruler from one grade to another as if they are civil service posts in a cadre.

If one were permitted to draw analogy, one would ask how a Governor would feel today if overnight his Deputy or Commissioner were "promoted" to enjoy the same rights and privileges as the Governor. You are witnesses to what has been happening on this score in the past three years.

In view of the situation I have just described and in order to be more specific on who, in fact, is a traditional ruler, I attempted a definition in the paper I circulated to my brother traditional rulers during my recent country-wide tour last October-November. Permit me to quote my suggested definition from that paper: "Traditional Ruler means the traditional head of an ethnic community whose stool conferred the highest traditional authority on the incumbent since the time before the beginning of British rule."

I drew attention in that paper to the similarity in this definition to the definition of antiquity in the National Commission for Museums and Monuments Act, 1979; that legislation defines "antiquity" as "any work of art or craft work, . . . if such work of art or craft work is of indigenous origin and was fashioned before the year 1918 or has been at any time in the performance and for the purposes of any traditional ceremony." It will be seen in this definition that what makes an object an antiquity is related to the time before the British or traditional usage. This was the cue for my suggested definition of traditional ruler; if the position did not exist as such before the British (thus setting a time limit to our phrase "from time immemorial") then to "create" it or "promote" it to that highest traditional authority thereafter is nothing short of the untraditional!

Ladies and Gentlemen, I realize I am to speak on the roles of Traditional Rulers in Local Government. But you will, I hope, agree with me that it is important we know whom we are talking about. Hence I have gone this length to try to establish that in my discussion, the term "Traditional Ruler" refers to those whom the Colonial Masters appointed sole authorities for local administration and termed traditional rulers within the definition in *Bendel State Traditional Rulers and Chiefs Law, 1979*, as modified by my definition just quoted.

THE ROLES OF TRADITIONAL RULER IN LOCAL GOVERNMENT
Now to the topic. What are the roles of the Traditional Ruler in Local

Government? We cannot answer the question meaningfully without once again going back to pre-colonial era; the position:

(a) Before the colonial

(b) During the colonial period; and

(c) Since Independence (taking the period from 1954 to 1960 to be the transition period).

Pre-colonial Period

To appreciate the position in the pre-colonial era, let us cast our minds back again to the extract I quoted earlier from Igbafe. Two other researchers have something more to say on this. I refer to Stride and Ifeka. In their work *Peoples and Empires of West Africa* they had this to say of the old Benin Empire:

> The empire was governed on the three levels. The Oba, who became an increasingly secluded and sacred figure during the seventeenth century, was at the top of the hierarchy. On the second level, there were the chiefs who formed the State Council in Benin City. The third level of government con-sisted of tribute units. A tribute unit corresponded roughly, but not exactly, to a village or petty chiefdom. Each unit was headed by an overlord who represented the interests of his people to the Oba, and told the people what the Oba's wishes were. However, the overlord did not live in his tribute unit but, instead, was represented there by a faithful servant. Overlords received deputations at the capital.
>
> Each overlord was appointed by the Oba. The Queen Mother, the Oba's first son and chiefs in Benin were usually heads of tribute units. The Oba had the right to re-distribute tribute units to prevent any chief from becoming too rich and influential, and to reward any trusty supporters. It was an overlord's duty to transmit appeals from the people in his unit to the Oba's court. He also had to organize the yearly or twice-yearly collection of tribute of yams, palm oil, meat, livestock and other food-stuffs to the Oba.

The finding in respect of the old Oyo Empire was not very different from this. So you see that in pre-colonial times, as Igbafe, Stride and Ifeka found, the traditional ruler of the caliber we are discussing was already at the head of a well-organized system of government. In that position, the Oba was the sole authority; he was the executive, the legislature and the judiciary. He had the power of life and death. That is not to say he was autocratic. He could not afford to be (without some serious repercussions) because checks and balances were built into the system and he had around him a body of senior chiefs who advised him; out in the districts, he assigned Enigie or district heads or, in modern parlance, Dukes (often children of the Royal Family), and Odionwere or village heads (usually the oldest person in his village).

This then was the three tier system of government in Benin Empire in pre-colonial era the Oba with the senior chiefs or Oba-in-Council, who were responsible for the affairs of the whole State; the Enigie or district heads who looked after specified areas (usually a group of villages) and responsible to the Oba; and the village heads who looked after their individual villages and were responsible to the Oba through the Enigie. But somewhere in between were the okakuo (army-generals) who took charge of certain border areas and non-Benin communities that had been subdued. It is a well-known fact that the pattern I have just described obtained in many parts of this country before 1914, and this was the pattern that Sir Frederick Lugard polished into his "Indirect Rule System."

The Colonial Era (1900–1954)

And so we move to the Colonial era. Between 1900 and 1914, the organs of local government in the area now known as Bendel State were the Native Courts which combined executive and judicial functions. In both member-ship and area of authority, the British did not, in all cases, follow strictly the existing traditional pattern of government although they preferred, wherever it existed, to appoint the true traditional authorities to these courts. With the amalgamation of the Southern and Northern Provinces of Nigeria in 1914, the enactment of the *Native Court Ordinance of 1914 and the Native Authority Ordinance of 1916*, the "Indirect Rule System" was introduced.

Many of you know that the essence of the Lugard (Indirect Rule) system was what the phrase implied; the British administrators administered the community indirectly through the recognized (or paramount) head of the community. Thus, all the organs, as I had earlier described in the case of

Benin, were allowed to remain but the Oba's sole authority immediately became curtailed (but only slightly): because he was now made responsible and accountable to the British Resident Administrator. But the situation was not intolerable at all for, as we shall see, the traditional ruler enjoyed far greater respect and recognition then than he came to do in the hands of his own people after Independence.

With the introduction of the Native Administration, the traditional ruler still held on to all his pre-colonial roles except that he lost his sovereignty to the British Monarch and operated under the guidance (or as the Masters put it, the advice) of the British officials. Although the Oba had lost the power of life and death he wielded over his subjects, he still exercised a great measure of his executive, judicial and legislative powers, in all aspects of local administration, particularly in matters of customs and traditions which the British Administrators recognized could not be wiped off outright. Many of you will recollect that in judicial matters the Oba (or Traditional Ruler) was both a court of first instance as well as Court of Appeal, and appeal lay from the Oba's Court to the Resident. The new situation did not affect his legislative powers, for custom was custom and the Oba's role here was to ensure its observance. His executive powers were affected only to the extent that he did nothing in conflict with the British Colonial Government policy. It was the "Sole Authority" that gave way to the Native Authority which subsequently gave way to our modern form of Local Government-modern in the sense that it was imported to us.

So, we may be able to draw some conclusions from what has been said thus far. First, it must not be thought that "Local Government" began with the country's attainment of Independence, for in pre-colonial era many of the traditional rulers, especially those whom the colonial masters identified and recognized as First Class Chiefs, sat at the head of very well organized system of three-tier of government and exercised executive, legislative and judicial functions. Secondly, the colonial government introduced the "Indirect Rule" system under which the traditional rider still exercised much of the pre-colonial powers except that he lost his sovereignty to the British Crown and carried on local administration under the guidance or advice of the new-found British Administrator. Thirdly, the new Native Authority system introduced taxation and the traditional ruler became the principal tax collector.

Period of Transition to Independence (1954–1960)

That then was the position of Traditional Rulers up to the eve of attainment of Independence in 1960, but we must remember that Independence started creeping in from about 1954; the Native Authority was gradually fading away until the English type of Local Government was imported for us to absorb hook, line and sinker. In the then Western Nigeria, the Local Government Law of 1952 was enacted. The principal effect of the law was to replace the Native Authority, which was basically the traditional ruler-in-council, with the British type representative Local Government. This law changed, drastically, the role of the traditional ruler and his chiefs in Local Government. Section 14 of the law provides that membership of the council may include a President and Traditional Members who must be holders of recognized chieftaincy titles and must not exceed, in number, one-third of the elected members.

As stated earlier, the then Western Region Chiefs Law made no distinction between traditional rulers and chiefs appointed by them; they were grouped together and classified as "recognized" or "minor" chiefs. The provisions in the Local Government Law for a recognized chief to be appointed as President or as a Traditional Member of a Council could therefore not be said to have created any specific roles for the traditional ruler as such roles could also be assigned to his chief, if recognized by Government. Nevertheless, those I can remember to have held the office of President of Local Government Councils were Traditional Rulers. Even in those cases, they were mere ceremonial Presidents as they could not participate in the deliberations of the Councils unless they were invited by their Councils to preside over the particular meetings at which they were present. *(Vide Section 39 (2) of the Local Government Law, Cap. 68 of the Laws of Western Region.)* As if to ensure that Traditional Rulers were excluded from active participation in local administration, the Local Government Law was amended by Western Region Legal Notice 40 of 1959 by the addition of sub-section (6) to Section 29 thereof under which no traditional ruler (or any other recognized chief) appointed as President of the Council could be appointed Chairman of the Council whereas any other person appointed as President under Sub-section (2) of Section 17 of the same law, could be appointed.

Apart from presiding over Council meeting when invited to do so by resolution of Council, the other roles left for the Traditional Ruler as President of the Council were the issuing of the letter of appointment of the Chairman within 24 hours after his election by the Council and power to summon a meeting of the Council. *(Vide Sections 30 (h) and 33 (l) of Cap. 68 of the Laws of Western Nigeria.)* These changes which were introduced during the period of decolonization (between 1952 and 1960) were the outcome of the pressures mounted by our politicians for more representative and democratic government. In addition to these minor roles, mention must also be made of the part he had to play as a member of the chieftaincy committee of the Local Government Council constituted under Section 5 of the Western Region Chiefs Law, 1957, Cap. 19 of the Laws of Western Region to make declaration under Section 4 of the same law "stating the customary law which regulates the selection of a person to be the holder of a recognized chieftaincy." The chieftaincy committee under Sub-section 2 of Section 5 of the law "shall be composed of the President, if any, and all the traditional members of the Ciybcuk." Under that law, power to determine the qualification and method of selection of a person for a recognized chieftaincy was vested in the Local Government Council, although the declaration made by the Local Government Council was subject to approval by the State Government.

After Independence and Before Military Intervention (1960–1966)

We cannot really say that at this stage in the development of Local Government the traditional ruler had any role to play beyond that of being a ceremonial President. On the attainment of Independence, and throughout the period before Military intervention of January, 1966, the position remain basically the same as described for the decolonization period except that the 1963 Constitution of the Federal Republic of Nigeria made provisions in the Constitution of each state for a House of Chiefs as a second chamber or Upper House to the House of Assembly with which it shared the legislative power of the state. Here again, because of the grouping of Traditional rulers with Chiefs, it was possible and, in fact it did happen in some cases, that a Chief was appointed to the House of Chiefs while his Traditional Ruler was left out. Perhaps I should mention here a ridiculous case where a Chief was gazetted as a "recognized Chief" while his Traditional Ruler who conferred his chieftaincy title on him was classified as a "minor Chief" by those in power then!

Period of Military Rule (1966–1979)

I think we may conveniently jump the period of the military regime because there was nothing outstanding in the roles of traditional rulers in the administration of that period.

After Military Rule (1979–)

When, towards the end of the military era, local government was re-activated, a completely new role was fashioned out for traditional rulers. The Federal Military Government issued guidelines for the formation of local government councils and traditional councils in the country. In this regard, the *Local Government Edict, 1976* and the *Traditional Rulers and Chiefs Edict, 1976* were promulgated in Bendel State. Like its predecessor, the *Local Government edict, 1976* made provision for a President of a Council where the instrument so provides but, in this case, the President must be a Traditional Ruler and not just a recognized chief or any other person as allowed by the earlier *Local Government Law*. Under the 1976 Law the President is also a ceremonial President with no specific role to play. The role which he had to play regarding the appointment of the elected Chairman was removed and vested in the Military Governor by Section 27 of the *Local Government Edict, 1976*. Although the *Local Government Edict, 1976* has since been replaced by the *Bendel State Local Government Law, 1980*, the provisions relating to the roles of traditional rulers remain unaltered.

Under the new arrangement, the important roles to be performed by the Traditional Ruler in local administration are *principally* as a member of a Traditional Council, and they are spelt out in the *Bendel State Traditional Rulers and Chiefs Law, 1979*. Under Section 45 (2) of Part VII of the law, a traditional council established under this section shall consist of:

(a). The President who shall be a Traditional Ruler in the local government area;

(b). All the other traditional rulers in the local government area where applicable;

(c). Other traditional chiefs whose titles are associated with the local government area or areas as the case may be," etc.

Section 47 of the same part of the law lists out many functions for a traditional council which include, inter alia,

(a). Formulation of general proposals by law of advice to the government or to all local government in its area;

(b). Harmonization of the activities of such local government councils and co-ordination through discussion of their development plans;

(c). Support for arts and culture, assisting in the maintenance of law and order;

(d). Generally, to advice on any matter referred to it by the state or federal government; and

(e). To advise on questions relating to chieftaincy matters and control of traditional titles

Also, section 51 of part VII of the traditional Rulers and Chiefs law of 1979 enjoins the Secretary of the Local Government to furnish the President of the Traditional council with copies of all minutes of the local government council meetings, copies of all agenda, memoranda, etc, so as to afford the president the opportunity to be fully conversant with all proceedings. The same law gives the president of the Traditional council the power to inspect any books of the local government council as would enable him obtain information that would facilitate the discharge of his own functions. Notwithstanding these provisions, the traditional ruler has been effectively excluded from involvement in local government since the enactment of the relevant laws, mainly because the role of the traditional council in local government is only advisory. The same law also provides for a state council of Traditional Rulers comprising the presidents of all the local government Traditional councils. This Council also has no specific roles other than to advise the state Executive Council or the commissioner for local government on matters referred to it. This is the situation up to this moment I am speaking. Since the military administration's guidelines were of country-wide application, the new pattern of local government was expected to be the same throughout the whole country. No doubt with slight modifications here and there to suit local conditions in different states in the country. These councils of traditional rulers do not exercise any executive, legislative or judicial functions.

From what has been described, I leave you to compare the position of the traditional ruler before and after independence. It can be said without any fear of contradiction that since independence, traditional rulers no longer have any roles whatever to play in local government, except what the community's customs and traditions enjoin them to do. The new system became intolerable, at any rate in Bendel State, because the traditional council, through which the traditional ruler gets his stipend, is dependent on the purse (and sometimes goodwill) of the local government council. In effect, since independence, traditional rulers gradually got relegated to the background and became "underutilized," to use a phrase that a newspaper attributed to a legislator recently. On the other hand, the councilor, be he elected or nominated, began to assume greater recognition and importance in the public eye, not only because they have now become more affluent than their traditional rulers but also because the local people now look up to them as the "government" men to meet for their needs while the traditional rulers remain mere ceremonial heads.

You can now appreciate why in recent times many prominent traditional rulers have been calling on the president of the country to amend the constitution to create roles for traditional rulers. The topic for this conference is "The Roles of Traditional Rulers in Local Government." This, to my mind, would give the impression that it is only in the field of local government that traditional rulers have seen that in practical terms the traditional rulers do not now feature at all, or at best only partially, in present-day local government.

REAPPRAISAL OF THE POSITION OF TRADITIONAL RULER

So let us examine their position again and re-assess it in the present scheme of things. I, for my part, do not subscribe to the suggestion that roles be found for traditional rulers in the Constitution. Our functions are already clearly laid down for us in our community's customs and traditions, and traditional rulers must strive to perform them without fear or favor, and as fathers of their people. But, alas the Executive order of suspension or deposition hangs over every traditional ruler like the sword of Damocles. What I advocate is that traditional ruler be given protection in the Constitution so that they can perform their traditional functions according to the dictates of the community's customs. The kind of constitutional protection I have in mind is the type given to the member of the judiciary and Auditors-general: the Constitution does not allow them to be pushed around. If this was done, the traditional ruler would have his hands full in the daily affairs of his people. Instances are known where a citizen had a misunderstanding with his traditional ruler; that citizen by chance gets into a political office or circle, and the first thing he seeks to do is how to depose that his traditional ruler! As many of you know, the political office holder often wins. The traditional ruler must be constitutionally protected against this and other kinds of abuse of power.

ROLES AT OTHER LEVELS OF GOVERNMENT (1979 CONSTITUTION)

Those who drafted, our 1979 Constitution did not altogether shut their eyes against traditional rulers. As you know, traditional rulers were provided for in two places, and in these places, they were referred to (derogatorily) as "Chiefs." One place is section 3 of part II of the third Schedule to the Constitution which provides for a State Council of Chiefs whose functions are to advise the Governor on matters "relating to customary affairs, inter-communal relations and chieftaincy matters" and on other matter at the request of the Governor. Here again, this Council, like the Local Government Traditional Council, is purely advisory. The second place is Section 1 of part 1 of the Third Schedule where it is stated that membership of the Council of state shall include a member of each State Council of Chiefs. But even in this august national body I believe the traditional ruler is ineffective for he is inhibited by the presence of his Governor in two respects: he may express opinion at variance with that of his Governor and the Executive is not likely to take kindly to that; or, against his better judgment, he would try to be in line with his Governor; in which case the traditional ruler cannot be expressing his honest opinion. So, to me, including the traditional ruler in the National Council of State is really not giving them any worthwhile role commensurate with their statues.

PROPOSALS FOR A NATIONAL COUNCIL OF TRADITIONAL RULERS.

This leads us on to the next point. If, in my view, traditional rulers are mere ceremonial heads, observers, and advisers in the local government set-up without any specific function, and they are ineffective in the National Council of State, what then? Well, we are still experimenting with different types of Constitutions, and we must continue with the experiment until we find a constitutional arrangement that meets the nation's diversified culture and temperament. As far as I know, there is no political philosophy, or political theory or political science that says every nation must have only either unicameral or bicameral legislative body. That being so, I am advocating that we in this country should give the world an example of three-chamber legislature, comprising the House of Representatives, the Senate and a National Council of Traditional Rulers.

The first two will be legislative (as at present) while the third, the council of Traditional Rulers, will be advisory to Head of State and the two lower chambers. The National Council of Traditional Rulers nominated by their own members. Though it will still essentially be advisory, such body will be free (or more free) to express independent opinion on the actions of the legislatures at the *national level* for it will be constitutionally protected. Is there reason why we cannot try this, whether the Country retains the present Presidential system or eventually reverts to the former Westminster system?

CUSTOMARY COURTS

Another area where tradition rulers can participate in government is the judiciary. As the custodian, in fact, the embodiment, of his people's customs and traditions, he is best suspicion or accusation that they set up Customary Courts for the oppression of their political opponents, they should not find it difficult to concede this idea. The membership of the Courts should comprise traditional chiefs, and the Traditional Ruler himself should be Court of Appeal. As stated before, this was the situation before our people took over from the British. I leave you to dwell on this idea.

I have already said that I am personally not in support of the suggestion that role be found for traditional rulers in the Constitution. I think, ladies and gentlemen, this is both an admirable time and place to publicly commend our respected President Shehu Shagari for the role he has carved out for traditional rulers in making them head institutions of higher learning as Chancellors and Pro-Chancellors. There are many now in this position. I myself was offered such a position which I regrettable had to decline for personal reasons. The president had been able to create this new role for traditional rulers without going through the tedious business of amending this our complex Constitution.

I am sure all traditional rulers are grateful to the President. If we cannot function in local government, and it is unwise to take part in partisan politics, we can at least make our contribution as heads of Institutions whose function is to breed good citizens. It is my hope that President Shagari or any other future President will, in the years ahead, find more new roles for traditional rulers, without having to interfere with the Constitution. I appreciate that some of you may say this part of my discussion is not local government. Yes; but what I am trying to show is that the topic is restricted in giving the impression that it is only in local government that traditional rulers can play any roles; and we have found in any case that they have not been given an effective place in that set-up.

SUMMARY

Ladies and gentlemen, I have been speaking on "The roles of traditional rulers in local government." I believe what I have succeeded in doing is to show that local government is not the only field in which traditional rulers can play any roles, and that as at now traditional rulers do not even have any roles at all to play in local, government, certainly nothing comparable to the functions they had in the colonial Native Authority system.

Secondly, traditional rulers can be put to better use within and outside the local government set-up, as the attempt in the National Council of State. It is, however, rather invidious, for reasons earlier stated, to join the traditional rulers with their Governors in the National Council of State.

Therefore, thirdly, in order to give traditional rulers greater opportunity and freedom to express independent opinion on national issues (and since we are still in experimental stage in constitutional development) we must have a third House to be called the National Council of Traditional Rulers over and above the existing two legislative House whose membership would be drawn from State Councils of Traditional Rulers and which would be a watch-dog, albeit in an advisory capacity, to the lower chambers, and the Head of State or President, as the case may be.

Fourthly, as the custodian, in fact, the embodiment, of his people's customs and traditions, the traditional rulers is best placed to constitute customary courts in his domain. The membership of the courts should comprise traditional chiefs and the traditional ruler himself should be court of Appeal as was the position in some parts of the country in the colonial era.

Fifthly, there is no need to create any legislative or executive roles for traditional rulers in the constitution because their roles are clearly laid down in the community's customs and traditions, and these have helped in no small measure in creating peaceful and proper atmosphere for good government. Rather, what is required is a constitutional protection for traditional rulers similar to that given to members of the judiciary and Auditors General so they can freely perform their traditional functions without fear of suspension or deposition by mere stroke of the official pen!

Sixthly, more opportunities should be created for traditional rulers to render national service not tied exclusively to local administration or local government. President Shehu Shagari has already started action in this direction for which we are very grateful, while hoping that he will do more!

Ladies and gentlemen, I trust I have given you some materials to think about in the course of your deliberations. There is nothing I have said that many of you do not already know. I wish I could have given you more contentious point to exercise your academic mind! I am grateful to the organizers of the Conference for giving me the opportunity to participate.

I wish the Conference successful deliberations, while looking forward to reading your conclusions at a later date.

Thank you.

||||||||||||||||||||||||||||||||||||||||||||||||

EXCERPTS FROM AN ADDRESS ON THE OCCASION OF OMO N'OBA'S Coronation as the 38th Oba of Benin on March 23rd, 1979

Things and times are changing fast and Traditional Rulers cannot afford to be left behind. Gradually, by political evolution and series of legislations, traditional powers have been whittled down; first, the legislative, then the judicial and finally the administrative. In more recent times it has become fashionable for some people to preach and advocate the abolition of the institution of the traditional ruler. Some of these people even went to the extent of describing traditional ruler as "a dying race," while some want to follow the example of India: All these in utter disregard for the Federal Military Government's constant pronouncement of its intention to up-hold the dignity of traditional rulers and enhance their status.

We think that traditional rulers must begin now to read the handwriting on the wall. We pray *earnestly to* Almighty God to our ancestors to create a change of heart in these people and show them the light so they can see for themselves that in the countries where traditional institutions have been abolished nothing but anarchy has followed, as we all see today. On the other hand, one can also point to a country that abolished monarchy and passed through a long period of anarchy but is now settling down to peace following the restoration of the monarchy by the people. We would therefore like to plead with the Federal and State Governments to live up to their public pronouncements as regards the status of traditional rulers and give these servants of the people (for truly they are servants of the people) their due place of honor in the scheme of things, and so put to shame those who advocate abolition of the institution.

Partisan politics has now commenced and very soon civilian government will return to the country. In the last civilian regime the traditional ruler was hard put to it in knowing precisely which way to go. There were the options open to him: to support the government of the day; to be one with his subject; or to be the father of his subjects and remain neutral to partisan politics. You are all witnesses to the fact that each of these three options placed the ruler in a dilemma at one time or the other. If he chose to support the Government Council, to be on the other side, the traditional ruler was in trouble from his own people. If he was one with his subjects but this happened to be in opposition to the government of the day, again, the traditional ruler was in trouble from the government.

Thirdly, if he decided as a father of his people that he could not be partisan he still found himself in a dilemma for he was accused of indifference. And, yet, with all these uncertainty in his position, the traditional ruler was often a tool in the hands of those who wanted to use him to catch election votes. Will traditional rulers be exposed to this dilemma and uncertainty in the next civilian regime? The answer must come from the traditional rulers themselves.

A lot has been said in recent times about insulating traditional rulers from partisan politics, and various means of doing this have been suggested. For example, that they should not be provided for in the country's Constitution or that the House of Chiefs, being legislative, should be discontinued or that matters of traditional rulers should be removed from the portfolio of a Ministry to that of the Governor.

In our view, none of these suggested measures will adequately serve the purpose because if examined closely it would be seen that in the attempt to insulate traditional rulers from partisan politics, they have been subjected to some form of disability. Our advice, therefore, is that, Traditional Rulers should at all cost avoid partisan politics and do their best to be father to all of their subjects, a position which the newly established Traditional Councils admirably place them. Government on its part should ensure that the constitution of the unpleasant reprisals for giving advice which may sometimes be unpalatable to the party in power. If the Traditional Council must act in advisory capacity to government, they should be placed in a position to give such advice without fear or favor. This is the only way, in our view, they can be insulated from partisan politics. We pray that the coming generation of politicians and the civilian government will allow the Traditional Rulers to play this non-partisan role.

In the coming regime, Traditional Ruler must be seen to be pulling different ways and enjoying unequal privileges. In this connection, we submit that there is a lot to be said about what used to be known in the 1930s in some parts of this country as Oba's Conference. This was an annual gathering at which all Traditional Rulers (or Natural Rulers as they were then called) exchanged views and discussed matters of national interest for presentation to the government. We very much like to pass this through on to all Traditional Rulers of today. Traditional Rulers ought not to wait for government to convene their meeting for them, but should take the initiative.

It is appropriate at this juncture, following the appeal we made earlier on to the government and what we have just said to traditional Rulers, to address a few words on the same subject to our Edo people. For ages, certainly since the time of Oba Eweka I, the institution of the Oba of Benin has held with great awe and reverence. In contemporary times non-Edo people throughout the length and breadth of this country look at our institution with great admiration and respect. The respect and dignity which others accord our institution has been due to the way our own people have held it. We pray that the present and future generations will continue to uphold this ancient and worthy traditional institution. We firmly believe that in any society the monarchy or traditional ruler is the hub that holds up the wheel, the tap root of the system. You may modify the role of the traditional institution but its total abolition cannot but have serious repercussions.

Chapter 4

On a New Political Order, The Judiciary, Tri-Cameral Legislature, Civil Service, Provincial Government, and Public Accountability.

Twenty-five years of experiment have shown conclusively that no foreign type of political structure or government will succeed with us, having regard to the country's diversity in historical evolution, customs, traditions, religions and temperament . . . We have to adapt the foreign system to suit our peculiar make-up or diversities as known today.
— Omo N'Oba Erediauwa, May 26, 1986

As far as I know, there is no political philosophy, or political theory or political science that says every nation must have only either uni-cameral or bi-cameral legislative body. That being so, I am advocating . . . a three-chamber legislature, comprising the House of Representatives, the Senate and a National Council of Traditional Rulers . . . Is there any reason why we cannot try this, whether the country retains the present Presidential system or eventually reverts to the former Westminster system?"
— Omo N'Oba Erediauwa, May 26, 1986

|||||||||||||||||||||||||||||||||||||||||||

"The Search for a New Political Order-Some Thoughts," A Paper Being a Memorandum Submitted to the Political Bureau, May 26, 1986

INTRODUCTION
Major-General I. B. Babangida, President of the Federal Republic and

Commander-in-Chief of the Armed Forces of Nigeria, in his famous October 1, 1985, broadcast, called on Nigerians to begin the search for a new political order that would ensure the stability of the country. The General was at a loss to understand why our great country had remained unstable (politically) in the (then) 25 years of independence. He then invited all Nigerians to come out with ideas. In his words:

> What really lies at the bottom of our past dilemma is the absence of a viable political arrangement. The political history of this nation is partly one of disillusionment with politics and with politicians. Intermittent bad government have left us a legacy of economic mis-management and a chain of political instability.
>
> We are convinced that the apparently more immediate problem of salvaging the economy and creating a disciplined social order are the result of the lack of a coherent national ethos based on shared ideals and values. These ideals and values have already been articulated clearly in the fundamental objectives and directive principles of state policy as enshrined in the 1979 Constitution. "I, therefore, reaffirm this Administration's commitment to the realization of these principles and objectives.
>
> Furthermore, we must begin a most vigorous search for a new political order capable of ensuring sustained economic growth and social development. It is only within such a framework that we can properly address these and other urgent tasks that lie ahead. With this in mind, we shall, in the course of 1986, announce a political program for the country.

President Babangida directed that the "political debate" (as the President's invitation came to be known) shall end with the end of 1986. He then set up a political bureau with assignment to monitor the trend of the debate and make recommendations therefrom to the Armed Forces Ruling Council. The bureau is charged with responsibility to

> gather, collate and synthesize the contributions of Nigerians to the search for a new political system; organize public discussion through debates, seminars, symposia, on questions relevant to the search for a new political order;

deliberate on political problem that may be referred to it by the President; and evaluate contributions and make proposal to the government.

Although the political bureau has, as one of its terms of reference, to propose a time-table for the return to civil rule, the President has already indicated that the country would return to civil rule by 1990.

All this is very interesting. As far as my memory goes (and that spans a period in the civil service covering two years of colonial government, six years of self-government, and thirteen years of independence, to the present day), General Babangida is the first Head of State to draw attention to the need for a new political order as a way to ensuring stability that has eluded us these 25 years. In my view, there is a difference between devising a new constitution and a new political order. Following the constitutional breakdown which caused the crisis that led to the civil war, General Gowon, in 1966, set up what was termed Ad Hoc Constitutional Committee whose task was to fashion out a new constitution to stem the impending crisis. I was at the inauguration of that Committee. After welcoming all "in the name of God Almighty," he went on to say, inter alia, that events of the recent past had shown that there was "no basis for a unitary form of government" any more. He then called on the committee members to fashion out a new constitution to meet the situation. It suited those who wanted to break up the country at the time to misquote General Gowon as having said there was no basis for unity.

As is well known, the Ad Hoc Committee flopped. Then came General Murtala Mohammed who set up another constitution drafting body. I was opportuned to listen to and watch him on the "TV" as he inaugurated the body. I heard him say that the Committee should consider all kinds of constitutions, including executive presidency. For reasons known only to the members of the Committee, they took it that General Mohammed enjoined then to give us a constitution for executive presidency, and they gave us in 1979, a kind of cross-breed between British and American brands of constitution. And yet no answer to the country's problem of instability! But I know there were some members of the committee who, in their Constitution Assembly days thought there was nothing wrong with the British type that we had operated, and that all we needed to do was to update it in light of past experience.

What, in effect, I am saying is that a new constitution had in the past been considered but not a new political order. Our independence was built on a very weak foundation-ethnic sentiments-as events have now shown, as we shall discuss later. It was that weak foundation on which our independence was built that has been the bane of our society, and it was not surprising that six years later the constitution broke down after two coups d'etat (military/civilian and military/military). I am grateful that General Babangida has drawn attention to the need for a new political order for reasons that he adequately adduced. I have myself advocated a new order, and I am glad I am in good (Babangida's) company. Or, perhaps, he is in (my) good company, for I began to make my pronouncements as far back as 1982 in the course of my country-wide tour.

In 1982 I circulated a memorandum to every traditional ruler I visited on that tour in which I advocated that there should be a new Political System in which traditional rulers must play a more effective role in national affairs. And when, in my capacity as Chancellor of the University of Ibadan I addressed Congregation in 1985, I said, inter alia:

> if there are reservations of our success as a nation, it is not because we lack
> the human and material resources to have done well. In my view, our real
> problem lies in the search for a viable political system and the right leadership
> which would harness our God-given resources for the attainment of a just
> and egalitarian society short of the blatant abuses of the political elite and
> the unbridled acquisitiveness of the generality of our people.

I like to elaborate a bit on what I have just said about the problem of viable political system and the right leadership. Since the Country attained independence 25 years ago, we have witnessed fierce, sometimes bloody elections, and military coup-de-tat, sometimes said to be bloodless. As between the dramatis personae in these elections and coups on the one hand, and the populace on the other, the elections and coups have had one feature in common: as soon as the previous government was dislodged the in-coming government listed all the ills of the outgoing that would be righted. The populace found themselves agreeing with the condemnation of the old, and the in-coming government was ushered in with great acclamation as the saviour. Before long that government was toppled; the new government used almost the same list of ills to condemn the condemnation while rejoicing with the new arrival. This has been the pattern to this day and we now have a nation that always shouted halleluyah yesterday and crucify him (or them) today. So, the question arises: what exactly is wrong with Nigeria? What is it in our system that produces the kind of leadership we have had?

Now, there are three main political ideologies in the world: Socialism, Capitalism, and Mixed-economy. It would appear that, tacitly, Nigeria is for mixed-economy, though some of our leaders have talked glibly about being socialists; but the country has never been better for it economically; otherwise, we would not be dissipating energy today debating the IMF. Again, there are two major political systems in the World: Parliamentary and Presidential, each with the traditional Lower and Upper House. Nigeria has tried both, and the country is none the wiser.

In such a situation the time has come for the country to fashion out a new political order. I wish, therefore, to repeat a proposal I have made in my previous papers that Nigeria should give the world an entirely new political system.

I propose that this new system should be Parliamentary in nature (as opposed to Presidential) and it should consist of a Three-tier Chamber made up of the Lower, Upper and the Uppermost, this last comprising traditional rulers. At the Local Government level the present Traditional (or Emirate) Council should form the base to build on. This is not the appropriate place to elaborate on this proposal. But for now I like to call on the pundits in this university and other universities to take up the call by the President that we must begin the search for a new political order. The time has come for us to realize that the history of what is now Nigeria (before the British), having regard to our people's inherent culture and temperament, are such that the European (or American) brand of political order will be difficult (if not impossible) to work with us. Twenty-five years have adequately proved this.

For my part, our experts should now have been debating a new political order rather than IMF, or how much comes from our internal resources; our money will continue to be squandered and our economic position shaky unless we have a political order that will not wish to tarnish their good name; who will bake the cake well for equitable sharing rather than rush to share it half-baked for themselves. Be that as it may, there is still hope for the future."

Having said all that, the question now is whether President Babangida is right in his assessment of the country's political structure in the 25 years of independence. There are many who are living witnesses and none can disagree.

CAUSES OF INSTABILITY

The next question obviously is what has been responsible for this instability? Why has unity of purpose eluded us, or why has the much talked about "unity in diversity" proved meaningless? These are the questions President Babangida wants his countrymen to find answers to. What is wrong with our system?

Ethnic Sentiments

The answer, I submit, is to be found in the poor foundation for our Independence-ethnic identification. During the Independence Talks held in London in the 1950s, Nigerians had three spokesmen: Abubakar Tafawa Balewa for the Northern (Hausa) block that came to be called Northern Region, Obafemi Awolowo for the Western (Yoruba) group that became known as Western Region, and Nnamdi Azikiwe for the Eastern (Ibo) group that evolved into the Eastern Region. Whether by accident or design, the ethnic communities from which these three champions of our Independent country or Premier of their ethnic community. Thus, our Independence was based on the three Regions that corresponded to the Hausa, Ibo, Yoruba ethnic groups.

It soon became clear, however, that these were not the only ethnic groupings in the country: the Midwest showed they had little in common with the Yoruba West; the Middle Belt nothing in common with the Hausa North. The Eastern Region was even more complex comprising other major

ethnic groups of Efiks/Annangs (Cross River State), Ikwerre/Kalabaris/
Ijaws (Rivers State) along with the Ibo heartland of Onitsha and Owerri
(Anambra and Imo States).

Unity in Diversity?

At the early stages of our Independence our political leaders led the
citizenry to applaud what was described as our unity in diversity. But events
up to the present day have proved clearly that the nation had remained not
only in geographical feature, but also in its culture and religion and natural
temperament. But since Independence these diversities have become more
accentuated, and ethnic sentiment has become a very strong weapon not
only in partisan politics but also in sharing the so-called national cake.
Even the coups have smelt of this cankerworm of ethnic pressure called
ethnic balancing. That the country is more diverse and unstable, and many
minority ethnic groups writhing under feeling of blatant oppression was
brought very much to the fore when the Shagari Administration (1979–83)
made a move to create more States. Had that exercise gone through, the
emergent States (Heaven knows how many would have resulted) would have
corresponded almost exactly to the provinces under the Colonial Administration, and clamor for States in the (Shagari) exercise was motivated by
one consideration only, i.e., self-preservation, the feeling by the minority
ethnic groups to be given a place in the sun to manage their own destiny
rather than being dictated to and controlled by the majority ethnic groups
that invariably corresponded with the political parties.

Thus, functionaries in every successive Government (national and state)
have made it their bounden duty to project their own ethnic group or, in
common parlance, their "kith and kin." Even if they have to resort to force
where all other strategies failed.

Federal Character

It would appear that this was the fear (of majority domination of mi-
nority ethnic group) that the drafters of the 1979 Constitution and the
Federal Military Government at the time tried to allay by providing in the
Constitution what in popular parlance is now known as "Federal Character."

Federal Character was to ensure by constitutional means that every state had a share of the national cake-in distribution of Federal amenities, job opportunities and Board appointments. As a constitutional provision it sounded well to the reader, but in practice it in no way solved the problems which had grown worse for minorities.

Some examples will illustrate this. All the nineteen states were represented in Shagari's Council of States and the Economic Council. When the "cake" was to be shared or political issue debated, the whole exercise always ended up in the three ethnic groups that dominated the three major political parties (of defunct NPN,UPN, and NPP) having the largest shares. This was not by any design but by the operation of the "Federal Character" which enabled the four Yoruba states, seven or eight Hausa states and two Ibo states to always team up according to their respective ethnic groups. It dawned on the original minority groups represented by Bendel, Rivers, Cross River, Plateau and Benue that they were still outnumbered and out voted even by the parties in whose band-wagon some of them were. This was particularly true of Bendel, Cross River and Rivers who, though associated with the other major parties, found themselves by force of circumstance coming together to scramble for their piece of the "cake." Thus, the practical application of the so-called "Federal Character" was that where appointments were too few or the booty too small to be divided into nineteen, then ethnic grouping came into play and the largest had it.

I was opportuned once to have a private audience with (President) Shagari, and I expressed my misgivings about the operation of "Federal Character," saying that the drafters of the Constitutions merely gave a constitutional backing to ethnic feelings that had hitherto been practised clandestinely. Shagari saw the point. He thought that "Federal Character" was introduced to keep a tribalistic Head of State in check, and there would be no problem if he was broadminded enough to apply it objectively and equitably. Recalling how much he strained himself at every meeting of the National Council of State to keep a topic out of the realm of ethnic sentiments, I had to tell him that the country might not always be blessed with a broad-minded head as he was, and that even if there was, the experience of debates at the time showed that the "Federal Character" in practice was incapable of allaying the fears of the minorities. We closed the discussion when he said, "let us see how things go."

Another example of the ineffectiveness of "Federal Character" is Bendel State. "Federal Character" had come to be a formula for sharing amenities in areas where there was multiplicity of ethnic groups. Bendel State, usually referred to as "miniature Nigeria," has nineteen Local Government Areas. But whenever it came to sharing anything, the outcome invariably ended in ethnic grouping-three Local Government Areas in Benin teamed up as Benin; two local government areas in Ishan teamed up as Ishan; Urhobo (three) and Ibo (two) local government areas teamed up, respectively. Yet a third example of ethnic feelings at work. A new political development was rearing its head during 1979–83 when someone mooted the idea of the minority elements within the three major parties coming together to form an entirely new party in a bid and hope to present the 1983 Presidential candidate. These minority elements in the major political parties came from Bendel, Rivers, Cross River, Plateau and Benue States. The idea turned out to be still-born. Although as a political strategy those concerned saw the reasonableness of the proposal, it got into deep waters over the question of which section would produce the group's first Presidential candidate-diverse as the components of the group were.

I have brought this lengthy discussion to show that Nigeria has no other problem but that of misapplied ethnic considerations or the emphasis our political leaders placed (or rather misplaced) on these considerations. The founding of our political system (in 1950–54) on ethnic grouping was a step in the right direction but the failure to relate the grouping to the appropriate ethnographical regions) in present-day Nigeria. Perhaps we did not realize it then but we see it clearly today. Ethnographically, our people are so diverse in customs, traditions, temperament and historical evolution that no foreign type of political system or arbitrary union can bind us together without correct re-alignment.

All the political blood that has been shed (in coups and in politics) has been shed not so much for political ideology (which the generality of our people never knew or discussed any way) but solely that the party and its leader are "our own." As it is at the national level so it is at the state or local level. Thus, people have bribed, rigged and committed arson and murder, all to keep "our man" there so he can speak for "our people." And yours truly, "our man" gets there (at the Centre, state or local) and his first duty is to his ethnic community; he gets his kith and kin into positions, and diverts development projects to his area even if such projects proved economically unviable in the area. We are all witnesses to the blatant truth that in 25 years of Independence, the minority ethnic communities have been greatest losers in the game, not because they lacked the human resources but because they lacked the numerical strength to struggle with the large groups.

It is appreciated that the problem of minority cannot be totally solved as there will always be minority within a minority. What is needed is a measure to protect the minority group against the overbearing influence of the predominant ethnic groups.

It has already been pointed out above (and the assertion is incontrovertible) that the only reason for the demand for the creation of states is self-preservation-the protection of individual ethnic communities, particularly those who see themselves as minority within the larger group.

When in 1914 Lugard introduced his indirect rule system, he used ethnic community with its paramount ruler as the unit of the Administration. The colonial "Provincial system" that evolved from the system coincided almost to the last inch with the ethnic identity. The list of colonial provinces from a 1944 map is shown hereunder:

PROVINCES IN NIGERIA IN 1944

	Colonial Provinces	*Present State.*	*Major Language*
1.	Abeokuta	Ogun	Yoruba
2.	Adamawa	Gongola	Hausa/Fulfulde
3.	Bauchi	Bauchi	Kanuri/Fulfulde
4.	Benin	Bendel	Edo
5.	Benue	Benue	Tiv/Idoma/Igala
6.	Borno	Borno	Kanuri/Fulfulde
7.	Calabar	Cross River	Efik/Ibibio
8.	Colony	Lagos	Yoruba
9.	Ijebu	Ogun	Yoruba

10.	Ilorin	Kwara	Yoruba.Nupe
11.	Kabba	Kwara	Ebira
12.	Kano	Kano	Hausa
13.	Katsina	Kaduna	Hausa/Gwari
14.	Niger	Niger	Hausa/Gwari
15.	Ogoja	Cross River	Efik/Ibibio
16.	Ondo	Ondo	Yoruba
17.	Onitsha	Anambra	Igbo
18.	Owerri	Imo/Rivers	Igbo/Ezon
19.	Oyo	Oyo	Yoruba
20.	Plateau	Plateau	Angas/Tiv
21.	Sokoto	Sokoto	Hausa/Fulfulde
22.	Warri	Bendel	Urhobo/Itsekiri
23.	Zaria	Kaduna	Hausa/Gwari

These 23 former provinces encompass some nine to twelve major ethnic (linguistic) communities as shown in the above table.

Each of the provinces or present States has other minor languages, but I have picked the largest two where there are more than two. Owerri (Imo/Rivers) in No. 18 calls for some explanations. The colonial provinces were Onitsha province and Owerri province. The Owerri provinces at that time included the areas that now form Rivers State and had its headquarters in Port Harcourt. It is the Rivers areas of what was Owerri province that now form Rivers State, hence the combination in the second column.

There are important observations to be made in respect of these provinces and ethnic groupings. Although the Northern Provinces appear to have "Hausa" as the ethnic group, the truth is that most of these areas had distinct indigenous ethnic communities (later described as "pagan" with the advent of Othman Dan Fodio in the Western half, El Kanemi in the Eastern half, Christian missionaries in the "Middle Belt" provinces). The whole of the Yoruba provinces have always remained as homogenous as they are today. Of the two provinces that make up present-day Bendel, only Benin province, with the possible exception of a small Ibo group, has homogenous Edo ethnic community. Warri province consists of Itsekiri,

Urhobo and Ijaw. The Eastern province comprise the Ibos, Kalabaris, Efiks, Ibibios, Annangs, Ijaws and Ikweres. These Eastern ethnic groups also had varied traditional governments. Originally, with perhaps the exception of Onitsha and the Kalabari/Amayanabo Kingdoms, the real Ibo heartland had no "king" comparable to Oba in the West and Emir in the North. To make up for this the colonial masters created "Chiefs" that came to be known as "Warrant Chiefs," most of whom later metamorphosed to "traditional rulers" as known today.

These were some of the factors considered by the National Conference of Traditional Rulers' in Kaduna in November, 1983, that led to the unanimous adoption of the following definition for "traditional rulers":

> A traditional Ruler is the person who by virtue of his ancestry oc-
> cupies the throne or stool of an area and who has been appointed to it in
> accordance with the customs and traditions of the area and whose throne
> has been in existence before the advent of the British in Nigeria. The area
> over which he and his forebears before him have ruled or reigned must
> have at least a Native Authority created for it in 1910 or the date of the
> introduction of Native Authority to area concerned provided that in the
> case of the former Eastern Region of Nigeria, traditional stools established
> according to the custom and tradition of the people and recognized by the
> Governments in those areas and occupied at the date of this resolution
> will not by virtue of this definition be disqualified; provided also that
> in respect of other parts of the Federation of Nigeria, traditional stools
> similarly established prior to the 1st of October, 1979, will not by virtue
> of this definition be disqualified.

TRADITIONAL INSTITUTION IN THE POLITICAL ORDER

Lord Lugard in 1914 recognized the inherent diversities in our cultures, hence he built his system of Administration around the traditional heads of these diverse cultures. At the early state of British rule the policy of indirect rule was adopted. The British ruled through paramount (traditional) rulers and where there were no effective systems of traditional government, influ-ential and powerful persons within the communities were appointed and given powers to function in the same manner as existing traditional rulers. This category of persons assumed titles which have through the years been recognized and accepted by the communities concerned as traditional rulers. Traditional rulership properly belongs to the period before the advent of British rule. The institution survived the British rule because it was found to be indispensable for the implementation of the British policy of indirect rule and thus for the smooth running of Government and for the mainte- nance of law and order amongst the people whose loyalty to their culture remained unshaken. Traditional rulers have remained the unquestionable leaders of their people, a unifying force minimizing hostility and maintain- ing peace among people with divergent political beliefs. The institution of Traditional Rulers must be seen as something brought from the past, our cultural heritage, needed today for maintaining unity and peace amongst our people and for support to the institutions established by the Constitu- tion for operating democratic system of Government.

Why do our people listen to their traditional rulers? The answer is simple-the traditional institution is rooted in the customs and traditions of the community; the customs/traditions of our Nigerian people (indeed Africans) derive their strength and sanctions from natural (God's) law which, if examined, are not different from the Christians' Ten Commandments or the Islamic Sha'aria. The only difference is the language and form in which they are expressed. It is because our people realize that these customs/tra- ditions derive their force from God's commandments that our people in the rural areas yet unspoiled by "civilization" and "modernity" live in peace to this day. Even to this day, when there is a disturbance anywhere in the country the "Administration" calls on traditional rulers to intervene and people listen to them if partisan political leader or an overbearing governor allows them handle it their own way. One can cite several examples of this from different parts of the country.

PROPOSALS FOR A NEW POLITICAL ORDER.

Having said all that, we now proceed to consider proposals for a new political order. In doing this, we must accept the fact that 25 years of experi- ment have shown conclusively that no foreign type of political structure or government will succeed with us, having regard to the country's diversity in historical evolution, customs traditions, religions and temperament. These are the elements in our "diversity" which we were made to believe "united" us but which, in fact, have been fragmenting the country in the name of "creation of States" because the diversifying factors were initially not properly managed. Taking all factors into consideration the solution to the country's instability lies in allaying the fears of minorities and recognizing the effective position of traditional rulers in the ethnic communities. We must therefore do the following:

Nigeria must give the world an example of a tri-cameral legislature comprising:

• Lower House (elective):

• Middle House (elective); and

• Upper House (of traditional rulers nominated by themselves).

There is nothing sacrosanct in a single or bi-cameral legislature (that have failed us in 25 years).

We must recognize that our "diversity" or "Federal character" is nothing but our individual ethnic sentiments, and that ethnic sentiment is linguistic and cannot be controlled by arbitrary geographical union.

We must revert as nearly as possible to the Colonial Provinces as listed earlier above, in view of the fact that each of such provinces in the old days almost corresponded to one or two ethnic groups within it. We must eliminate, or at least, reduce to the barest minimum, our areas of conflict by reducing the number of elections, apart from high maintenance costs of services necessary to make the system truly "presidential." Although our experience (1979–83) was only a "skeleton" of a presidential system, its cost weighed heavily on an impoverished nation.

We need to return to Westminster type of government to reduce areas of conflict both in operation and during elections. Our own presidential system had too many captains, and the country has never had it so bad. The military must return to the barracks and concentrate on their traditional function of keeping the security of the nation.

NIGERIA MUST REMAIN A FEDERATION

We will now try to elaborate on some of these ideas.

The historical evolution of the component parts of present-day Nigeria is such that the subsequent unification of these pieces as three "Regions," far away from what Lord Lugard did, is nothing short of putting together "birds of different feathers" in the Regions. Attention has already been directed to our diversity in many facets of human endeavour that in totality form a nation's (or a community's) culture. Nevertheless, we can and should remain a federation and not a confederation, provided the various cultures and traditions of our people are respected as was done in Lugard days.

The United States of America, regarded by some as the greatest power today, fought their civil war over the choice between confederacy and federation, and is today a Federation. The Soviet Union was a multinational, *federal* state uniting over a hundred different peoples. In a manner of speaking (because they do not use the word to describe themselves) the United Kingdom is a Federation (of England, Wales, Scotland and Ireland). I believe it is correct to assert that everyone of the commonwealth countries is a Federation. It is a fact of history that prior to the Lugard experiment many of our independent "kingdoms" (which also corresponded to our ethnic, or tribal, communities) were often at war with one another. Something similar to those inter-tribal wars are still with us today as inter-ethnic boundary clashes. The Nigerian civil war was nothing but inter-ethnic conflict and the "Republic of Biafra" crumbled perhaps not so much due to the Federal might but for the breakaway of the non-Ibo ethnic communities. If these things are happening before our very eyes today, why do some people think that our salvation lies in a confederation particularly after our experience of the use (or misuse) by politicians of "Road Traffic wardens" and "security men." Our choice lies in the better of two evils, and since the chances of inter-ethnic conflicts will be far less in a Federation, we should choose the lesser of the two evils, viz Federation.

We propose a Federation with a strong Centre but with increased functions to the State. We are not advocating existence of "States" any longer, but we have used the expression here because it is appropriate at this juncture to mention the kind of Federal Centre we are advocating. We are proposing that the "State" system, as presently structured, should be abolished.

Instead, the pre-independence Provinces (about 23 in number) shall form the Federation. Each of such Provinces shall be an autonomous province.

The Federal Parliament

We should return to the British Parliamentary system for reasons already adduced earlier. In addition to those reasons, the British type has one great merit to commend it. It is that before any general election Parliament is dissolved and the Prime Minister, with his Cabinet, resigns. This ensures that the Prime Minister no longer has access to government machinery with which to prosecute the elections to his advantage. Here in Nigeria, even in States, the head of government remains in office throughout the duration of elections exercising all his constitutional powers. It is, therefore, not surprising that a head of state (or governor) once in power becomes difficult, if not impossible, to dislodge. Little wonder that all sides engage in all kinds of evil deed to remain in office or to dislodge the incumbent.

On the other hand, the U.S.A is a classic example of the Presidential system. But it is a known fact that how well (or badly) it works depends very much on the caliber, the strength, the "foxiness" of the incumbent President or Presidential candidate. Today, "lobbying," which is a less ugly word (euphemistically) than our "bribery," has over the years in the U.S.A. developed into a profession, and they now have recognized "professional lobbyists" whose assignment ranges from "explaining policy" to buying "conscience" with anything, including threat and providing "lovers" (call-girls).

Similarly, our experiment in the Presidential System (1979–83) resulted in the institutionalization of bribery and corruption. Furthermore, it simply "legalized" what our politicians had done "underhand" in the past, and our system of lobby became open racket. Those holding public offices practised the evil without any qualms and it assumed the proportion of daylight robbery. So we became a nation of money worshipers. Of course, one must concede that there is lobbying in the U.K., but because of their system they still do it in the quiet, and those caught while in office have been honorable enough to "call it quits"—in disgrace. At election time, their system, especially the mass resignation of the Cabinet, creates so much uncertainly that down-right bribery is discouraged. Hence it is done not only with finesse but with some circumspection. Take, for example, the celebrated case of the British Minister of trade who had to resign simply because it was thought that his decision might have been influenced by a dinner party he attended which was hosted by a business man! It is common sense that we cannot swallow the British system hook, line and sinker, as was done in the First Republic. For reasons that will come out later in the light of our (bitter) experience to date, we have to adapt the British system to suit our peculiar make-up or diversities as known today.

The Federal Legislature shall consist of three chambers as follows: *Lower House, Middle House, and Upper House to be known as National Council of Traditional Rulers.*

ELECTIONS

The Lower House: For elections to the Lower House each Province (or multiple Provinces as the case may be) shall be divided into specified number of electoral districts, equal number for every ethnic group, irrespective of geographical size or population of each province or group of provinces. This means that where an ethnic community occupies more than one province, such group of provinces will be divided into the specified number of electoral districts in the same way as a province "housing" an ethnic group. Thus, the largest ethnic group will have the same number of electoral districts as the smallest. In this way, large and small ethnic communities will have equal representation in the lower house. We propose 25 of such districts for each autonomous province or group of provinces that constitute an ethnic group. Each district will elect one person. Thus, Benin Province, or Benue Province, for example, with one ethnic group (or one predominant group), will have the same number of representation as the combined Onitsha Province and Owerri Province that jointly have one ethnic group. Based on that figure of 25 electoral districts per ethnic group the Lower House will have something like 25 multiplied by Y members (y being number of ethnic groups). We have identified earlier on at least nine and at most twelve major ethnic (linguistic) groups. Because each autonomous province corresponds roughly to an ethnic group, consideration of interests of different ethnic communities will initially commence at this level.

The Middle House: Elections to the Middle House shall be based on numerical constituencies, i.e., the whole country shall be divided into electoral districts, each with a specified number of population. If we take the country's population to be 100 million by 1990, we propose 200 electoral districts, each of 500,000 citizens. Thus, the Middle House, based on "one man one vote," will have 200 members.

The difference between the formula for election to the Lower House and that for election to the Middle House is that representation to the latter is purely on general population basis as it applied to the country as a whole, while the former is designed to cater purely for ethnic representation. And since there is equal number of districts for every ethnic group in the lower house, no one "tribe" will be at advantage over the other in that house. The aim of this arrangement is that what the larger ethnic group loses by having the same representation as the smaller group in the house is gained in the middle house where the smaller group loses on account of population.

The Upper House: The National Council of Traditional Rulers shall comprise two representatives from each Provincial Council of traditional rulers. The two representatives shall include the Chairman of the provincial Council and a second representative elected by members of the Provincial Council of Traditional Rulers from amongst themselves to serve in the Upper House. The latter shall serve in the Upper House for a period of not less than two or more terms of three years at a time. The tenure of the Chairman of the Provincial Council of Traditional Rulers in the Upper House (National Council of Traditional Rulers) shall be governed by his tenure as chairman of the Provincial Council of Traditional Rulers. For 23 provinces the National Council will have a minimum of 45 members; membership here is based on provinces (as opposed to ethnic grouping) because they are not elected, and being "fathers of the people," they are expected to objectively oversee the Lower House, advise and check abuses of recklessness where necessary.

LEGISLATIVE PROCESS

Each of the three Houses (Lower, Middle and Upper) is free to propose a legislation by way of Bill; the consideration of every bill with the exception of those relating to matters listed below, shall commence in the lower house and end in the middle house. Bills and resolutions of the two lower Houses on matters listed below must receive the approval of the Upper House before they can become law or effective. Where there is disagreement between the Lower and Middle Houses, the issue in disagreement shall be referred to the Upper House for consideration and the views of the Upper House shall be referred to a joint committee of both lower Houses. Agreement reached by simple majority of vote shall be binding on all the three houses. The matters in respect of which no bill or resolution shall become law or be effective unless such bill or resolution is passed by the upper house are as follows:

- Fundamental human rights of citizens
- Amendment of the Constitution
- Provincial boundary adjustment
- Land use and tenure system
- Declaration of war
- Religious matters
- Impeachment

This list is not exhaustive. There shall be no difference in treatment between "Money Bill," and other Bills. All Bills shall be subjected to the procedure outlined above.

The Upper House shall meet not less than twice a year. A meeting of the House shall be convened at any time to consider urgent matters of national interest at the request of any one of the following:

- Not less than one third of the members
- The Chairman
- The Prime Minister
- Any of the lower house by resolution

The Upper House shall be empowered to intervene at any time a situation to be clearly described in the constitution arises in which in the opinion of two-thirds of the members it will be in the interest of the nation to dissolve the Lower House, or to impeach the head of government for abuses, corruption, recklessness and other vices such as led to military intervention in the past. It is the absence of effective machinery for checking the excesses of the elected government in previous constitutions that left military intervention the only option. (For the avoidance of doubt, it is proposed that where the third in this and preceding paragraph results in a fraction the figure shall be rounded up to the next whole number).

When the two lower Houses are dissolved, an interim Government shall be appointed by the chairman of the Upper House-National Council of Traditional Rulers-to carry on Government business and organize elections to the Houses within a period of three months at the end of which the interim Government shall automatically fold up, provided that the Upper House shall have power to grant the interim Government an extension of a further period not exceeding three months to enable it complete its assignment. The interim Government shall consist of:

- The Chief Justice of the Federation as Chairman
- The Grand Khadi as member
- The Chief of Army Staff as member
- The Chief of Naval Staff as member
- The Chief of Air Staff as member and
- The Inspector-General of Police as member

The Chairman of each of the House shall be elected by its members, and he shall hold office for one session of the House in the case of the Lower House, and for one year in the case of the Upper House unless, in each case, he is re-elected, provided that he does not hold office for more than two terms.

Since traditional rulers are permanent by God's Grace in their positions, the National Council of Traditional Rulers, with its initial composition, shall be a permanent body unless otherwise altered by changes emanating from the Provincial Council of Traditional Rulers that did the nomination. The composition of the National Council of Traditional Rulers will therefore not be affected by general elections.

THE HEAD OF STATE/GOVERNMENT

Since Independence, these two positions have been combined in one holder or separated. Either way their position have created problems for the country. One of the factors that were thought by some to have led to the fall of the First Republic was the alleged refusal by the then president (Nnamdi Azikiwe) to "take over" the Government from the Prime Minister,

Abubakar Tafawa Balawa. The military regime have known one incumbent holding both positions, but then there was trouble because it was thought that one part of the country monopolized it.

Prime Minister

There is no special merit in having a separate "Head of state"—the position is ceremonial. So we submit that it can conveniently be combined with the position of Head of Government which really is the functioning position. The combined position shall be held by and known as the Prime Minister (or any suitable name). The position shall rotate among the ethnic groups as described below.

The Prime Minister (Head of State/Head of Government) shall be elected by a joint meeting of the Lower and Middle Houses from among the members of the two Houses which belong to the ethnic group whose turn it is at the time to produce the Prime Minister. In this regard, the major ethnic groups earlier identified and numbering between 9 and 12 have been zoned as listed below and the first zone on list shall produce the first Prime Minister under the new dispensation. Subsequent Prime Ministers shall be appointed in turn according to the order on the list.

ETHNIC LANGUAGE GROUPS

Zone	Provinces	Principal Languages
1.	Adamawa	Hausa/Fulfulde/Gwari
	Bauchi	Hausa/Fulfulde/Gwari
	Sokoto	Hausa/Fulfulde/Gwari
	Kaduna	Hausa/Fulfulde/Gwari
	Katsina	Hausa/Fulfulde/Gwari
	Zaria	Hausa/Fulfulde/Gwari
2.	Abeokuta	Yoruba
	Ijebu	Yoruba
	Colony	Yoruba
	Ondo	Yoruba
	Oyo	Yoruba

3. Ilorin . . . . Nupe/Ibira
    Kabba. . . . . Nupe/Ibira
    Niger . . . . Nupe/Ibira
    Abuja . . . . Nupe/Ibira

4. Benin . . . . Edo/Urhobo/Itsekiri
    Delta . . . . Edo/Urhobo/Itsekiri

5. Calabar . . . . Efik/Ibibio
    Ogoja. . . . . Efik/Ibibio

6. Onitsha . . . . Ibo
    Owerri . . . . Ibo

7. Benue. . . . . Tiv/Idoma
8. Plateau . . . . Angas/Tiv
9. Rivers . . . . Ezon

(This list has been compiled with due regard to ethnic grouping, and the ranking is according to the number of province including in each zone).

His functions shall be similar to the traditional function of Head of State and Head of the Prime Minister at the time of taking office shall not be less than 45 years or more than 65 years old.

There shall be a Deputy Prime Minister. For amity and smooth running of government, it is only reasonable to allow the Prime Minister have a "Deputy" he can work with. Therefore, the Prime Minister shall be free to appoint a "Deputy" but subject to the following:

The Deputy shall not come from the Prime Minister's own ethnic group: he shall be chosen from the list of zones described above for the appointment of Prime Minister but in reverse order beginning with the last zones on the list.

The Prime Minister shall choose his "Deputy" from either of the lower Houses: and the "Deputy" shall be given a portfolio in addition to such other functions as are assigned to him by the Prime Minister.

Federal Cabinet

The Prime Minister shall be free to appoint his cabinet from the two lower Houses, provided, however, that no ethnic group represented in each province (or multiple province) shall have more than two persons. The Prime Minister with his cabinet shall be responsible and answerable to the populace through the lower House, he and his cabinet shall be eligible to defend any Government action in any of the three Houses. At the end of the four-year term or on the dissolution of the two lower Houses, he and his cabinet shall resign. If, however, circumstances force it before the dissolution of parliament, they shall resign or be removed from office provided such resignation or removal will not affect the individual's membership of either of the two lower Houses and provided further that the zone that produced the removed Prime Minister shall retain the right to serve the remaining period of life of that parliament. A new cabinet will also be formed in accordance with the procedure.

THE PROVINCES

"States" as presently structured should be abolished. We have advocated that the Federal shall comprise the 23 colonial provinces, each or multiple of which correspond to definite ethnic communities. Thus there were 23 such provinces but, ethnographically speaking, they traversed only about twelve different major ethnic groups. To these 23 colonial provinces, Abuja, the Federal capital Territory, should be added as a new province. It had already been incorporated in the zones listed above.

For administrative purpose each province shall be administered by:

Provincial Resident who shall be an indigene of the Province and shall be nominated by the Provincial Assembly from amongst its member in rotation according to the list of Local Government Area arranged in order of population based on figures in force at the time of introduction of the new arrangement.

Provincial Council of Traditional Rulers which shall be the upper "legislative" House in the province;

The provincial Assembly to comprise elected members; and

Village Council headed by the village (or district) head with the "edion" or elders as members. In most parts of the country there is a customary procedure for selecting and making these "edion" (amale as sometimes called in Ibo areas or Bale in Yoruba areas).

The *Provincial Resident* (or any other name chosen) shall be nominated by a meeting of the Provincial Assembly and appointed by the Chairman of the Provincial Council of Traditional Rulers. The President shall perform functions similar to those of the Premier under the 1963 Constitution.

The Resident shall hold office for four years only and shall relinquish his post before any general election to the Provincial Assembly. He shall function, in relation to the provincial Government, in much the same way as the Prime Minister in the center. His remuneration shall be on the provincial Budget.

Provincial Cabinet

The Provincial Resident shall be free to choose his cabinet comprising the Deputy Resident and commissioners from among members of the provincial Assembly, provided that the Deputy Resident shall not come from the provincial Resident's ethnic group if the province is heterogeneous or from his local government council area where the province is heterogeneous. He shall be selected from the ethnic group or the local government area whose turn it is to have the Deputy Resident according to a predetermined order. For this purpose, there shall be a predetermined list showing the order in which the ethnic groups or the local government areas in the province are to produce the Resident and his Deputy, and while the Provincial Resident shall be appointed starting with the first on the list, the Deputy Resident shall be appointed starting from the last on the list.

When appointing his commissioners, the Provincial Resident shall ensure equitable representation of the ethnic groups or of the local government areas depending on which is applicable.

The Provincial Council of Traditional Rulers

The Provincial Council of Traditional Rulers shall be made up of traditional rulers in the province in accordance with the law in force in the area concerned for the present State Council of Chiefs. Its Chairman shall be appointed and he shall hold office in accordance with the existing law for the Council of Chiefs in the area. It shall be a permanent body like the National Council of Traditional Rulers, and for the same reason, its functions shall be similar to those of the National Council, except that they shall be in relation to province and the institutions therein.

The Provincial Assembly is the elective chamber and the lower House. Whereas at the center the Middle House is the "People's House," at the provincial level this is the Provincial Assembly. Elections to Provincial Assembly shall be on the same pattern as to the Middle House, i.e., on the principle of election districts based on population.

Local Government

The existing local government system based on the local government reforms of 1976 shall be retained. There shall, therefore, continue to be in each local government area: a local government council made up of elected members as at present and a Traditional Council made up of all the traditional rulers in the local government areas or of the Traditional Rulers and a given number of his chiefs where there is only one Traditional ruler in the area. As at present also, where there are two or more local government areas in the domain of a Traditional Ruler, a Traditional Council or Emirate Council shall be constituted for the group of local government areas.

Functions

Local Government Councils shall be assigned specific functions which shall be exclusive to them. The practice of assigning concurrent subjects to them and the provincial Government shall be discontinued as suggested in respect of the assignment of responsibilities of the Federal and Provincial Governments.

Functionally, Traditional Councils shall relate to Local Government Councils in a manner similar to the relationship between the Provincial Assembly and the Provincial Council of Traditional Rulers. Thus, in addition to its existing functions, all bye-laws shall be referred to the Traditional Council for approval before they are issued.

The local government council budget and development plans shall also be subject to approval by the Traditional Council. No bye-law or measure affecting traditional institutions or the custom and tradition of the people shall be effective without the prior approval of the Traditional Council. The Traditional Council shall also be empowered to initiate proposals for bye laws, development plans and other issues within the competence of the Local Government Council. All matters within the purview of local government council initiated by the Traditional Council shall be referred to the Local Government Council for initial consideration. The Traditional Council shall have its own secretariat, and its budget that shall be subject to approval by the ministry of Local Government shall be a direct charge to the revenue fund of the Local Government Council (s) concerned but shall be payable direct to the Traditional Council by the Provincial Government.

The Village (or District) Committee

It suits our politicians and government functionaries to talk about those at the "grass-root level" without telling us where they are and how to reach them. I submit that the "grass-root" is at the village level and not necessarily the so-called "common man." When the Bendel State Government launched the Development Fund, Government decided that the disbursement of the fund shall be determined by the villagers, and it has worked out very satisfactorily. In my view, this is the first step at bringing the village communities into the governmental processes and in the political (not necessarily partisan) system.

I do not know of any village in country that has not got a village council of elders. It is usually headed by the eldest man going down the line in order of age seniority. The age at which one becomes an "edion" (Benin word meaning "elder") is determined by the custom of the governs age-group. My proposal here is that the village committee should be constitutionally recognized on the lines described above as the lowest level in the range of government.

The village committee shall be constituted/appointed by the Traditional

Ruler in accordance with the custom and tradition of the people. The functions of the village committee shall include promotion of self help development projects; formulation of proposals to the Traditional Rulers for community development; assisting as and when required in the collection of taxes, levies, rates; etc; maintenance of law and order; security; and the usual traditional functions applicable in the community.

The area of conflict could arise from what has been said about the legislative chambers that there are only four elective houses (the lower and the middle House at the Centre, and the Provincial Assembly and the Local Government Council in the Province) out of a total of seven different chambers throughout the country, viz: three at the center (National Council of Traditional Rulers, the Lower and Middle Houses) and four at the province (Provincial Council of Traditional Rulers, Provincial Assembly, Local Government Council and Village Committee).

We propose that polling for the four elective House shall be completed within seven days avoiding interval between elections which, in the past, created time for the contestants and their supporters to engage in fighting and other irregularities. The Traditional Rulers and the Village elders are the chosen ones of their people; also, they do not require any elections.

The Legislative lists have been a sure area of conflict. We propose the abolition of the "Concurrent Legislative List" so that functions are divided distinctly between the Centre and Province on the one hand, and between the Province and the Local Government on the other. We propose, however, that in future there should be increase in the functions of the Province without necessarily weakening the powers of the Centre; e.g., on Education, the Federal Government could have responsibility for National Policy on Education, Establish institution at post-secondary or tertiary level, while Provinces are assigned responsibility for secondary institutions and Local Government take on primary institutions. Regarding health, National Policy on Health, Teaching and Specialist Hospitals could be assigned to the Federal Government, while the other institutions are assigned to the Provinces and Local Governments.

Critics of Traditional Rulers

It is pertinent at this point to answer the critics of the third chamber comprising traditional rulers. I have read some of the criticisms in various newspapers, and they fall into two main categories:

Some traditional rulers were picked out who are said either to have "misbehaved" or made public statement that the critics saw as not progressive; and some traditional rulers were picked out as having supported politicians during the civilian past.

If these seeming "shortcoming" are all the critics can adduce for disqualifying traditional rulers from the governance of the country. Then all organizations or groups of persons, be they public or private, in which there have been the proverbial "bad eggs" would have to be banned from participating in the political system of the country. Show me the political party since independence that has been free of murders, arsonists, frauds, even treason offenders. Must the country do away with the civil service, the police force, the universities, or any other arm of the government, simply because some of their members have committed offences that range from civil to criminal?

Some critics accuse traditional rulers of taking sides in partisan politics. This is no fault of ours. The politicians themselves drive us unto taking sides. Those who are criticising us must know that during the first and second civilian regimes, the creation of traditional rulers where there were none or the promotion of junior ones was one weapon that politicians used very effectively to secure votes. A traditional ruler is also human being,. And like living creatures, the instinct of "self preservation" is also in him. I did, as far back as 1979, in my coronation address, make an analysis of our political order (or disorder?) and did indicate the stabilizing influence that traditional rulers could bring to bear on the country's body polity if given the opportunity by partisan politicians. The disorder is still with us today as it was in first civilian regime and on the eve of the re-introduction of party politics in 1979. Can anyone blame traditional rulers for trying, like all others, to keep afloat? How would you feel as a traditional to wake up one morning to hear that the governor has partitioned your domain and given each fraction a "traditional rulers" or promoted your chief to your rank?

At this point one would like to draw attention to the current trend in the position of Monarchs in Europe. A very illuminating article appeared in the American *Newsweek* magazine of November 19, 1984, on the opposition of Europe's monarchs. The article is captioned, "Europe's modern Monarchs: Royalty is once again influential in matter of State, commerce and style." Two statements from introductory paragraphs reproduced below will suffice for our purpose here:

Yet the astonishing fact is that in this final quarter of the 20th century, monarchies are flourishing in Western Europe.

All of the royal houses of Europe are seen by their people as revered symbols of stability, continuity and national unity.

Political Parties

We recommend the abolition of political parties: it is an area of conflict and should not find a place in the new political order. Before the introduction of political parties or foreign system of government, our different communities had and still have their systems. Thus, when a matter of common interest had to be decided, the village head summoned all age groups to the village square where decisions were taken by simple show of hands. Where representative have to be nominated, for example, to go to the court of the traditional ruler, they are nominated and voted for by show of hand. That is "election," and everybody knows everybody else. For reasons I shall state below, I do not support one-party system. If elections can be held in a one-party system, then there is no reason why they cannot hold in a no-party system. But if we must have two political parties, there is advantage in having three: one is bound to be the least and that will hold the balance of power between the bigger two.

The "opposition" in parliament in a political party system is a useful body, and it should be retained for the minority of the parties. One evil of the presidential system (at any rate as practiced here in 1979–83) was that nobody, not even the participants, were the leaders or the authority, the government or opposition. It was not clear who controlled whom those within or outside the government. It is to be hoped that the opposition does not go beyond constructive criticism to subversion.

ONE-PARTY SYSTEM

Some people have advocated one-party as a means of ensuring stability. Those who advocate this are only exhibiting their latent support for dictatorship. It is a natural phenomenon that when opposing view is repressed the holders go "underground." This is invariably so in one-party system which is usually the result of the majority forcibly swallowing up the left-over of the minority. The latter fear to express contrary views to the "leader" and talk "sweet something" to him but behave differently behind him. So, a one-party system is not as healthy or stability-guaranteed as the proponents will want us to believe.

ELECTION PROCEDURES

Our intention is to try as much as possible to reduce areas of conflict. The 1979–83 era with five political parties was the worst period the country has ever passed through at election times; not only did different parties fight with one another, but members of the same party fought themselves. We propose that for elections into the Lower and Middle House at the centre and the Provincial Assembly, the communities in the electoral districts (already described) will select or elect their representatives in the following manner:

Any member of the community in the district will nominate a candidate. Any person wishing to go may also nominate himself (or herself). After candidate have been nominated and seconded, the list will be published— thanks to news media—or pasted at public square of community hall or any other suitable place.

Each of those eligible to vote will simply do so by dropping the ballot paper in the box bearing the photograph of the candidate. The cost of the exercise will be entirely borne by the Federal government.

The electoral Committee for the different electoral districts shall be constituted by the interim government earlier referred to in this chapter, membership of which shall be drawn from such organizations as trade union, market union, cooperative societies, associations of teachers and teachers in other educational institutions, provided that those to be appointed were not involved in partisan politics in the past ten years preceding military take-over. Members of the electoral committee shall be precluded from contesting any election for eight years after serving on the committee.

No member of the legislative house will be paid any stipend or remuneration for being as member other than sitting fee and traveling allowance if he uses his personal car. No official vehicles but group transport will be provided for members who do not own personal vehicles for duration of sitting. There will be no permanent residential quarters.

The effect of the foregoing process is that every member will be in the house of his choice on his own merit as an individual and representing his community. As president Babangida observed in his October 1, 1985 speech, "the political history of this nation is partly one of disillusionment with politics and politicians." In 25 years, our political leaders who (by act of providence) were also our earliest Western educated elites have caused nothing but disillusionment, unfulfilled promises, self-aggrandizement and national instability. In developed countries politics is not a "money chasing affair." It is engaged in by persons who approach it with a sense of commitment to service and duty to society "behind some pillar of ideals." Such sense of commitment to service and duty to society can only be brought out in a system, such as we have advocated, in which every aspirant to a legislature does so under his own steam and on his own merit knowing full well that there is no huge salary and unnecessary perquisites and luxury flats, and, above all, there is always his own personal vocation to return to. Too often, one heard it said by persons with self-respect and good family name to cherish that they could not fight to go into a legislative house or local government council so they do not have mud smeared on them.

PERIOD OF ELECTIONS:

Each Electoral District will be divided into wards at least two months before the polls. The electoral register will be published at least 45 days before election day. The list of nominated candidates must be published in public places at least 14 days before the polls. Polling should be done in one day, preferably on a weekend unless the day is declared a public holiday. Polling stations will open at 6 a.m. and close at midnight, followed immediately by counting and publication of results.

TRI-CAMERAL LEGISLATURE:

Some critics have argued that a third chamber would make the cost of government more expensive. It is interesting to observe that some of these same critics are advocating a presidential system which is comparatively cheap. It will be seen from our proposals that a third chamber will not add extra cost. In fact, we have proposed that "parliamentarians" of the future will get nothing but "siting allowance" and no official residence and many of the present extravagant perquisites. And except what every traditional ruler gets in his doman as traditional ruler, he will not get anything extra by being in the Third House.

As for the 23 provinces, the idea of reverting to the colonial provinces is actually not new. One or two elder statesmen had made the suggestion in the past. They were criticized on ground of cost. But the cost of increasing from 19 States to 23 provinces will not be "the last straw." In fact, in the final analysis, 23 provinces will be cheaper for, if as we argue, these provinces are virtually coterminous with ethnic spread and if our proposals do take care of fear of domination, then there will be no need for the demand for more provinces by "minorities," whereas for as long as we retain states in their present form so long will there be demand by minorities for more states ad infinitum. We are, therefore, convinced that a tri-cameral chamber will not necessarily be more expensive to run.

DIARCHY

Some have advocated a system termed "diarchy" (or a mixture of civilian and military in government). If a total military government failed to give stability, what is there to suppose that their presence in diarchy is the answer? What is required for the military is contentment. The future political system should make adequate provision for the comfort of the military personnel in terms of adequate remunerations, good accommodation and other perquisites for themselves and families. People whose nature of services is "to kill or be killed" must be given all the comfort they deserve.

THE CIVIL SERVICE

The desire of the minority ethnic groups or the so-called less advantaged areas of the country to have their needs catered for by the system was what led to the formula known as "Federal Character"; but, as we have already argued, the expression was ill-defined. With every state now having at least one or two institutions of higher learning for several years and several grammar schools for decades, there should now be no "less advantaged area" nor the need for "Federal character." In the new political order, all appointments to the Federal and Provincial Civil Services shall be strictly on merit by competitive examination of the appointing body.

THE CIVIL SERVICE COMMISSION

This shall be the "appointing body" for all Federal posts, including those designated Permanent Secretaries and heads of non-ministerial departments. All appointments shall be made by the Commission through process of advertisement or departmental recommendation. No one who has served as a member of Civil Service Commission shall be eligible for appointment to any post in the Civil Service thereafter. The secretary shall be appointed from the rank of Permanent Secretaries.

THE JUDICIARY

The Judiciary is, regrettably, one arm of government in which the nation has had a lot of problem. If there had been any doubt that state governments used (or misused) the judiciary, the events of 1979–83 removed any such doubt because some judges were patently seen to be not entirely "impartial." If we concede that such allegations were baseless but made against judges by detractors, the fact that their actions gave room for such allegations at all already dented the image of the judiciary, and the results were clearly seen in the manner politicians and government functionaries alike defiled or ignored court orders.

The method of selection of judges in the state leaves much to be desired. There were cases that evoked a spate of criticisms and petitions from the Bar on the ground that the candidate was either "unstable" or "much junior" to some others.

There is no doubt too that some Judges do dance to the tune of politicians, especially where the appointment was controversial.

I am therefore proposing that the appointment of all judges shall be made by a judicial Service Commission comprising the Chief Justice of the Federation as the Chairman, the Chairman of the committee of Benchers and not more than four retired Chief Justices of the Federation. Recommendations will be initiated at the Provincial level by a committee comprising the Chief Judge, and not more than five retired judges including chief judges if any, of the Province concerned.

The Federal Government shall set out the guidelines for appointment that shall apply equally to the Federal and Provincials Judicial Service Commissions. In particular, the judiciary shall be granted financial autonomy so that expenditure of approved vote shall not be subject to approval by any external authority. The vote shall be a direct charge to the consolidated revenue fund and in case of deficit budget the judiciary shall be entitled to the proportion of available funds in the consolidated revenue fund appropriate to its vote in relation to the total budget. We see this as a necessary measure to ensure the much needed independence of the judiciary.

RELIGION AND POLITICS

A lot of questions have been raised in recent times as to whether Nigeria is or not a "secular country." A distinction should be made between the people and the state in this context. The historical evolution of the usage of word "secular" restricted its correct application to the power, i.e. the government or state. There is no people in the world, primitive or civilized, that does not have a kind of religion that forms the basis of the people's belief. The religion indigenous to this country was originally referred to by expatriates as paganism. Islam and Christianity were later imported into the country. So, today this country has three principal religions that suit the belief of its people; they are our traditional religion, Islam and Christianity.

The Federal Government on the other hand is a secular power in the sense that as a matter of constitutional issues successive government since independence declared that they do not tie themselves to any one particular religion. Hence a head of State worship in the Church or mosque depending on his religious belief. At joint worship, leaders of Islam and Christianity officiate. The traditional religion has not reached such height. With three religions open to the populace it is only politically wise that the government as distinct from the people should remain secular, i.e. not adopting any religion as state religion.

Christian/Muslim Relations

I think it is appropriate, at this juncture, to say something about the relationship between the Christians and Muslims in the country. We cannot now run away from the naked truth that the relationship is deteriorating every day and there is no knowing to what level it will go or whether it will ever improve again. I submit that the time has come for some positive step to be taken to arrest the worsening situation which even if it ever improves will still leaves both sides suspicious of each other. I am proposing that the joint (Christian/Muslim) Committee appointed recently by President Babangida to handle the Organization of Islamic Countries (OIC) affair be retained as a permanent organ to monitor and supervise the activities of Christians and Muslims all over the country. Every one of their organizations anywhere in the country should bear the responsibility of reporting one party or the other to this joint body of any unsatisfactory or suspicious movement, and the joint committee shall take immediate step to nip it in the bud. It should be the responsibility of the committee to invite the law enforcement agency to deal with the party the joint committee found guilty if it is beyond the committee.

I would repeat, for emphasis, my suggestion that President Babangida's joint committee on the OIC be converted to a permanent organ subject to the Christians and Muslims retaining or changing their representatives from time to time. There should be joint secretaries of a Christian and a Muslim. Something like this was suggested to the Shagari Administration. But instead of constituting a committee, he decided to appoint a civil servant in the President's office for the purpose, and the whole idea got politicized even before the appointment was made.

My whole idea (and hope) is that proposed joint committee will have responsibility for dealing with any suspicious religion movement and invite law enforcement agency, if necessary, we do not know yet what the Federal Government will decide on the committee's report on the OIC; but if that committee has achieved nothing else, it has least succeeded, even if for a while, to defuse the mounting tension over the OIC, and I have no doubt it can also do so as proposed in other religious matters.

Finally, since the subject is in the context of the future political order, I would advocate that any future government should hands-off pilgrimage and leave any Christian or Muslim aspiring to fulfill that mission to make his own arrangement (as his forefathers did) subject to all travel and foreign exchange requirements.

PUBLIC ACCOUNTABILITY

To promote the culture of public accountability, it is necessary to:

- Strengthen the independence of the Auditor-General so that he could work without fear of highly placed persons. In addition to the provisions in the 1979 Constitution in that regard, the removal of the Auditor-General shall be subject to the approval (by two third vote in support) of the Upper House-the National Council of Traditional Rulers. His report shall be submitted not only to the Prime Minister and the Public Accounts Committee but also to the Legislatures. It was useful in those days when Auditor-General discovered faults and queried, and the Public Accounts Committee called on officers affected to explain or give account. The Auditor-General's report and the report of the Public Accounts Committee will be useful to the Upper House in monitoring the management of the finances of Government.

- Make public the assets declared by public officers so that members of the public could have the opportunity of pointing out the asset of any public officer known to them which the public officer might not have declared. The innovation of declaration of assets by public officers was good, but the secrecy that surrounded it made it not very useful.

SUMMARY

The proposals we have put forward are designed to ensure stability of the country through the elimination, as mush as possible, of areas of conflict. The principal area of conflict arises from the fear of domination by the majority ethnic group over the minority ethnic group. That this fear is very genuine and founded is evidenced by the plight of the minority groups in the scheme of things at the Federal, State and even Local Government level. All other evils in the body politic (appointments to positions, dispersal of amenities, even bribery and corruption) trace their root to ethnic imbalance.

Another area of conflict is the relegation of the traditional institution to the background and away from the scheme of things. And yet, that these personalities are the ones closest to the communities at the "grass-root" level and therefore cannot be brushed aside is not in doubt. Evidence for this abounds: During political campaigns, politicians try to woo traditional rulers (many who have withstood their wooing to avoid being dragged into partisanship have done so to their detriment). Government often appeals to traditional rulers in times of crisis between the citizens and government, and thank God our people have often respected our appeal, and even the military regimes recognized the need to have traditional rulers with us.

The moment politicians/governments dissociated themselves from the traditional institutions, they always courted trouble as evidence in areas where politicians/governmental action slighted the traditional ruler. Traditional Rulers, in the context of these proposals, is as defined by the National Conference of Traditional Rulers held in 1983 and reproduced earlier in this memorandum.

Our proposals are designed:
- To make every ethnic community feel wanted and have a say in the governance of the country;
- To give a place to the traditional institution in the scheme of things because traditional rulers are not only closest to their people and the keepers of their customs, but they (traditional rulers) are in fact ordained by God as proclaimed in First Peter 2:17 and Koran 2:247;
- To harness through the traditional institution, the customs/traditions of the people which derive from nature's law or God's Ordinance,

very much similar to the ten commandments and which people have ignored in the name of politics and material wealth.

The new political order we have proposed takes the following form:

- A federation with 23 Provinces whose geographical boundaries shall reflect the Colonial Province plus Abuja, the Federal Capital Territory, carved out of the old Niger, Kabba and Ilorin Province.

- A system whereby each ethnic group represented by each Province or multiple provinces shall have a say in equal proportion on the sharing of the national cake.

- Tri-cameral legislature at Federal level of which the lower two are elective and the third is the National Council of Traditional Rulers which is empowered to intervene in circumstances that justified military coups in the past.

- The Provincial Government shall have increase in functions but without weakening the powers of the Centre, as a strong Centre is desirable both in keeping the Federation together and in the country's external relations.

- Each of the tri-cameral chambers shall appoint its chairman from its members.

- In the Province there shall be a three-tier system, the first tier being the Provincial Government with two chambers, one (Provincial Assembly) elective and the other the Provincial Council of Traditional Rulers; the second tier being the local government, also with chambers: one elected local government council and the other the traditional council comprising all traditional rulers in the local government area; and the third tier being the village committee composed of village head and elders in accordance with relevant customs and tradition of the people.

- The Office of Head of State or Government shall be combined in the office of Prime Minister. The Prime Minister shall be elected by a joint meeting of the two elected legislatures at the Federal Level from among their members in rotation around the ethnic groups in the pre-determined order proposed earlier on.

- In order to allay fears (which are genuine) of minorities, "Federal

Character" shall be interpreted in terms of ethnic groups, rather than mere geographical boundaries as at present.

- Elections to the two lower House at the Centre and to the Provincial Assembly and the Local Government Council shall be done by dividing the country, the province and the local government area into electoral districts. Electorate will openly nominate candidates and vote openly; and an aspirant may nominate himself or herself. Each Electoral District will be divided into wards at least two months before the polls. Electoral register to be published at least 45 days before election, and lists of nominated candidates at least 14 days to the polling day.

- Polling is to be done in one day, and polling station will open at 6 a.m. and close at midnight; counting and the publication of results follows immediately. Prime Minister and all elective office holders at Centre and at the Provinces shall resign their appointments on the dissolution of the Legislative Houses.

- When the two Lower Houses at the Centre are dissolved and the Prime Minister and his Cabinet are relieved of their appointments, an Interim Government comprising the underlisted will be appointed by the Chairman of the National Council of Traditional Rulers to carry on the government business and organize/supervise elections into the dissolved Houses and the appointment of a new Prime Minister and his Cabinet within a period of three months at the end of which interim government shall fold up automatically.

    The Chief Justice of the Federation as Chairman
    The Grand Khadi as member
    The Chief of Staff (Army) as member
    The Chief of Air Staff as member
    The Chief of Naval Staff as member
    The Inspector-General of Police as member

- While advocating the disengagement of the military from the political system, it is strongly recommended that future government should make adequate provision for the comfort of military personnel in terms of adequate remuneration, good accommodation and other perquisites for themselves and families.

- On religion and politics, it is emphasized that Nigeria is a secular state in so far as the Government has not adopted any religion as the State religion. This position should remain so, though it allows its people to practice one or other of the three main religions—Islam, Christianity and the Traditional—in their own ways.

Future Government should hands-off arrangement for pilgrimage and let any Muslim or Christian wishing to perform to make his or her own arrangement.

May God help us all. Long Live Nigeria.

Chapter 5

On Abrogation of the Land Use Act, 1978, and a Review of the Local Government System

I maintain that the Land Use Act is no use to anyone: it is no use to the government (whether Federal or State), to industrialists and to the so-called common man . . . I submit that it is unrealistic to make any legislation against what has been described as land speculation when there is no objection to an affluent person speculation with his money in business at the Stock Exchange.

— Omo N'Oba Erediauwa, June 25, 1982

. . . We feel the time has come for measures to be taken to attract persons of high caliber to the Local Government Councils; not persons, as in the past, who failed all else and then found their way as Councillors. In this regard, we would suggest that a level of honest affluence and respectability be added as a qualification for becoming a Councillor . . . for we have heard it said by some respectable persons that the Local Government Council is no place for a person with self-respect.

— Omo N'Oba Erediauwa, June 25, 1982

IIIIIIIIIIIIIIIIIIIIIIIIIIIIIIIIIIIIIIIIIIII

"The Land Use Act: Dead or Alive," a Commentary by the OMO N'OBA, Made Available to the Press on June 25, 1982

It is very interesting to observe that the legal pros and cons in respect of the Land Use Decree (now Land Use Act) have now surfaced, causing serious open disagreement between learned Judges of our High Courts. Two Chief Judges have been reported by the news media to have declared the Act dead and of no effect. On the other hand, two High Court Judges, "with respect," have disgreed with the Chief Judges and have held that the Act is very much alive and operative.

The *New Nigerian* (alone so far of all the news media) seems to have stood firmly for the retention of this obnoxious Land Use Act and has also given its own interpretation to the disagreement between the Judges. It is for our High Courts to interpret our laws. Now that High Court Judges and Chief Judges are disagreeing, the ordinary man (but certainly not the *New Nigerian*) will eventually turn out to be the arbiter between Judges.

I have decided to express my opinion on this subject on the pages of newspapers, now that Judges have disagreed, because I have on a number of occasions called for the abrogation of this Act on the ground that it has turned out to be an ill-wind that blows no one good. Because of my pronouncements, the *New Nigerian*, in its editorial of Wednesday, May 12, 1982, took it up itself to openly insult me by calling on me to "swear" that Traditional Rulers have not abused land whose ownership was vested in them. I am prepared to ignore the insult implicit in the Acting Editor's call on me "to swear" and deal with the subject at issue. I will, however, say that the *New Nigerian* is one newspaper I normally respect for its mature publications and its choice of words. I did not expect that there could be any one on its Editorial Board who would not know that it is an insult to call on a Traditional Ruler to "swear," when "to assert" or such like phrase would equally have conveyed his thought! Perhaps if the Acting Editor had applied himself he would have appreciated the difference between "to swear" and "to prove." One can only hope that no matter how strongly the *New Nigerian* may feel on a subject, the editor would be temperate in his language.

I seize this opportunity to congratulate Mr. Dan Ochima Agbese, the newly appointed substantive editor of that newspaper (NN) June 3rd, 1982.

The Land Use Decree (or Act) is now a matter of controversy among four eminent judges. It is to hoped that sooner or later our Supreme Court will have the opportunity to pronounce on the issue. Since the Acting Editor of the *New Nigerian* has attempted to interprete the law on this subject, it would not be out of place for someone not on an Editorial Board or on the Bench to venture an opinion on the same issue.

The legal practice in the country has been that whenever there is a constitutional change which has the effect of changing the names or titles of certain government functionaries, a law is immediately also made to enable the functionaries, by their new titles or names, to assume the functions of the former functionaries. The most recent of such legislations that immediately comes to mind (though it is currently being challenged in Court by some State Governments) is the Constitution of the Federal Republic of Nigeria (Adaptation of Public Order Act) Order 1981, changing "Military Administrator" to "Commissioner of Police." In the case of the Land Use Act, Sections 274 and 276 of the 1979 Constitution have been dealt with extensively, including the definition given to the expression "former authority," by those who wish to have the Act retained. Their argument may be correct but, "with respect," it is not valid.

Section 274 says many things about "existing law" but for the purpose of this commentary, I need only refer to sub-section (5) of that section which lists out four "existing" legislations of which Land Use Decree, now Act, is one that have been specifically made part of the 1979 Constitution. This section 274 then ends with the words that the provisions of those (four) enactments "shall not be altered or repealed except in accordance with the provisions of section 9 (2) of this Constitution." It is obvious from the last words of Section 274 just quoted that any alteration to the Land Use Act must inevitably mean an amendment to the constitution, the procedure for which is set out in the Constitution itself.

Section 276, dealing with "succession," defines "former authority of a State to include references . . . to the former government of a State . . . or any person who exercises any authority on its behalf, (italics mine). Now, here, in my opinion, lies the crux of the matter. By the Constitution (Basic Provisions Transitional Measures) Decree (now Act) 1978 all the Constitution (Basic Provisions Transitional Measures) Decree (now Act) 1978 all functions conferred upon the "Military Governor" of the State became exercisable by the "Military Administrator," the last "former authority" of the State in the Military regime. The Land Use Decree came into effect in

March, 1978; the Transitional Measures Act came into effect in July, 1978. The 1979 Constitution came into effect in October 1979. At this point there is an intriguing observation worth making in the definition of the expression "former authority" in section 276: that section defines "former authority of a state" as referring to the "former government of a state." Grammatically, this clearly something of the past; but, when it comes to individual persons who acted for the "former authority," that same section talks of "any person who exercises . . ." Now, why did the section talk of the former government in the past tense but when it comes to the individual persons, it used the present tense ("exercises") when it could have completed the same definition in the past tense since it was referring to the past government? My answer is that the law-makers must have had at the back of their mind that the "government" may change, as indeed it has, but the individual functionaries, by whatever name known, would be in post at the time the Constitution came into effect. Thus, for example, of the four "existing" legislations in Section 274(5) the "Director" of the National Youth Service Corps is still as he was before the Constitution; so is the Public Complaints "Commissioner," and the "Director General" of the Nigerian Security Organization is still as he was-all these immediately before and after the Constitution came into effect.

But is the "Military Governor" or "Military Administrator" still there for the Land Use Act? We all know that this functionary disappeared with the coming into effect of the Constitution. Hence, that "person" is no longer there and was not envisaged to be there for Section 276 to speak of him in the present tense as "any person who exercises" authority for the former Government. For this to be done effectively now in relation to the civilian Governor (who is not the same either in name or authority as the Military Governor or Military Administrator), the Land Use Decree (or Act) has to be suitably amended such as was done by the Adaptation of Public Order Act Order 1981 earlier cited which changed "Military Administrator" to "Commissioner of Police." But Section 274 says such amendment can only be done in accordance with Section 9(2) of the Constitution. In so far as this has not been done and in so far as Military Governor or Military Administrator disappeared when the Constitution came into effect, where then lies the "operativeness" of the Land Use Decree or Act? It is to be hoped that our Supreme Court will have the opportunity at the earliest date to answer this question. Having said all that, one must ask: who are we lay-men to proffer an opinion an a legal technicality when Judges have disagreed with Chief Judges? But a layman may be correct, for after all, the law is said to be an ass and common law is common sense, as they say!

Now to come to the Land Use Act it self. I am strongly advocating the repeal of this Act, whether the Judges find it dead or alive, because the Act is detrimental to the governments themselves, to the industrialists and, worst of all, to the so-called ordinary man in the street. This is not a matter one needs to be sentimental about, like the Acting Editor of *New Nigerian* because we see daily the practical ill-effect of this Act. But to be able to appreciate my points, I will like to take readers back to the months before the decree was passed by the Military Government.

Shortly before the Decree was promulgated by the Military Administration, the then Chief of Staff (Supreme Headquarters), then Brigadier Shehu Musa Yar' Adua, came to Bendel State to brief the Bendel State Traditional Rulers on the impending legislation. I represented my father at the meeting, which was held in then Military Governor's Office. Before proceeding to explain the provisions of the Decree, Brigadier Yar' Adua (now a retired Major-General) informed the Traditional Rulers of the reasons he gave for the Military Government's decision. Put briefly, the reasons he gave were, first, to save the common man from the oppressive hands of the powerful land-owners. According to him, the Military Government had been afraid that if the situation (i.e the oppression of the common man) was not arrested, those Brigadier Yar' Adua termed the proletariat would one day rise against the powerful land-owners and there could be considerable bloodshed. The Military Government did not wish to be indifferent to such a possibility.

Specifically, the reasons given by Brigadier Yar' Adua fell under the following three headings:

a) Traditional land-ownership had constituted a barrier to National Development Programs and Governments were having difficulty in acquiring land for its development projects;

b) Government could not be indifferent to a system where only the rich and powerful owned land; and

c) Land racketeering and unending litigations in land transactions had become the order of the day.

To know whether the Land Use Act has been successful one must examine from personal knowledge of today's events how the Act has answered each of the three problems.

1. Traditional Land-ownership as a barrier to National Development Programs:

Has the Land Use Act made things easier for the Government? Before the Military regime and throughout the Military period the Federal and State Governments could acquire land anywhere in the country for its development projects under the Public Land Acquisition legislations, but since the promulgation of the Land Use Act, do we not see evidence daily of the inability of the Federal Government to reach the States and of the frustration in certain States for the Federal Government? Has the Federal Government Development Program not been frustrated by Some State Governments? Even within the State have there not been instances of clashes between the Government and the local community, in spite of the Act, due to indiscriminate acquisition of private properties? Is this the work of the so-called traditional land-owners? Of course, the Act has now been found to be a good political weapon and it suits some people to have it in the statue book. What about the industrialists and prospective investors who have not been able to use land to secure a bank loan because a Certificate of Occupancy is not forthcoming, and some industrialists have been hard put to it because of the excessive fees and delays they are subjected to while, in the meantime, their costing keeps escalating. Is all this a merit of the Act?

2. A system where only the rich and powerful own land:

This was what the law was designed to put right so as to protect the so-called common man. But has this common man benefited in any way from the Act? The answer is no! he has not benefited in any way. One can cite situations in which the Act operates or can be made to operate to the detriment of the citizen or the so-called common man:

(i) Under the Act a governor could revoke a Certificate of Occupancy in respect of land on which a house stands on the ground of "over-riding public interest." An Islamic scholar has pointed out that under Islamic law, a Governor or a constituted authority has no power to acquire land belonging to people unless such owners voluntarily consent to sell it.

(ii) Under the Act land cannot be allocated to a person under the age of 21 years. The same Islamic scholar pointed out that Islamic law provides no limitation to age in respect of allocation of land for residential or agricultural purposes.

(iii) Furthermore, if the provisions of the law were to be truly enforced, the Governor or any public officer authorized by him can enter upon and inspect anybody's land granted under the right of occupancy or building standing on it, and he does not need to seek the owner's consent to do so. Again, we are told that under Islamic law a person is forbidden to enter into another's house in the absence of the person's permission.

(iv) In many rural areas in the Southern States, at any rate, one thing that most impecunious man could boast of as his own was a piece of land, no matter how small, developed or underdeveloped, very often undeveloped. On his death such a piece of land was usually inherited by his child or children. Now, under the Act, a man's child cannot now succeed to such inheritance and, of course, if he is below 21 years he is completely ruled out.

(v) Under the Land Use Act, the right of a citizen over a parcel of his land is now restricted in that whereas under the customary law, an individual having been given a parcel of land by his Natural Ruler, acting on the advice of his duly appointed "Committee" possesses the land for life. This represents the English land tenure system of fee simple absolute. Now, a grant under the Land Use Act makes the recipient more of a leasee, while the government, acting through its Committee or Board, is the leasor. This, in my view, has derogated from the right of the citizen generally, and it is in contradiction of the asserted intention to improve the lot of the citizen by the promulgation of the Land Use Act.

(vi) Much as one should not be pessimistic in considering the long time effect and the manner in which the Land Use Act could be manipulated by either the Government or its agents now or in the future, there is nothing wrong in reasoning and thinking ahead with a view to having solution or at least relief, where malice dictates the basis of the application of the Land Use Act, to the detriment of any citizen. For example, what happens where a politically elected Government, having nominated its party supporters or Committee or Board members charged with the responsibilities of exercising its power under the Land Use Act, decides for political reasons to revoke a Certificate of Occupancy for reasons of over-riding public interest? Here, it may be argued that the citizen has a right to go to court to argue that the Certificate of Occupancy granted to him has been revoked maliciously for political reasons and not "for over-riding public interest." That right is available only where the citizen is in a financial position to pursue a land matter to court. Where the citizen has the means to go to court and he finally succeeded against his adversaries, the opportunity to embarrass him by attempted revocation of the Certificate of Occupancy has been created to his disadvantage. Of course, his time and money has also been expended against his will. This is where the citizen has the means to fight for his right.

(vii) Blackmail is known to be very dangerous and a powerful weapon, politically. The danger of blackmail inherent in the Land Use Act can be envisaged where a political party in power threatens to revoke the Certificate of Occupancy of an opponent with a view to intimidating this opponent to submission (in the interest of his property and on the land). This blackmail is not inherent in our old system of allocation of land under either custom or Public Lands Acquisition, for once land has been allocated and developed, it is hard for any government to acquire it compulsorily for any public interest. An attempt to do that will attract sumptuous compensation as has been decided by the highest court of our land.

(viii) Where any land acquired compulsorily is not used for public interest, the right of reversion rests in the community which originally owned the land. But in the case of revocation of a Certificate of Occupancy under the Land Use Act, the reversion seems to rest on the Government automatically, nor is there provision for compensation as in the case of compulsory acquisition.

So, with all these disabilities, how does the Land Use Act help the so-called common man?

3. Land racketeering and unending litigations:

Again, the Act has not helped to eradicate these, for cases are still rampant in courts everywhere. What is even worse is that the Act now makes it possible (as I have personally found out) for someone to "steal" somebody else's piece of land and to acquire the ownership of that land by using influence (I hesitate to say fraud) to obtain a Certificate of Occupancy. Is this what the Land Use Act is designed to do? And is it not the persons of influence who are twisting the law to their advantage in this manner? The cases that caused the High Court Judges to disagree among themselves are all part of the "unending litigations" in land transactions! So, what has the Act done to improve the situation?

THE TRUE POSITION:

The Idigbe Panel that investigated the desirability of promulgating this Land Use Act had four terms of reference, one of which was "to examine the feasibility of a uniform land policy for the entire country, make necessary recommendations and propose guidelines for implementation." It is an open secret that a large majority of the Panel recommended against a uniform land policy and favored action under existing legislations. It is also on record that at the time of the Idigbe Panel, some Military Governors of the royal family stock in some Northern States opposed the move. But Military Government decided to go ahead with it all the same on the basis of a minority recommendation. There is a wide difference between the land tenure system in the Northern States and in the Southern States. Traditional Rulers in the Northern States are still very much in the system of land allocation which is not the case in the Southern States.

The *New Nigerian* asked in its editorial of May 12, 1982 whether Traditional Rulers have not abused land whose ownership was vested in them. I would have liked to answer the Acting Editor if I knew what he meant by abusing land vested in Traditional Rulers. A generalized statement such as that is dangerous, for the fact that there may have been some instances over land is not enough basis to generalize. Everywhere in the Southern States, before the promulgation of the Land Use Act, a Traditional Ruler was entitled to and did have his own personal land just like any other citizen. Here in Benin, before the Act, the Oba of Benin was said to hold all Benin land in trust for his people; but when the Oba wanted as little as half acre for his personal use, he had to "apply" to the ward or village for allocation. Of course, the Oba's request was never refused but what he got thereby became personal. That some "big men," not traditional rulers, used the Act to their own best advantage is revealed by the spate of newspaper accounts immediately after demise of the military regime, of some communities taking umbrage against some erstwhile "big men" in uniform who, in spite of the Act, had acquired extensive areas of their land almost the size of the whole community. Those "big men" were no Traditional Rulers. We also know that under the Land Use Act whereas the Traditional Ruler in the South has practically been eliminated from the system I am yet to see a local government in the Northern States that would recommend land allocation without the knowledge at least (if not consent) of the Traditional Ruler of the area.

Now that two Judges have disagreed with two Chief Judges, I will urge that the matter be referred without further delay to the Supreme Court for further pronouncement.

I happen to know that at the instance of the Federal Attorney-General a meeting of all Attorneys-General took place to consider the desirability of repealing the Act or at least of reviewing it. It is an open secret that on the instructions of their governments many of the Attorneys-General opposed any review or abrogation of the Act. They had seen it as a useful political weapon! There is the question of the constitutional provision that anyone whose property is taken must be adequately compensated for it. I do not know how much compensation is being paid to acquire land by other State Governments, but it is common knowledge that here in Bendel State the value of land acquired now runs into several millions of Naira-unpaid. One wonders whether there is no conflict here between the Land Use Act which has deprived everybody of his land and the provision of the Constitution regarding payment of compensation for property-as distinct from "crops"!

I still maintain that the Land Use Act is no use to anyone: it is no use to the Government (whether Federal or State), to industrialists and to the so-called common man. I appeal to the President of the Federation, the State Governors, the National and State Assemblies to take steps to expunge this Act from our Constitution. I submit that the legislation in existence prior to the Land Use Act, namely, the Public Land Acquisition Law and relevant legislations contain adequate and effective provisions for acquisition of land by Governments, and similarly there are legislations against undue influence in the allocation of land. I submit that it is unrealistic to make any legislation against what has been described as land speculation when there is no objection to an affluent person speculating with his money in business at the Stock Exchange.

The Act will be abrogated or reviewed for the better, for Allah gave land to the rich and poor to use freely and to get his daily bread out of it.

IIIIIIIIIIIIIIIIIIIIIIIIIIIIIIIIIIIIIIIIIIIIIIIIII

Excerpts From a Memorandum Submitted by the Omo N'Oba on the Review of Local Government System During the Review Committee's Visit to the Palace, August 1984

We commend the Head of the Federal Military Government for setting up this Committee and in particular for putting the position of Traditional Rulers in the Local Government set up as one of your terms of reference. Both the Local Government system and the institution of the Traditional Ruler touch the day-to-day lives of our people. In many parts of this country, the ordinary man (or woman) in the town or village in search of redress takes pride in putting his problem first to his village/district head and from there to his Traditional Ruler. We believe that it is in appreciation of this fact that the present Administration has drawn Traditional Rulers close to itself. We Traditional Rulers have pledged, and will continue to pledge, our unflinching support to this administration. Unfortunately, a section of our so-called educated elite do not see why the Federal Military Government should bring the Traditional Rulers to the forefront. Such uncivilized person who arrogate "education" to themselves have used the pages of newspapers to castigate the Federal Military Government and show the highest discourtesy to Traditional Rulers. It is our hope that the setting up of your Committee and the result of your work will once and for all silence such persons by establishing that the traditional institution is a force to reckon with in our society.

TRADITIONAL RULERS IN THE LOCAL GOVERNMENT SYSTEM

The present Local Government System is based on the 1976 guidelines. Prior to 1976, Traditional Rulers had reached such a low ebb in the scheme of things that they were only seen but no longer heard. The establishment of the State Council of Traditional Rulers and the Local Government Traditional Council gave Traditional Rulers a new position, though this arrangement did not go far enough. It did not go far enough because these bodies were only advisory to the Governor and, in Bendel State, the State Council itself did not, in fact, cannot, meet unless a matter was referred to it from the Government side. The Local Government Traditional Council, on the other hand, had no means of coercing the Local Government Council to action. We have done a lot of writing on this subject, and we would like to hand over to you for careful study copies of our writings on the position of Traditional Rulers. These papers are:

(i) "The Role of Traditional Rulers in Local Government," being a special lecture I was invited to deliver at a National Conference under the auspices of the Department of Public Administration of the University of Ife.

(ii) "The Traditional Ruler in the scheme of things," being my memorandum to the National Conference of Traditional Rulers held in Kaduna in November, 1983.

(iii) Memorandum to the same National Conference held in Kaduna in November, 1983, covering:

(a) Definition of Traditional Ruler.

(b) The question of security of tenure of office of Traditional Rulers.

(c) What should constitute the proper functions of Traditional Rulers in our present society; and

(d) The question of political and social stability in our country.

(iv) "Establishment of a National Council of Traditional Rulers," being a memorandum to the same Conference in November, 1983."

In all these papers, I tried to discuss who is a Traditional Ruler and to give a definition; then I discussed what I consider should be the roles of Traditional Rulers in Local Government-what these were before and after independence, during and after the military regime, that is, the military regime that preceded the recently ousted civilian government. The subject titles listed in the memorandum in (iii) above show the topics that were discussed in the memorandum, and finally, the proposal for the establishment of such a body as a third chamber of our Legislative Houses. I appeal to your Committee to read these papers as annexures to this memorandum.

The National Conference of Traditional Rulers with delegates from each of the 19 States met in November, 1983, in Kaduna to consider those papers and many others from Traditional Rulers. At the end of our two-day meeting, we reached very vital conclusions aimed at giving Traditional Rulers their proper place in National and Local Government affairs.

A delegation led by the Chairman, His Royal Highness, the Emir of Kastina, presented the text of our decisions to then President Shehu Shagari some time in December, 1983. As soon as the appointment of your Committee was announced, I proposed to the Emir of Kastina to make the text available to your Committee. I hope he has done so, and I am sure you will find it worthwhile to study our conclusions.

The sum total of all our views boils down to this:

(a) It is derogatory for the 1976 Constitution (and repeated by Decree No. 1, of 1984) to refer to Traditional Rulers as "Chiefs" when those on whom Traditional Rulers confer traditional titles are also referred to as "Chiefs." Therefore, the term "State Council of Traditional Rulers" should be put in the Constitution with the definition proposed by the Kaduna National Conference of Traditional Rulers and the term "Chief" used for the recipient of traditional title from his Traditional Ruler.

(b) The State Council of Traditional Rulers, even though it is advisory, is a good forum for Traditional Rulers and it should be repeated at the National level as a third chamber in a three-chamber parliament; the State Council of Traditional Rulers, or the Local Government Traditional Council, as the case may be, should be responsible for the appointment of and disciplinary action against any Traditional Ruler, Traditional Rulers, being the custodians of their people's customs and traditions, should be involved in the establishment and running of Customary Courts. Also, Traditional Rulers, being the custodians of their people's customs and traditions, to which land tenure and inheritance are tied, should be the proper authority to receive recommendations from Local Government Land Use and Allocation Committee; dealing with urban areas, go direct to the Governor. Since experience has shown that some Local Government Councils deliberately hold Traditional Councils to ransom by not releasing funds for the payment of stipend of Traditional Rulers and his Chiefs, the funds for the Traditional Council should be a direct charge to the Local Government Joint Account, and should be paid direct to the Traditional Council and not to the Local Government Council.

The foregoing are only a few of the highlights of the topics discussed and of the recommendations made in Kaduna, my own arguments for which will be found in the papers I have given to you. So much for the Traditional Ruler in the Local Government System.

On the Local Government System Itself

I would like to draw attention to the three Local Government Council Areas in my domain known as Oredo, Ovia and Orhionmwon Local Government Councils. Each of these has a population of about 585,472; 306,372; and 206,236 respectively by the State Ministry of Economic Development figures in July, 1981. By ground area they are so extensive that going from one corner to the other is quite a journey, even where the roads are good; but the roads are so bad in most cases that it can be a test of human and mechanical endurance to go from the Headquarters on an inspection to some of the corners, and the officer in charge will have to be genuinely dedicated to have to undertake such a task. The last Civilian Administration made a move in the right direction to break up some of the larger areas but then, the whole thing became politicized and by the time the exercise was over, nearly every village or hamlet had become a Local Government Area of its own. The total number was such that Bendel State would have required nearly half of the "Oil money" to be able to run the system. I recently took our Commissioner for Local Government on a tour of parts of one of my Local Government Council Areas, and he will confirm the distance and the difficulties in reaching some places. I wish, therefore to propose to your Committee to recommend that, as soon as it is economically feasible, permission should be given for more Local Government Councils to be carved out of the present Oredo, Ovia and Orhionmwon Local Government Areas in order to spread out development more evenly and to make for easy accessibility. Each of the three areas at present can be broken up into at least two Local Government Council Areas to make a total of six Local Government Council Areas in the Benin Area, as was the case prior to 1974.

CALIBRE OF COUNCILLORS

We do not know whether this Administration intends to nominate Councillors to management committees or retain the Sole Administrator system. Whatever the case, we feel the time has come for measures to be taken to attract persons of high caliber to the Local Government Councils; not persons, as in the past, who failed all else and then found their ways as Councillors. In this regard, we would suggest that a level of honest affluence and respectability be added as a qualification for becoming a Councillor. We feel that a person who has already "made it" in life, contented in himself and has a family name to protect from blemish, will be more able to render selfless service and eschew the corrupt practices that debased most Local Government Councils (and, indeed, most legislatures) in the past and made Local Government Council an unclean place for a person with self-respect, for we have heard it said by some respectable persons that the Local Government Council is no place for a person with self-respect.

I trust it is not out of place here to deal with the remunerations of the Traditional Rules and his Chiefs. The Traditional Ruler is not a Traditional Ruler without his Chiefs and here in Bendel State, as in other parts of the country, Traditional Rulers attach great importance to their Chiefs. Taking the Traditional Ruler first, except for three of us, all the other Traditional Rulers in this state are each on a stipend of only N6,000 per annum, thanks to Alli Administration. I argued for it and the rationable for my argument was that it was unthinkable for a Traditional Ruler to earn less than a part-time Councilor and at that time part-time Councillor was on N6,000 per annum here in Bendel State, while Supervisory Councilor and Chairman were on N9,000 to N10,000 respectively. I wish to propose to your committee to recommend to the authorities that even the N6,000 per annum is now too meager for a Traditional Ruler and that it should be reviewed upwards. If the approval is given in principle the details could be worked out with the state authorities as the circumstances of each Local Government Area may warrant.

Once more, we thank your Committee for calling on us. We appeal to you to endeavour to study the documents I have submitted to you. We pray the result of your work will give us a more virile and respectable Local Government system and give a place of greater honor to the Traditional Rulers and their Chiefs.

Thank you.

Chapter 6

On Corruption, Moral Rejuvenation, Elections, Politics and Our Politicians

I am unable to resist drawing attention to a social malaise, a canker-worm eating deep into the fabric of our national life which, if not abated, is capable of rendering all the good intentions and efforts of Government an exercise in futility. I am referring to the high degree of bribery and corruption, which is apparent in particularly every aspect of life in this country. Where corruption thrives there can be no social justice, there can be no free and fair elections; . . . it erodes into the management of national economy . . .
— Omo N'Oba Erediauwa, October 10,1989

People who easily win the admiration of the public these days are those who have money and display it. It does not matter how that money is obtained . . . the acquisition of money has assumed such importance that our moral values are easily compromised in favor for money and the respect for money which is a virtue.
— Omo N'Oba Erediauwa, December 17, 1984

||||||||||||||||||||||||||||||||||||||||||||||

An Address to the National Conference on Moral Development, December 17, 1984

It is a pleasure, and I welcome the opportunity, to be able to say a few words to this National Conference on moral development. An inter-disciplinary national conference of this nature is certainly a welcome move that has come too soon; indeed, it has come too late! For several years now we haves been witnessing the moral standards of our nation degenerating. Church leaders have talked about it; traditional rulers have talked about it; the government also talked about it And yet, we never seemed to get an answer to what is responsible for the falling standard in the country's moral values.

In June this year, when I was opportuned to address the Benin Anglican Diocesan Synod, I observed that our country, Nigeria, and indeed the whole world, is today in a State of turmoil. I attributed this to the fact that four estates of the realm-Lords Spiritual (the Church), Lords Temporal (the Judiciary), the Commons (Parliament) and the press (news media)-have failed the nations of world.

I gave illustrations, which we need not repeat here for time. Even military weapons have failed to engender peace and stability!

What then is wrong with our system, with the system of the whole world, that produces the kind of leaderships that we and this world have had that seem unable to give us a stable world? The answer, to my mind, is simple and is to be found in our shunning of our traditional values, leading to our turning away from God.

Here in Nigeria, whether in the Christian, Muslim or traditional communities, our traditional values, our customs and traditions, centered round God, the Supreme Being—no murder, no covetousness, no adultery, no greed, respect for one's fellow man, etc.—we here in Benin Kingdom have our own vernacular expressions for these values, and there are sanctions for their violation. Above all, it is believed that God will punish or reward according to how each person performed here, and those who performed well or badly will return to this world again to meet the good or evil he left behind. Children are taught these beliefs from childhood and in time our people grow up with the fear of God in them. The teaching is usually done through attendance at customary rituals and folklores.

The European world, on the other hand, claimed to be the embodiment of Christian teaching; at least, so they made us believe when they first came out of these shores. And our people followed them. When, according to Alan Ryder, a French Capuchin mission came to our ancient city in the 1640s, its leader wrote: "In these Kingdoms live a great multitude of people who are truly gentile, civilized, friendly to priests, exemplary in their behavior and receptive to all good teaching."

Why will there not be moral decadence; why will there not be turmoil in the world, when all the traditional, Christian and Islamic values have been thrown overboard in preference for the love and the amassing of money—physical cash—and people have sunk to any depth in search of money?

The interpretation of civilization and modernity has spoilt things for the world. People who easily win the admiration of the public these days are those who have money and display it. It doses not matter how that money is obtained. Here in Nigeria the acquisition of money has assumed such importance that our moral values are easily compromised in favor of money and the citizenry can no longer draw the distinction between the love for money (which is the root of all evil therefore condemnable) and the respect for money which is a virtue. It is in this latter context that our Benin philosophy sees money when we say "t'aguan N'Igho, Igho itoboreguan," which is another way of saying that money should be seen as a means to an end, and not an end in itself.

Little wonder then that even the Vatican was dragged into monetary mess a couple of years ago by some of its staff out of love for money! Can the older persons honestly blame our young persons who today will perpetuate any crime in their inordinate bid to get rich quickly and live like the older people?

Next, the Government came and abolished missionary schools and all forms of religious instructions that those schools (Roman Catholic, the Anglican and the Muslim) used to impart to our children. To me the takeover of missionary schools in some parts of the country with the consequent abolition of the teaching of the Bible and Koran has left a vacuum in the moral development of our people. It is equally regrettable, as I have had occasion to say publicly elsewhere, for the Church leaders to have resigned themselves to the situation and unable to prevail on the Government even through judiciary process to reverse the order. It is no use to say, as some parents. That was so years ago. But not so now when father and mother, for economic reasons, go to work, while the children go to school and return home to the house servant. Then the TV with increasing volume of films of violence and pornography take over the Traditional folklore telling and traditional games. These are some of the factors that militate against the teaching of morals in the home.

In those countries that we in Africa usually refer to as "white-man's country,' permissiveness has become the order of the day where the child is given unlimited freedom at such tender age to do what he/she likes oblivious of the consequences of the act, and ends up a drug addict, armed robber or victim of other social ills. The situation in the world, and in our country in particular, shows beyond any doubt that there is urgent need for moral rejuvenation not only in the adults but also in the young persons, more so in the latter who tend to emulate their elders.

The defunct civilian Government tried to improve the situation by setting up a committee on ethical re-orientation. The present Administration is facing the problem in a military manner with various phases of "War Against Indiscipline" (WAI). All over the world some years ago there was the movement known as Moral Re-armament whose aims/objectives were to stem the decline in moral standards, as the promoters saw it then.

But the world is none-the-better; not more stable; Young persons become unruly and violent. So, your conference has a great task ahead-to find an answer to the question: what exactly is wrong with Nigeria-nay, the world? What is it in our system mat produces the kind of leadership we have had that seem unable to maintain ethics and morals and keep the nation stable and prevent violence in business communities, violence in the campuses of educational institutions, violence even in Christian and Islamic organizations and, also, prevent the modern man's inordinate craze for material wealth-money!

I am glad your conference is inter-disciplinary as I feel certain that you will need not only educationists, social-scientists, anthropologists, curriculum experts but certainly psychologists and, of course, Christian, Islamic and traditional religious leaders as well as service oriented bodies if you are going to attempt to answer the question I have posed. If the organizers have not already got representatives from these bodies, I strongly advise that you invite them.

I congratulate the organizers of this very important conference. I understand there is a plan to establish a center for Moral Development for which reason some donations are expected of us here. After all that I have been saying, I have no doubt that such a Center is long overdue to complement the present Administration's efforts in moral regenerating for our country.

I wish the conference successful deliberations.

Chapter 7

On Political Transition—
the Case of District Administration

Administration is the process through which public policies become apparent to citizens. Until it is administered, a policy is little more than words, and it may have good or bad effect, or no effect at all, depending on how the policy is administered by the various government functionaries. Here, then, lies the problem . . .

         — Omo N'Oba Erediauwa, April 1972

. . . The Civil Service has made immense contribution to the development and stability of the country. By its knowledge, resilience, loyalty, the service has kept the country together. Where politicians have been rash in taking a decision which would cause unpleasantness, the Civil Servant had displayed his knowledge and skill to smoothen things out. During the Nigerian Civil War, Civil Servants displayed Unprecedented loyalty and fortitude.

         — Omo N'Oba Erediauwa, April 1972

||||||||||||||||||||||||||||||||||||||||||

Chairman's Speech at the Opening Ceremony of the "National Conference on Social Transformation for Self Reliance and Social Justice," October 10, 1989

We thank God who, in His infinite Mercy, has seen us all here safely. May His Blessing abide with us at this opening ceremony and through the duration of this conference so that the outcome of the deliberations will lead to the greater transformation of our great country to the glory of God and the betterment of the people. And may He, as we disperse from the conference, lead us all safely back to our respective homes.

I am immensely grateful to the Directorate for Social Mobilization for having invited me not only just to participate in, but to preside over this august opening ceremony at which are present this galaxy of eminent personalities. When I received the letter of invitation from Professor Jerry Gana, and realizing how he literally took Bendel State by storm when he visited, I had to read the letter over and over again for three days to be able to answer my own inward question: "why me"? I finally decided to accept the invitation, and I am glad to be here. Glad to be here for the same reason, I think, you are all here-that we believe in the philosophy behind the program for "social mobilization."

The MASS MOBILIZATION for Economic Recovery, Self-Reliance and Social Justice (known by its less breath-sapping acronym, "MAMSER') has, since its inception, become a house-hold word because its policy, aims, objectives and modus operandi have been so well documented and articulated and the result is visible. One therefore need not dwell on that here. Suffice it to say that I, for my part, as earlier hinted, believe in the policy and philosophy of MAMSER. I will, by your indulgence, mention some of the objectives that have endeared the program to me.

a) Preparation for clean partisan politics

One is its program to give the country an enlightened and articulate followership as distinct from leadership. Since attainment of Independence and the introduction of partisan politics, civil rule in this country has known nothing but election rigging, violence, murder and arson, resulting from unwholesome manipulation of the followership.

In this connection, I recall a statement credited to a female [political activist in the United Kingdom (incidentally, a Nigerian) who, in comparing the practice overseas with what obtains in her country, Nigeria, observed that in developed countries politics is not "money-chasing affairs" as she put it. According to her, politics is engaged in by persons who approach it with a sense of commitment to service and duty to society "behind some pillar of ideals." That is how it ought to be. I earnestly hope and pray that MAMSER will be able to enlighten the electorate to give them the strength to resist being deceived and led by the nose any more. But considering what the so-called "political associations' have been doing so far one fears that MAMSER may have an up-hill task.

b) Integrated Rural Development

This is another very laudable activity of MAMSER (through the Directorate of Food, Roads, and Rural Infrastructures) that I admire very much. I donated a trophy some years ago to Bendel State Local Government Councils to be awarded to the Local Government Council that makes the greatest contribution to rural development. Bendel State Government kindly accepted the trophy and has been awarding it annually. When in 1987 I was privileged to address Congregation at the University of Ibadan, I spoke about rural development in the context of reducing ethnic sentiments and concluded in these words:

"In my view, the present Administration's determined policy of rural development, which happily is yielding good result, is one effective way of solving the problem of minorities and hence reducing ethnic tensions. It is my hope that the next breed of civil administrators will pursue this laudable policy with equal, if not greater, determination. It should not be allowed to be killed by partisan politics, come 1992."

If DFRRI carries its present momentum of rural development, and rural areas now enjoy motorable roads, potable water and electricity supply to assist cottage/medium scale industries, I venture to suggest that future politicians will have to devise new promises with which to entice those in rural and minority areas. It is to be hoped that by the end of this Conference, useful suggestion would have emerged for the sustenance of this program after the initiators have quit the scene.

c) Rural Women

In connection with rural development, one must commend the very successful efforts to give the rural women a "face lift' beginning from when some rural women set eyes on Lagos and Abuja for the first time in their lives to what is being done now to give rural women economic base and make them self-sufficient. One prays, however, that rural women will not now refuse to accompany their dear husbands to the farm, contending that they now use machines to make garri at home! But this is not to say we do not support the program.

d) Efforts to instill discipline, inspire patriotism and nationalism

Permit me once more to repeat part of what I said to Congregation in Ibadan in 1987. I said then, and I still hold to it, that another weakness in the nation's polity is the inability to evolve a national ethos; that the nearest to it had been the code of conduct in the 1979 Constitution but which applied only to public officers. Apart from that, not much attention has been given to finding a simple philosophy that will guide the people's behavior, attitude and relationship with one another according to the rules of natural justice.

We need to have, so I said then, a yardstick for a broader application of MAMSER. Some themes in this Conference program are quite relevant and timely and the listening public await the outcome of the deliberation as it concerns this matter of social justice and just society of which, to my mind, the tripartite evils of indiscipline, lack of patriotism and lack of nationalism form a part. Having made reference to the tripartite evils in our society, I am unable to resist drawing attentions to a social malaise, a cankerworm eating deep into the fabric of our national life (in fact, it is fast becoming part and parcel of the country' way of life) which, if not abated, is capable of rendering all the good intentions and efforts of Government through MAMSER an exercise in futility. I am referring to the high degree of bribery and corruption which is apparent in practically every aspect of life in this country. Where corruption thrives there can be no free and fair elections; corruption has rendered the fight against corruption and other social ills unsuccessful! It erodes into the foundation of social justice; it erodes into the management of national economy: all these as evidenced from reports of commissions of inquiry and Court proceedings published by the news media. This is why I am calling on the Directorate to mount a special campaign against corruption and enlighten the people on the need and the advantages of eschewing corruption in all its forms for the benefit of all. I urge those who will be discussing various topics in this Conference to avert their minds to this issue and come forward with ideas to clean up the society of this cancerous disease, as much as it is humanly possible! Again, I do not see how one can talk about "social transformation,' "social justice,' "patriotism and nationalism' in the Nigerian context without drawing attention to the role of the news media in our national affairs. What some section of our news media, especially the print media, publish about this nation is quite often most unpatriotic. One sometimes gets the impression that Nigeria is the most debased and polluted in the world. What is even more distressing is that some of the media repeat almost verbatim the disgraceful abuse that the foreign press heap on our country. I am aware that the speakers at this Conference have already concluded crossing the "t's and dotting the "i's in their papers.

But I cannot resist the urge to appeal to all the expert participant not to exclude the news media from their analysis of the nation's problems and the road to social transformation.

e) Attacking mass illiteracy

Finally on the selected programs of MAMSER, I want to commend the Directorate for what it is doing to combat mass illiteracy among the nation's population. What has been achieved in a short period in Bendel State has been most impressive and encouraging not to those who are already "literate' but also to the participants on the course. MAMSER and Government should not relent in their efforts.

Ladies and gentlemen, it is the hope of the Directorate that "the findings and recommendations of the Conference shall be placed before the Federal Military Government as well-articulated Advisory Memo on Structural Transformation." So may it be, and I pray that the Federal Military Government will give serious consideration to the package. I am very hopeful of the outcome of the Conference.

The themes for this Conference are wide and varied, and I conjecture that the end of it all, they would have covered not only SAP, and the national economy, but fields such as law, politics and religion; perhaps even the traditional institution, who knows! The themes are all topical. I have no doubt that the speakers will do justice to their respective subjects and give each and everyone in the country some food for thought. Above all, it is to be hoped that the Conference will answer the following questions, among others:

(i) How do we reconcile the two divergent camps of experts on whether or not there is a viable alternative to the Nigerian type of SAP?

(ii) What are the answers to some of the questions that our native people back home have often asked, e.g., if SAP has been all that successful, why is price of locally produced food stuff rising ceaselessly? And why are industries that retrenched prior to SAP not now recalling the retrenched staff?

(iii) How do we bridge the gap (for the sake of social justice) between the factions in the group traditionally known as "learned friends" who have been disagreeing (in varying degree of vitriol) on what to do with certain legislations, the Nigerian legal system, the rule of law, the judiciary, human right posture, democracy, etc.?

(iv) How do we achieve increased food production and bring down prices?

(v) Has the country's population in fact reached "explosion" point or is the cry of too many mouths to feed attributable to wrong approach to farming?

(vi) Can MAMSER (and perhaps the National Electoral Commission) be assisted to deal with the money-spinning banned politicians who have been functioning and will function as "king makers' behind the scene in the "political associations" or political parties in order to ensure that only honest and selfless politicians come into power in the next civilian regime?

One can list many more questions which one hopes this Conference will provide useful answers to.

Finally, I think it is appropriate that I (indeed we here) use this platform to express the poor man's gratitude to President Ibrahim Babangida for the very good news announced some days ago in the establishment of the People's Bank of Nigeria on the 4th October; we cannot hide from the fact that it is the category of persons to be served by this innovation in banking that bear the heaviest weight of social injustice. It is, therefore, not only an act of great foresight but also great magnanimity to establish the bank.

We will earnestly appeal to our countrymen and women to reciprocate the good gesture of the Government by repaying their loans promptly so that others who have not enjoyed the facility may have their opportunity. We will also appeal to the Bank Officials managing the fund but also in advising prospective clients. We wish the People's Bank every success in its task to improve the living conditions of the so-called "common man" or "man in the street" who invariably are the poor in the society.

Ladies and gentlemen, I am not on the list of speakers and I should not impose on your patience, especially when you will have the opportunity to listen to the distinguished experts. More importantly, there is the key-note Address from the President of the Federal Republic of Nigeria, I am sure you are all itching to be allowed to hear Mr. President in what some usually describe as his characteristic forthrightness and others term his diplomatic language. So, ladies and gentlemen, thank you for your attention; happy listening, while wishing the Directorate very successful deliberation.

Thank you.

‖‖‖‖‖‖‖‖‖‖‖‖‖‖‖‖‖‖‖‖‖‖‖‖‖‖‖‖‖‖‖‖‖

AN ADDRESS ON THE EVE OF THE REGISTRATION OF VOTERS, AUGUST 1982

I have invited you here today to address you on the current public enlightenment campaign for the registration of eligible voters for the 1983 elections. The FEDECO will commence registration of voters from 16th to 31st August. It is important that all citizens of the age of 18 years and above come out to register their names.

The need for every eligible person to be registered cannot be overemphasized. In the first place, only those who are registered can participate in the election of those to represent us at the three levels of government, that is, at the Local, state and Federal Government levels. The constitution of the Federal Republic of Nigeria 1979 grants every Nigerian of the age of 18 years and above the right to participate in determining who should represent him or her and their community in the government, either as a member of the Local Government Council or as a member of the State or

Federal Legislature or as a the Governor of his State or as the President of this country.

It is those in government who decides on how to apply the people's resources in satisfying the people's priorities and who gets what at any given time; they make the laws which regulate our day-to-day life, our business and our general movements. Therefore, any person of the age of 18 years and above who fails to register now is denying himself or herself the right to vote at the coming elections and choose those to govern the people. Nobody can deny an eligible voter the right to vote, but you will deny yourself that right if you fail to register.

Furthermore, although the registration exercise is principally for the 1983 elections, the figures of registered voters in the various areas could be useful to the government for other purposes such as for planning its development program, and providing amenities for the people of such areas. In the absence of any official census figures since the past 20 years (1963) the number of registered voters has proved a most reliable indication of the number of persons not below the age of 18 in the respective areas. Thus, this is another very important reason why those who have attained the age of 18 years and above must turn up for registration.

When, therefore, you come out to be registered from August 16 to August 31 you will be rendering service to yourself and community that is your village or town. First, you will be able to have a say in choosing the members of the National and State Assembly, the Governor and the President. Secondly, you will help the government with useful figures in planning for our development. I understand that some persons served at polling stations in the 1979 elections (presumably as polling agents or officials) had decided to abstain from participating in the forthcoming registration of voters because they had not been paid their fees for their 1979 services. This attitude is very wrong, and it shows the misconception some people have about the purpose of the registration of voters. They believe they are penalizing the government by refusing to be registered. You are wrong: those who wish to vent their grievance against the authorities by boycotting the registration exercise are doing a disservice only to themselves and to their community. The government does not lose anything by your refusal. If you were not paid for your (1979) election work, all you can do is to refuse to work again; but that should not make you refuse to exercise your own personal right to vote, and you cannot vote if you are not registered (now). I trust that such persons now understand the true position.

I hereby call on all qualified Nigerians, all Bendelites and particularly those resident in my domain to turn out massively between Monday, 16th and Tuesday, 31 st August, 1982 to register their names at the registration centres nearest to their respective homes. All those who have attain the age of 18 are qualified to register. No fees are payable and non-payment of tax is no disqualification. On the other hand, the registration is not to make people pay tax. It does not matter what political party you support or if you do not support any. You lose nothing by registering (now), whereas you lose a lot by not doing so; for you lose your constitutional right to elect those to govern you for the next four years. You may find, when the time comes, that you want a particular person elected; you will regret if you find that you cannot exercise your civic right to vote for him because your name is not in the register of voters.

I wish to seize this opportunity to answer the wicked allegation made against me by the *New Nigerian* of July 29, 1982, and the *Punch* of August 3, 1982. Both newspapers published that I was behind plan to exclude all non-Benins from the Governorship race. The *New Nigerian* claimed to have seen a letter signed by me, and the *Punch* made reference to a meeting it claimed I hurriedly summoned for the purpose. These publications are wicked and mischievous and calculated by enemies of progress to sow the seed of inter-ethnic discord. I say it boldly for all to hear that there is no such move by Binis to exclude non-Benins; or if there is, I am no party to it, and no newspaper should mischievously involve me in it.

On the other, the Binis, like all other ethnic groups, have a right to fight for the Governorship post or any other political positions and those doing the politics of it know how to set about it. I do admit that I talked to my people that if they wish to vie for the political office, they cannot afford to break into factions and end up by Binis fielding several contestants for one post. The Binis must copy the example of other ethnics groups who always present a united front in such matters by sinking their own domestic differences. I will want the *New Nigerian* and *Punch* to tell me that they do not know that other ethnic groups do this. I have not stopped with the Binis. In my present position which it has pleased God to place me I see things in the context of overall interest and not the restrictive context of the self-centered. Hence I have also, on a number of occasions, spoken to the State officials of the U.P.N. and the N.P.N. This is not to help any particular individual score points but to let the party leaders realize that the more factions they break into the greater the risk that peace of the nation would be disturbed. And I do not want the peace of this nation to be disturbed. I call on the *New Nigerian* and the "*Punch*," and all the news media to contact my secretary to check any information about me before they use it. Deliberate misinformation does not help your newspaper, and you do not help the country by fanning flames of discord.

I hope to be able to speak to all of you again before actual voting commences. But as I speak to you today I cannot help expressing my fears about what the voting has in store for the country. The 1979 campaigns and elections were conducted, as all know, under military supervision and, I believe there was tacit understanding among all political leaders to let the military go. That was probably responsible for the few unpleasant electioneering incidents. The coming elections will be first since the military handed over. Already the handwriting on the wall is getting bolder and bolder. There are newspaper reports of violent clashes between political factions; already bloody incidents have been reported from certain parts of this State and elsewhere in the country. As I address you on the registration, I must appeal to all our political leaders and aspirants for political posts to constantly refrain from acts that will break the country, especially utterances calculated to arouse inter-ethnic feeling for the sake of scoring political point. It is very sad that politicians cannot be unanimous even in the interpretation of their own Party Constitutions; factions behave as they like and no one seems to be able to discipline anyone. Political parties striving to control the affairs of this country must first ensure the continued existence of the country. I therefore appeal to all political leaders to keep their followers under control. Our country is bigger than any party or individual and in 1982 our politicians should have become mature enough to discard as child's play the practice of "you sack him, he sack you."

We wish the Chairman and Members of FEDECO God's guidance and every success in its very difficult assignment.

All Enigie, chiefs and ward leaders, market women, and all present here should carry this message to their respective areas and homes and ensure a most successful registration exercise. Begin now to preach peace and orderliness in the campaigns and elections to follow. "Enikaro Kevbe Osanobuwa ghe gie azusun zuwa hin-usunre; temwan gha muan vbe Evboima. Evboima ghi yeke.,"

God bless you all.

ııııııııııııııııııııııııııııııııııııı

AN ADDRESS TO THE EDO PEOPLE ON JULY 5, 1979, SHORTLY BEFORE THE 1979 ELECTIONS

Chiefs, Enigie, Ladies and Gentlemen.

I have invited you here today to transmit to you the message from the Military Administration of this state, Brigadier Abubakar Waziri, concerning the forth-coming series of general elections which will usher in Civilian Rule.

On the 2nd of July, the Military Administrator addressed all Traditional Rulers in this state and disclosed to us that the first of these elections will be held on the 7th of July, 1979, which is only the day after tomorrow and the last of them (if the need arises) on the 18th of August, 1979.

In his address, the Military Administrator made it quite clear the responsibility of traditional rulers during these elections:

First and foremost, we are to ensure that every qualified person in our community. Is encouraged to exercise his civic right and to vote for the person of his choice without fear or hindrance.

Secondly, we are to spread the message of love, understanding and cooperation among all our people so that the winners and losers will, at the end of it all, remain brother and friends.

It is nearly 15 years since elections were last held in this country. The elections that are about to begin are different from all previous ones in that they will mark the end of a long Military Rule. Every well-meaning person, every politician, every citizen must keep at the back of his mind during these elections that the Military Government is voluntarily, I emphasize voluntarily, handing over its power to Civilian Government. It is, therefore, a commendable action which no one in his right senses should do anything to disturb. There are very few places in the world where Military took over and voluntarily handed over. I would like to recall a passage in my coronation speech in which I appealed to the politicians to remember the years prior to 1966 and to eschew in the electioneering campaigns the unhealthy habits of the past which were characterized by mud-slinging, attack on personality, victimization, persecution, character assassination, and the worst of all physical violence.

If these elections go through in peace and tranquility and a Civilian Regime comes into power the credit will go to the generality of the Nigerians and in the Nigerian politics we would have scored another record. The first record that this country set in Nigerian politics was when we received our Independence in our palms: we did not have to fight for it. It would be another record if the coming elections could be conducted peacefully and successfully for the Military Regime, which out of its own volition, prepared the program to hand over peacefully. These two events are records because events the world over have shown that people have had to fight, at times bloodily, to attain Independence and on the other side where a Military Regime had been in power either the Regime closed the door permanently to Civil Rule or the Civilian again have had to fight to regain Civil power. God bless Nigeria we have not had to fight to attain these two positions.

I appeal to all of you in the name of posterity and in the name of our children who are watching us today that all of you who are involved in these elections should behave yourselves. In the interest of peace and tranquility let the winners be magnanimous and avoid victimization of their opponents; the losers on the other hand should accept the decision of the electorate with good heart for there is another day. I strongly appeal to all the political leaders amongst you to be firm in the discipline of your followers.

I must ask all the Chiefs, Enigie and Igie-ohen to pray earnestly that

God and our Ancestors may grant that these elections be held in a peaceful atmosphere. I expect you all to carry this message to our people.

I wish all the campaigners every success and may God give us the Party He knows will bring in peace and tranquility to our land.

||||||||||||||||||||||||||||||||||||||||

An Address on the Occasion of the New Year Get-Together Party Held at Ugha-Erha OBA in the Palace, Benin City, on Saturday, 10th January, 1981.

It is our great pleasure to welcome you all again to this our annual get-together. We hope you all had a pleasant holiday and merry-making.

The year 1980 is now gone. As we enter the new year 1981 let us offer thanks to God Almighty and our Ancestors for having seen each and every one of us through the old year and for the blessing received. Each and every one should pray that this new year may be better for us than the past year. In doing this it is proper that each citizen takes stock of his or her achievements during the past year to determine how and where to improve on past performance.

A year is good or bad depending on how much good people do to attract other known factors that govern or control human behavior. Someone once gave a formula for ascertaining how good you are: he advised that at the end of each day a man should take stock of his activities from waking to bed-time, and ask himself what good act or good turn he did in the course of the day. The average person should be able to count, at least one: but you will be surprised how many persons cannot count a single act of good turn to his fellow man in a whole day. We therefore, urge on all citizens to strive hard to do good, think good so as to make this year a good one for all.

We believe those of you here today adequately represent a respectable cross-section of our society. That being so, it is impossible to resist the urge to unfold to you our thinking on a few matters. So, bear with us for a while. To an august gathering such as we are privileged to have here, this is one occasion anyone in our position must be outspoken.

At a similar get-together last year we expressed our anxiety about the unstable state of the country. We expressed our disappointment at the brand of partisan politics that had come after 15 years of military rule. It is sad to observe that at the end of 1980 the situation has not changed for the better. The country is still treated to politics of abuse, mud-slinging and character assassination. It is even worse now, for in addition to all the unwholesome attacks, a new element has been introduced whereby the personal secrets of opponents are now dished out in the open market places! Almost daily the nation is treated to explosive utterances capable of inciting one community or ethnic group against another, all this in a bid to score political points. Even among the parties themselves there is so much dissension that it makes one shudder whither they are leading the nation. And the news media (we shall refer to them later) have not helped the situation either. May we therefore appeal to the older politicians to use their maturity, age and years of experience at the game to put things right.

Since we are now operating a semblance of the American type of Constitution, let us learn from the experience of that great country at their last election in the tussle between Carter, Reagan and Kennedy. According to our newspaper, Carter conceded victory even before the counting was over and has been doing what is required to get his successor into office. Kennedy, we are told, also conceded victory to his Partyman, but did not go to form a splinter group and start pouring abuses on his rival. We also know that in Britain a man of Callaghan's caliber conceded victory to a woman before counting was over. There are aspects of clean politics in other more advanced countries that we who are still learning can emulate. We therefore appeal to all concerned to let us have less of personal antagonism in our politics. Those who have the political power in their hands should use it not to destroy but to build a united and peaceful country.

As we have often pointed out you do not score a point over your opponent by leaving the statement or ideology he has propounded to go and abuse his person and parents or discredit his occupation. This is the pity of it all. And what is the cause of all this trouble? As we see it, the cause is due to disagreement over party ideologies or objectives.

Now the objectives of five political parties fall into four categories, namely:

- Food and water for all;
- Roof over everybody's head;
- Medical care within everybody's reach; and
- Education at all levels within everybody's reach.

These are all laudable amenities aimed at improving the standard of living which all Nigerians, the poor as well as the rich, are longing to enjoy. What is even more interesting is that they feature in different forms in each party's manifesto.

We have traveled extensively in this our country. We have been to practically all major towns in the northern parts from Lake Chad in the eastern boundary to Sokoto in the west; from Lagos in the south up country to Kastina and Niger boundary in the extreme north. Similarly, in the southern States from Cameroon border in the east to Idiroko in the western border. We traveled these places in pleasure cars, land-rovers, even bicycles or on foot in some places. We have given this description of our travels for you to appreciate that what we wish to say is not read from books but seen with the naked eyes.

We have been to areas where human beings use small cups to scoop out the last drops of water in a drying well or stream; where human beings surrendered the last drops of water to the cattle (their life-blood economically) rather than use it for themselves. We have been to areas where human beings can hardly have one full meal not to talk of three square meal a day. We have been to areas in the so-called towns, where families share not a room in the human sense but a cage built round with corrugated iron sheets; where people have used sheds, disused vehicles as sleeping apartments. We have been to areas where level of environmental sanitation is low that hospitals have been rendered meaningless; areas where level of education is so high and widespread that the educated elite hardly know what to do with themselves.

In short, distinguished guests, there is nothing in the objectives of each political party that is not in dire demand by the generality of our people. Our contention however, is that because of the diversity of the whole country it is unrealistic to make anyone of the objectives a priority for the whole country. In other words, what is the use of housing in an area where you cannot get food and water to keep body and soul together; what is the use of education when all that the so-called educated elite can get is a ramshackle room in a slum or what is medical care to people who drink from the bottom of wells or live in refuse dumps? We would not like to be misunderstood. All we are advocating is that each of our political parties today has something to offer, but since what may be in short supply in the east may not necessarily be a priority for those in the west or what is in demand in the north may already be in abundance in the south, our earnest appeal to our leaders is that they should please put the interest of the country above party score-board and come to an understanding which would enable different parts of the country to get the amenities they need most. In short, the programs of Federal and State Government should be given a chance to proceed without hindrance by opposing sides since, in the final analysis, it is the citizens who benefit. He would be a foolish man who would not accept or sleep in a house because it was built by a Government whose party he does not support or take advantage of free hospital service because it is not provided by the Government he supports.

We would, in this connection, like to make a passionate appeal to the press to help ease tension by emphasizing only those things that foster the unity of the country rather than the things that cause dissension. Too often many newspapers merely reproduce with prominence not only the divisive utterance of politicians, but degrading aspects of our National life. When these vices are said by word of mouth they have restricted area Of circulation than when printed in newspapers. A good image of the country is not being painted by circulating our vices or brand of politics all over the world. Some of us do read overseas papers, and observe that unless in Very extreme cases, and such are very rare, the type of matter that get blown up in our newspapers do not get a place in overseas ones.

We therefore must appeal to newsmen to endeavour to play down the degrading and disgraceful aspects of our country's image, and emphasize for the consumption of the reading public, only those things that unite and uplift the country. In this connection, one must commend the forthright admonition that the President of the Nigeria Guild of Editors issued recently to journalists as reported in the back page of the *New Nigerian* of January 6, 1981. After warning news media to report more of what unite Nigeria rather than pull it down, the President of the Guild then observed, according to the *New Nigerian*, that in the struggle to uphold editorial policy and score political points, some journalist had thrown professional ethics to the winds and ignore their code of conduct, and are drifting back to extreme partisan lines of media in the First Republic. How very true! We join the President of Guild of Editors to appeal to his members to correct this dangerous drift.

Finally, distinguished guests, we wish to draw attention to a matter that is perhaps new to discussions. We are in 1981, and by all indications this year should be a good one. As we had earlier observed it is human beings that make a year good (or bad) as reflected by the amount of good (or evil) done by the majority of the people. But it is also a well-known fact that human actions are governed by certain other factors.

This is evidenced by the well-known Roman adage: "Vox populi, vox Dei" (the voice of the people is the voice of God), or, as the Edo people put it, "Unuagbon ere eseye," meaning "it is man's tongue that gives rise to evil."

In the past two years one word became a favorite in the nation's vocabulary; it is the unsavory word "disaster." Suddenly, in daily occurrence every accident became a "national disaster." We wish to make this solemn appeal to all our Governors and newspapers in particular, and the general public, to erase this ugly word from their vocabulary in this year 1981. You must refrain from using the word. We are making this appeal solemnly and with a sense of responsibility. People who have suffered national disasters have been too overwhelmed to shout their misfortune on roof tops. By the Grace of God our country has not experienced any earthquakes, volcanoes, hurricanes, epidemics, heatwaves and famine. These are disasters from which it has pleased God Almighty to protect us. We must not willingly invite disaster, bearing in mind the Roman adage already quoted. We must urge it on all our leaders, economic planners and news media to find other words to describe the kind of localized unfortunate mishaps that have occurred in some sections of the economy, even if lives were lost. People must erase the word "disaster" from their vocabulary and their minds in this year 1981 so that the year which promises to be a good one may shower its blessings on mother earth. We repeat that we are today making this appeal solemnly and with all sense of responsibility. Please do not use the word this year.

In conclusion, we wish to thank you for your attention. The position of a traditional ruler places on him the responsibility to speak out when he sees or senses certain things. Not being an actor himself in respect of some of the things he speaks about, the traditional ruler can only point out things for the actors to take cognizance of. It is our earnest hope that what we said today, especially our warning on the use of the word "disaster," will go down well with our actors presently on the stage.

We thank you all for sparing time to honor our invitation. We pray that this year will make the bad people in society good persons, and the good persons better.

To those who have to return to their homes we wish you a safe journey back.

A very happy New Year to you all.

Thank you.

||||||||||||||||||||||||||||||||||||||||||||||

Excerpt from an Address by the Omo N'Oba on the Occasion of His Coronation as the 38th OBA of Benin, on March 23rd, 1979.

. . . We must, in the same breath, make a strong appeal to the politicians who have now commenced their campaigns to remember the years prior to 1966 and eschew in the coming electioneering campaigns the unhealthy habits of the past i.e. mud-slinging attack on personality, victimization, persecution, character assassination and violence. If you must reply your opponent, attack only his statement or policy, but never his name or person as the latter process does not make your reply more valid but only leads to personal animosity.

III

From "The Problems of the Transition From Colonial Status to Independence with Special Emphasis on District Administration," a Paper Presented at the Waigani Seminar in Australia, April 1972, While Still Prince S.I.A. Akenzua and Permanent Secretary, Federal Ministry of Health, Lagos.

Chairman, distinguished Ladies and Gentlemen,

May I begin by first expressing the appreciation of my Government to the organizers of the Seminar and the Australian Government that Nigeria has been invited to participate in the Waigani Seminar. I personally would like to record my grateful thanks to have been afforded the opportunity to participate, and to see something of this part of the world.

The subject of my paper is "The Problems of Transition from Colonial Status to Independence with Special emphasis on District Administration." There are four elements in this subject title:

- Colonial Status
- Attainment of Independence
- Problems associated with the transformation from Colonial Status to full independent state and
- District Administration

In discussing these elements, and in order to appreciate the problem that arise in the transition period between dependence and independence, it is necessary first to remind ourselves of the history of colonialism and examine the impact of Europe on the rest of the world.

Historians say that European expansion overseas began in the fifteenth century when Henry the Navigator's sailors went down the coast of Africa, Vasco Da Gama entering the India Ocean, and Columbus re-discovering America. Then followed the activities of Spanish and Portuguese Powers which divided the Americas, settled colonies on the coast of India, Africa and the East Indies. They were followed by the Dutch, the British and the French.

The motives which led to the acquisition of colonies were both economic and nationalistic. It was nationalism on the part of those who pursued the cause, and these were usually determined minority groups, exerting considerable pressure on their governments, believing they were acting in the national interests. But the motives were also economic in that once the Colony had been acquired, its administration was governed by considerations of economic advantage to the Colonial Power. The Colony was expected to be self-supporting and the Colonial "Administrator," usually the leader of the trading company, had strict orders to produce only what could be turned into profit. Of course, this was easy because of the availability of natural resources and cheap labour. Because the "government" of the colony was in the hands of the commercial body, little or no wealth was left in the territory, profits and capital reverting to the colonial power, or the handful of capitalists who originally provided the capital. In this state of affairs, it is easy to appreciate the reluctance of the colonial powers to let go their colonial territories.

After the First World War, however, the international position of Europe began to grow weak. Throughout the areas under the political control of European powers, economic and social developments took place which in the long run were to undermine the whole colonial structure. By building schools, roads, hospitals, and factories in their colonies, Europeans were facilitating the transition to modern economies in these areas and were, perhaps unwittingly, also arousing in the inhabitants a feeling of self-realisation. What finally dealt a fatal blow to colonialism was the victory of Japan in the Second World War over America in the Philippines, over Britain in Malaya and Burma, over the Dutch in Indonesia. The Western Powers were not so invincible after all! The experience which Britain and other Western powers gained from the Japanese successes coupled with the significant contribution which soldiers from Africa and India made to British successes in the War led to a change of attitude towards the less developed territories.

Now, COLONIAL TERRITORIES CAN be grouped into four:
- What is left of the 16th-/17th-century Spanish, Portuguese, Netherlands, and French Empires in the East and West Indies and the Congo;
- Those communities of French Canada and Boer South Africa who tried to get away from the injustices of the industrial revolution;

- The non-European world of Africa and Asia;
- Colonial territories in Africa and Asia.

For the purpose of this paper, I shall confine my analysis to the fourth category-colonial territories in Africa and Asia. We know that in those areas, independence was won from the colonial power in one of two ways: by sheer force and violence, or "on a platter of gold" following amicable negotiations. In the former case, the revolt was due to harsh and unimaginative colonial administration; in the latter case, it was the result of the awaking of political consciousness coupled with the wind of change which had begun to blow over those territories similar to that which swept away slave trading. People and organizations had begun to express deep sympathy for the dependent territories. The problem of transition from colonial status to independence would be great or light depending on how independence was attained. If the transfer of power was by mutual understanding, some preparatory work would have been done, and it is conceivable that the new nation would continue to look up to the former master for guidance and assistance as in the former British territories. Where, however, independence was wrenched from the hands of the master, the latter could hardly be expected to show much interest (as happened with the former Congo, Brazzaville).

Now, what are these "problems of transition"? It is possible to identify a few of them:

The influence of (and antipathy towards) the new political leaders;

Political and economic instability;

Effect of an elite leadership who held a position as rulers but far removed from the ruled;

Imbalance in the growth of political institutions.

I will go briefly over the first three, but will, for the purpose of this paper, discuss item 4 at some length.

With the emergence of independence, political leaders were hailed as the "New Messiah" and were looked upon as the experts who alone could pilot the ship of State to the twin goal of full nation-hood and economic advancement. Soon, however, the erstwhile leaders who had been acclaimed for successfully pushing away the colonial masters now themselves became object of suspicion and vilification before those who wish either to retain the status quo, or that the leaders should accelerate the pace towards nationhood or simply to share in the eating of the national cake. These contradictions have led to civil strife, sometimes violent and bloody, resulting in political instability. Regrettably, the sections of some of the leaders have made the situation inevitable.

In extreme cases in more recent times, especially in Africa and Asia, violence has actually resulted into military regimes, with or without bloody coup d'etat, when the Army stepped in to restore order.

A third problem that faces the newly independent nations is the general attitude of the new governing elite. In the colonial era, this group was represented by the Colonial Administrators, who gave way, after independence, to the nationalists and the traditionalists both of whom, in some cases (as in Nigeria and India), have come into head-on collision with each other. Finally, there is the economic elite or resident foreign industrialists who are known to have exerted considerable influence on one section or the other of the community, an influence that sometimes generated internal unrest or aggravated it. This has created a problem because the new leaders remain on their ivory towers completely out of touch with the masses and therefore unable to feel their pulse.

You will have observed, at this juncture, that I have identified three problem areas. First, is the acceptance of the new political leaders followed by the emergency of contradictions, claims and counter-claims which have exposed the leaders to suspicion and accusation of selfishness. This situation has led to political instability resulting, in the extreme cases, in military coup d'etat. There is the consequence of the governing elite keeping out of touch with the masses. All of these have had the effect of slowing down the march to full nation-hood, and the influence of the economic elite has left the nation economically dependent, though apparently politically independent.

The most serious problem facing the developing countries, however, is, in my view, the problem of administration. Politicians and political parties may come and go but the Civil Service remains forever. I am aware this statement is not wholly true because there are few countries where Civil Servants change with the political party. I would not wish to speculate just now on a situation in which the Civil Service would be brushed aside with its political overlord! But I would hope, for the sake of the political leaders themselves, that such a situation never arises. I have used the expression "Civil Service" because of my background; I would like it to include any organ responsible for carrying out Government policies.

Administration is the process through which policies become apparent to citizens. Until it is administered, a policy is little more than words, and it may have good or bad effect, or no effect at all, depending on how the policy is administered by the various government functionaries. Here, then lies the problem and in order to appreciate its magnitude we must cast our minds back to the pre-independence period. The most significant legacy of colonialism is the existence of institutions in the newly independent states, which are based on levels of political development far in advance of those new States. These institutions, of which Administration is the most important, were devised to serve the purposes of the ruling power and not necessarily to improve the lot of the ruled. Thus, at independence, the new nation is left with an administrative structure modeled on that of the colonial power, but deficient in skilled manpower since most of the expatriates are withdrawn.

At this point, I must take you to my country, Nigeria, to illustrate the evolution in administrative processes with particular reference to District Administration. Nigeria, as known to-day, is an artificial creation of the British. Without going too far back into history, the present day Nigeria came into being in 1914 when the Colonial Governor amalgamated the Northern and Southern provinces.

I did say that because of the influence of the colonial power, the newly independent countries found themselves inheriting a system of administration modeled on that of the colonial power. Happily (or unhappily), this has not been the case with Nigeria. I say "unhappily" because as we shall see later, the indigenous administrative system which the architect of modern Nigeria (Lord Lugard) used to his Government's advantage was destroyed after independence and replaced by that imported from Britain.

Now, at the time Lugard was carving out Nigeria on the map, there already existed indigenous political institutions, which formed the basis of the now historically famous indirect rule system devised by Lugard. He found that, in his new assignment in the newly proclaimed Protectorate of

Northern Nigeria, there were well-established indigenous political institutions which could be made to serve the needs of local administration under the supervision of the few British Officers available. It was his view that both the British and the African would gain from colonial rule in that the material resources of the one would thereby be developed and made available to the colonizing power while the indigenous people would derive benefits of European civilization. The system, which Lugard found, was composed of the following elements:

(A) The Emir at the head of the administrative machinery assisted by a Council of family headmen;

(B) The Alkali and his Court as the judicial arm applying local customary laws;

(C) The treasury maintained by a system of taxation on cattle and landed property.

In practical terms, what Lugard did was to assign a British officer, known as Resident, to each large emirate or province whose function was to advise and to supervise the local administration. To each Division of the Emirate, he assigned a District Officer who assisted the Resident. He then chose District and Village Heads and made them directly responsible to their superiors for their respective areas of authority.

The Indirect Rule system having proved successful in the North was introduced into the Southern Provinces. It went very well in the Western parts of the country where there were indigenous institutions similar to those in the Northern Provinces. It was however, not so easily assimilated in the Eastern part because of the absence of the traditional tribal structures. The whole complex of Emir, Council, Court, Treasury, District and Village heads constituted the Native Authority System.

At the apex of the system was the Governor, assisted by Lieutenant-Governors in the Northern, Western and Eastern Provinces to whom the residents were responsible in the first instance. Practically, all the Residents and District Officers were, of course, expatriate employees of the Home Government. Such then was the position up to independence.

Actually, changes in Native Administration System began not at independence but with the introduction of home rule in the period between

1950–52. Politics and politicians had come on the scene as Nigerians assumed partial responsibility for the control of their affairs with the exception (until full independence) of Defence, Foreign Affairs and Justice. By 1954, the political structure had changed when the country was divided into three Regions: the Western, Eastern and Northern Regions. Full independence was attained in 1960.

In the Western and Eastern Regions, almost overnight, the existing Native Administration System was abolished and replaced by the new Local Government System which was patterned on the English System. This was what I referred to earlier on as an unhappy situation-because the new system bore no relationship with the traditional structure. The new system, as in England, provided for the establishment of a three-tier type of elected Council, County, Urban and District Councils under the general control of the Regional Ministry of Local Government. In the Northern Region, however, the existing Native Administration System still remained to a large extent but considerably modified and enhanced in status. The sole native authority represented by the Emir now became "Native Authority in Council" with the Emir exercising his power through the Chiefs-in Council.

Although changes have taken place in each of the three Regions, there is still one feature common to all. The District Officer of the Lugard era still has a pride of place-except that his role and functions have altered somewhat. These changes have presented problems which I shall now proceed to examine. As already indicated, the new system of administration, especially as practised in the Southern Provinces (or Regions) is alien to the people. In the Western Region, the power of the traditional chiefs, around whom Lugard's Indirect Rule System was built, had been whittled down considerably since by the various Local Government Laws, most of their functions, especially tax collection and land matters, were passed on to the new Local Government Councils. The traditional chiefs did not like this much but they could do nothing about it since they had come under the general control of the Ministry of Local Government and Chieftaincy Affairs which could make a law any time to contain an undesirable situation. In the Eastern Region, where there had been a traditional administrative structure different from that of the Western and Northern Regions (in that they did not have traditional chieftaincy institutions except in a few areas) the new system easily met with popular support as a means of weakening the powers of the British Administrative Officers which had obviously increased in the absence of traditional chiefs. The Northern Region was, however, more fortunate than the rest of the country in that the changes never reached the very foundation of their system with the result that even as of now the traditional chiefs still retain substantially their position.

The system of election inherent in the new development presented a problem. In a country where the electorate are illiterate or semi-literate, elections at the national level is a most difficult exercise. So you can imagine what it would be like in the rural areas that are served by the Local Government Council. In the first place, the people had to be educated in the new system, complicated as it is. The Local Councils were very much influenced by the national political parties with the result that where the most influential leader in the local area happened to be in the "opposition," the national party used all available means to break that influence and the district officer found himself confronted with the problem of the maintenance of law and order! The voters were not guided by any ideology or philosophy; this meant nothing to the illiterate. They simply looked out for the symbol of the National Political Party, and cast their vote as preached to them by their national leaders.

Councils have been elected and constituted, and what do we find in most of them-a bunch of illiterate or semi-literate Councilors. So, almost simultaneously with the introduction of the new system, there were established Local Government Service Training Courses of about nine months duration for the turning out of trained Local Government personnel, and of about three months duration for the training of Councilors themselves. The Local Government Training Courses in later years developed into permanent features as Institutes of Administration.

It is convenient, I think, at this juncture, to discuss "Indigenization" or "Africanization" or as we say in Nigeria, "Nigerianization." In the year immediately after independence, practically all the expatriates in the Administrative Service had been replaced by indigenous officers. (The country now still retains some expatriate professional staff). Nigerians held posts from Permanent Secretary down to District Officer.

Two factors caused the general exodus of the expatriate staff: the younger officers, who anticipated Nigerianization, voluntarily resigned to seek alternative careers elsewhere while the going was good; most of the more senior and experienced officers also left, but not all. The few remaining were used for a very brief period as Advisers.

Thus, from the point of view of District Administration, a number of the former (expatriate) Residents remained on their posts to look after a group of Divisions within his Province, otherwise the District Administration was taken over completely by Nigerians in which capacity they assumed responsibility for the functions previously performed by the expatriate District Officers; these included those of Police, Prison, Magistrate, Public Health. These were some of the matters which the young newly appointed Nigerian District Officers had to face. They learnt fast, and it is to their credit that, administratively, they did not bungle things up. Their headache came from the politicians and local councilors who, in the practical application of the new Local Government set-up, saw themselves as the new masters of the ship of State and the new officers as their sailors. Trouble often erupted when the District Officer had to play his role as adviser to the Council which had itself become the tool by which the politician strives to keep himself in power. It gladdens one's heart to know that these young officers stood firm; but in a few extreme cases, confrontation had to be resolved in the Ministry of Local Government or in the Office of the Premier. The commonest areas of friction were: irregularities in the award of contracts, staff appointments, allocation of market stalls and, sometimes, general financial mismanagement.

In discussing indigenization, one cannot forget the human relation's aspect of it. In Nigeria, the public tended to regard the indigenous field officer as a "local," as one of us, and the respect he enjoyed is derived from his own personal achievement. Whereas a mistake by an-expatriate officer would almost pass unnoticed (or rather unheeded), if made by a Nigerian officer would be magnified by the public to the utter embarrassment of the officer. The Nigerian officer, therefore, has to assert himself not by use of force but by display of outstanding intelligence and ability. The problems notwithstanding, the Civil Service has made immense contribution to the development and stability of the country. By its knowledge, resilience, loyalty, the service has kept the country together. Where politicians have been rash in taking a decision which would cause unpleasantness, the Civil Servant had displayed his knowledge and skill to smoothen things out. During the Nigerian Civil War, the Civil Servants displayed unprecedented loyalty and fortitude.

I hope that, in the course of this paper, I have been able to highlight some of the problems of the transition from Colonial States to Independence with special reference to District Administration. It is impossible in a paper like this to give a catalogue of them or to do more than highlighting the problem areas. But I hope what I have said will give you food for thought.

BIBLIOGRAPHY:

D.C. Watt/Frank Spencer/Neville Brown: *A History of the World in the 20th Century*

Ferrel Heady: *Public Administration: A Comparative Perspective*

Joseph La Palombara: *Bureaucracy and Political Development.*

Dr. T.O. Elias: *Nigeria.*

Chapter 8

On the Need for the Creation of Edo State

*We have, however, now reached a stage that we must say it loud
and clear and with every confidence that whether or not the other
proposed States in the present Bendel State are created, we, the Edo-
Speaking peoples of Agbazilo, Akoko-Edo, Etsako, Okpebho, Oredo,
Orhionmwon, Ovia and Owan Local Government Council Areas are
now demanding that we be constituted into a separate State of our
own. . . . The feedback I received after our last meeting in July indicated
that majority of our people favored a positive action for the eventual
creation of Edo State and the immediate establishment of an Edo State
Movement, one of whose primary objectives would be not to oppose the
creation of other States but to ensure that no one encroaches on the territory of the Edo speaking people.*
                        — Omo N'Oba Erediauwa, November 30, 1980

IIIIIIIIIIIIIIIIIIIIIIIIIIIIIIIIIIIIIIIIII

**An Address on the Occasion of the Launching of the Ibadan Chapter of
the Movement for Creation of Edo State on Saturday, 31 July, 1982**

Beloved Edo-speaking Peoples, Distinguished Ladies and Gentlemen.
Just about two months ago we gathered in Lagos for the launching
of the Lagos Chapter of our Movement for the creation of Edo State, I
believed all Edo-speaking people were satisfied that the Lagos launching
was a great success. We were particularly happy that we were privileged
to meet with the Speaker of the House of Representatives to whom we
were able to make a special appeal, face to face, for support and as he

humorously told us that day, he saw the possibility of the Edo State being created, as he put it, either by omission or commission. May the Good Lord say Amen to that.

As I said in Lagos it is the intention of the Steering Committee of our Movement to declare in the major cities our aspiration for the creation of an Edo State out of the present Bendel State. Hence, today, we find ourselves here in the City of Ibadan. In putting our views across today I seek my people's indulgence to repeat almost verbatim what I said in Lagos about two months ago.

As I have often said since we began this movement, we the Edo-Speaking peoples of Bendel State, are rather late-comers in this race for the creation of States, for other ethnic groups in Bendel State had practically concluded their own actions before we began. When I spoke at the launching of the Movement in Benin City in November last year, I gave four reasons which different peoples or ethnic groups have advanced for wanting to constitute themselves into a new State. Since I repeated these in Lagos, I think there is no need to go through all that again. We mention them only to enable us to say that it is not we, the Edo-Speaking peoples, who initiated the call for the break-up of Bendel State into more States. I like to be making this point because of the frustration we nearly suffered at the hands of certain persons who tried to impute partisan political motives into our action. We have, however, now reached a stage that we must say it loud and clear and with every confidence that whether or not the other proposed States in the present Bendel State are created we, the Edo-speaking peoples of Agbazilo, Akoko-Edo, Etsako, Okpebho, Oredo, Orhionmwon, Ovia and Owan Local Government Council Areas, are now demanding that we be constituted into a separate State of our own.

We have very strong reasons for this proposition. First, we the Edo-speaking people in the eight Local Government Areas have been accused in some quarters of dominating the score in Bendel. But, in point of fact, this has never been so, as all those who have followed with open mind the development of Bendel State can substantiate. For our part, if the first comers into the race got their own States, we the Edo-speaking people in the eight Local Government Areas stand the risk of having our territory dismembered unless we come together to declare and define our own State and territorial area.

The second reason why we must have the Edo State from the ethnic composition of the present Bendel State. The State is usually referred to as "Miniature Nigeria" because it has as many diverse tongues and cultures as Nigeria itself. But, of all the ethnic groups that form Bendel State, the Edo-speaking peoples comprising of the eight Local Government Councils of Agbazilo, Akoko-Edo, Etsako, Okpebho, Oredo, Orhionmwon, Ovia and Owan are the only ethnic group today that communicate among themselves in English. You never find a Benin man, Esan, Akoko-Edo, Owan conversing in a common vernacular language! Ethnographically, we are all Edo-speaking, with Edo as our parent tongue. But owing to inter-mixing with other neighboring languages on our eastern and northern sides the original Edo language now takes different forms and with the result that the Edo of the Benin man in South now sounds slightly different from the Ishan or Etsako man in the middle or the Akoko-Edo man in the far north. Yet by listening attentively, one easily identifies the similarity. Furthermore, while there is a difference of some sort in the language there is hardly any difference in the customs of the people. This is why we are appealing to the National and State Assemblies that, taking into consideration the factor of ethnicity, cultural affinity and ancestral heritage, these eight Local Government Councils deserve to be constituted into a new State. Added to these are the current factors of economic viability, population and landmass. So our demand for the Edo State is not a partisan political issue but one of cultural identity and survival. We want to come together so that our children, if not we their fathers, can speak in our original mother-tongue from Oredo to Akoko-Edo as one ethnic group. We, the peoples of these areas, are quite alive to our historical antecedent and we are conscious of our own heritage. The proposed Edo State will live at peace with its neighbors and with other new States in Bendel State.

I must state, at this juncture, (permit me if I do so with a feeling of pride in our people!) that we the Edo-speaking people of Agbazilo, Akoko-Edo, Etsako, Okpebho, Oredo, Orhionmwon, Ovia and Owan, by the fact of our being offsprings of the great Benin Empire, can justly claim to be an ethnic group that has been known through the ages. We have never lagged behind, and, God willing, we will not. We are an ethnic group with history, and clear distinct culture and tradition of our own. Unfortunately, by historical accident our own group had become fragmented and disunited with the result that other ethnic groups less homogenous and of more recent history tend to take advantage to lord it over the Edo-speaking people. We must have the Edo State so this wrong can be righted.

The Edo State will be for all of us. We who are presently championing the cause cannot, at present, promise anyone any office. The Steering Committee itself comprises representatives of all the political parties functioning in the Edo-speaking areas, in addition to prominent citizens and Traditional Rulers. As you all know, a time will come when a political party will take over all that we have been doing. It is that political party that will be responsible for sharing the booty when the time comes. Our own concern, at this stage, is to ensure that we successfully fulfill all the constitutional requirements for the creation of a new State and that is why I am appealing to all of you to join hands in achieving our objectives. We hope and pray that those who will be at the helm of affairs when the time comes will be men of honor who will exercise such independence of mind as will enable them to put the interest of the state first before their personal interest.

I am sure I speak the mind of all Traditional Rulers and our people from home when say we are very encouraged by this large turnout of our sons and daughters, friends and well-wishers of the people of the proposed State. The launching here today, in addition to spreading the gospel of the Edo State, is also a fund-raising affair. As I indicated in Lagos, the demand for the creation of the then Midwestern State will recall. You can well imagine the high cost now that we are doing it in a Presidential System! Ibadan is the second of the major towns in which we hope to have a Chapter, outside Bendel State.

The Edo State Movement plans to go places in the interest of the proposed Edo State. It is expected that there would be a referendum and we have to be well prepared for it. Bearing in mind that in a society where people like to reap where they did not sow, some persons who put black balls in the ballot boxes in 1963 were among the first beneficiaries of the new Mid-Western State.

There will certainly be massive secretarial and publicity work. All these will cost money. We are aware that a number of prominent sons and daughters in Lagos State and environs, as well as many friends of Edo-speaking peoples, were unable to come to Benin for the main launching on 28th November 1981. We know also that our daughters in Ibadan and environs prefer to do theirs as to beat Lagos. It is my earnest hope that all such persons will use this occasion to demonstrate their support for the Movement and faith in the proposed Edo State. I therefore appeal to all to donate generously now or any day hereafter. Receipts are issued for substantial donations and as it is proposed to publish list of donors. I assure you that your donations will be thankfully received and faithfully applied for the purpose.

Before I close I like to announce with great happiness the launching in Benin City on the 24th July the Women's Wing of our Movement. Our women have rallied themselves together to back up the men in this great task. You all know how powerful women can be.

Their representatives are here with us, and we give them hearty cheers for making it a point of duty to come to Ibadan. It is my hope that women in the two Chapters we have launched will give their full support to the Women organizers at home by following their example.

Finally, I like, on behalf of all of us from home, to express our deep appreciation to our sons and daughters who have organized this launching and put up this magnificent show. I wish to say a very big thank you to His Excellency, Chief Bola Ige, Governor of Oyo State, for all the co-operation he gave the Organising Committee. My thanks also to His Highness, the Olubadan and people of Ibadan for the hospitality our own people enjoy among the indigenes. Ibadan has scored a significant point in that this is his first launching our own Governor, His Excellency, Chief A. F. Alli has been chanced to be physically present. We are happy to have him with us today.

In conclusion, may I call on all here present to support the cause for which we are gathered here, and donate generously. If you cannot put all down now, we will accept your spreading out a big purse rather than giving what you can just afford today; but, of course, nothing will be too small for us, not even the proverbial widow's mite or I.O.U.

God bless you all.

||||||||||||||||||||||||||||||||||||||||||||||

A Speech to Traditional Rulers and Leaders of Thought in the Northern Senatorial District of Bendel State on the Need for the Creation of Edo State, 26–27 June, 1981

I am grateful to all the Traditional Rulers who have made it possible for me to come to address this august gathering of leaders of thought from these parts of the Northern Senatorial District. I thank all of you present for coming to hear me.

You are no doubt aware by now of my active involvement in the movement for the creation of Edo State. Since we began last year, I have had occasions to address in Benin City meetings of Traditional Rulers and prominent citizens drawn from the eight Local Government Councils of Agbazilo, Akoko-Edo, Etsako, Okpebho, Oredo, Orhionmwon, Ovia and Owan. I have also addressed letters and sent emissaries to individual Traditional Rulers. I have been doing all this with a view to putting across the reason why the creation of the State is necessary.

I have found, however, that my motive in initiating the move for the creation of Edo State has been very seriously misconstrued, misrepresented and misunderstood by people. In particular, people in the Northern Senatorial District have been fed with wrong information as to my motive, and certain allegations have begun to be made against my person. The result is that what I believed I was doing in the interest of all of us is now being thwarted. It is in view of the seriousness of the situation that I have decided to speak to you myself, having in mind the old Edo saying" "Aguanomwan eghiye vbe emwen nu'nuomwan" (to speak for yourself is quite different from someone else speaking for you). This is why I am happy and grateful that you have all come to hear me.

I would like to address you from the three perspectives: first, how I came to initiate the move for the creation of Edo State; secondly, I will enumerate the allegations that have been made and where my action has been misunderstood and, thirdly, I will try to give answers to the allegations and clear the areas of misunderstanding.

For a start, I like to state that my call for the creation of Edo State has been necessitated by the activities of the other major ethnic groups in this State, namely: those who want the Anioma State, the Delta State and the Coast State. You all know the ethnic groups that form these areas. If these three areas were to be constituted into three new States, what would remain of the present Bendel State would be only the eight Local Government Council Areas occupied by the Edo-speaking peoples.

My initial reaction, and the reaction of many persons whose opinion I sounded, was that since only the Edo-speaking areas would be left, we should let those who are asking for their States to go. We thought that what would remain would become a State of its own. Two factors, however, came to light which made us change our stand and which motivated us to action. First, there is enough evidence that the other ethnic groups to which I have referred are not only asking to be constituted into new States, but are hoping that parts of Okpebho, Orhionmwon and Ovia Local Government Councils would join them. Outside Bendel State, the proposed State of Kogi and Okura are hoping to take parts of the Etsako area.

Among the older States, our neighbors in Kwara State are having their eyes on Ukpilla. It therefore, became obvious to me that if we folded our arms, not only would these other ethnic groups have their States, but the ethnic group known as the Edo-speaking peoples, to which we belong, could completely be wiped out because what would be left in the present Bendel State would have been shared out! I felt that no Edo-speaking person would allow his heritage to wipe out in this manner.

This is why I consulted a few individuals, many of whom I have known and worked with, picked at random from each of the eight Local Government Councils. After sounding their opinion, the consensus was that we should take definite action to prevent our territory from disappearing. It was on this basis that I initiated the setting up of the Steering Committee. The membership was nominated by Traditional Rulers and citizens from each of eight Local Government Councils is an open meeting held in the Conference Room of the Oredo Local Government Council on the 30th of November 1980.

The second reason why action had to be taken for the creation of Edo State arises from the realization that under the Constitution no area can automatically be declared a State. The people in that area have to fulfill the conditions laid down by the Constitution.

These are:

(i) Application by the citizens of the area to the National Assembly. This must be supported by;

(ii) Two-third majority of the members of the National Assembly who are from the area;

(iii) Two-third majority of the members of the House of Assembly of the area; and

(iv) Two-third majority of the members of the Local Government Councils of the area.

It is obvious that if the eight Local Government Councils did not fulfill the constitutional conditions, the fact of the other three groups forming their own States would not automatically constitute the Edo-speaking area into a State. Hence it became necessary for something to be done.

I hope you will agree from what I have said so far that my primary aim has been to ensure that the ethnic group known as the Edo-speaking peoples is not dismembered and carried away by our neighbors who want to constitute themselves into new States. Of course, since a part of my own domain is affected I could very well have invited my own people to stand firm to resist any move by those other ethnic groups to encroach on my territory. Not minding what happened elsewhere. I felt, however, that because of our historical connection that would be selfish of me. I also felt that in my position I can speak on behalf of all of us in the eight Local Government Council areas, if I am convinced that what I am doing is to the benefit of all of us.

Before I proceed further, I think I ought to explain here why I believe I can speak on your behalf in this matter. I believe that we of the eight Local Government Councils grouped as the Edo-speaking peoples have a common heritage that makes us one people. In the midst of modern politics, unbridled ambition and falsification of history, there would be those who would ask for my authority that we in these parts have a common heritage. There is no citing authority from traditional history which educated people easily brush aside these days. I will, therefore, quote from two eminent University writers.

First is Dr. R.E. Bradbury, who was an eminent historian and ethnographer. In his work entitled The Benin Kingdom and the Edo-speaking Peoples of South-Western Nigeria, he defined the term "Edo-speaking peoples" as applying to those who speak either Edo proper or closely related dialect as a first language. He pointed out that the term is derived from "Edo," the vernacular name of Benin City. He then went on to state that the Edo-speaking peoples fall into four main territorial groups as follows:

(i) The Edo proper of the Benin Kingdom;

(ii) The Ishan to the North-East of the Benin Kingdom;

(iii) The Northern Edo; and

(iv) The Urhobo and Isoko.

Bradbury went further, and this is relevant to my address to you, to identify the groups that form the Northern Edo, thus;

(a) Ivbiosakon;

(b) Etsako

(c) The North-West Edo; and

(d) The Ineme.

It is interesting to note that outside Benin proper, Bradbury had enough evidence to show that all the other ethnic groups he identified within the Edo-speaking peoples migrated from Benin City at some time or the other to where they are to be found today.

What I have quoted is from the work of a European. An eminent Nigerian Professor, who is himself an Etsako son, has done some work on this. He is Professor P. A. Igbafe of the University of Benin. He has this to say in his lecture titled "Bendel State History: Its Peoples and Resources." I will quote him at some length because he is one of us.

"Historically speaking," Dr. Igbafe says, "since the Bendel State is made up of diverse peoples, its history is a history of those peoples. In this connection, it is relevant to stress at this stage that the history of the Bendel State is the history of the Diaspora of the Edo-speaking peoples of South-Western Nigeria whose antecedents lie deep in the history of Benin through various transformation phases from Kingdom to Empire dating from around the 9th century A.D. and possibly beyond."

Dr. Igbafe went further to say: "The Bendel State is part of the famed Benin Empire which was an outgrowth from the Benin Kingdom whose nerve center was its dynastic and monarchical traditions. For a proper understanding of the history of the Bendel State, its peoples, culture, present-day relationships, the chieftaincy institutions, the arts and crafts and the general outlook of the people in the area, a brief analysis of the history of the Benin Kingdom and Empire is inescapable. This is partly because, in the history of the Bendel State and its peoples, it can be said that the Benin ruling house is a cultural water-shed. Most of the traditional rulers of the State-the Enigie in Benin East and West Divisions, the Enigie in the Esan (Ishan) chiefdoms, the Obis in Ika and Aniocha divisions especially those in the Ezechime group, the Ivie in Urhobo land, the Olu of Warri and most of the clan heads in the several divisions of the State trace their origins and history either partly or wholly to the Benin dynasty. In addition, large sections of the various ethnic groups of Esan, Etsako, Owan, Akoko-Edo, Urhobo, Itsekiri, Aniocha, Ika, Isoko, Aboh as well as Ijaw possess a history of various migrations from Benin at different periods of the imperial expansion when powerful rulers at the center with their effective and at times intolerable rule created conditions for the dispersal of their subjects." This is Professor Igbafe.

So even if we were to disregard our own traditional history, which I dare-say, we honestly cannot do, there is enough modern history to testify to the fact that there is in this Bendel State certain communities for which the term "Edo-speaking peoples" is most appropriate. It is only those who wish to erase their ancestry and name from history who will deny this fact.

I believe that, from what I have said, you will agree with me that I am in a position to fight for the progress of all the Edo-speaking peoples. It is in this spirit that I initiated the move for the creation of Edo State, having regard to what is happening around us, in order to preserve our common heritage as the Edo-speaking peoples. Of course, if any other traditional ruler had initiated the move for the creation of Edo State, I would gladly have gone along with him. It is in the light of what I have said thus far that I have found it most disappointing that certain persons have gone out of their way to misrepresent my intention to you. I find it even more disappointing to know that those who engage in this act were some of the people whom I took into confidence in forming the Steering Committee of the Movement for the creation of Edo State, an action aimed at preserving our unity and territorial heritage.

I now come to the allegations/misrepresentations that they have made:
- Some Traditional Rulers have been told that I am advocating the creation of the Edo State in order to revive the old Benin Empire and that after the creation of the Edo State I would compel all Traditional Rulers to be paying tribute to me;
- It has been said that I am doing it for the support of the N.P.N. and so the opposing party felt the initiative taken from them;
- The Etsako people say they are opposed to the creation of the State for fear that it would intensify the existing hostility which the Binis have against them;

To crown it all, the U.P.N. of the Northern Senatorial District, comprising the five Local Government Councils in this part, met on the question of the creation of Edo State. They then sent a delegation to inform me that the U.P.N. of the Northern Senatorial District would support the creation of Edo State if I granted the following five demands to them. They want me to:

(i) agree on a new name for the proposed State;

(ii) agree on where to site the headquarters of the proposed State;

(iii) say how major public offices would be shared

(iv) agree on the principle of equality among the component ethnic groups; and

(v) stop the activities of certain Benin organizations likely to cause disaffection among the ethnic groups, two of such organizations NEDOGHAMA and ADUWA were specifically mentioned.

As I heard these accusations and demands it became quite obvious to me that a great deal of damage had been done to my reputation and intention. That is why I decided to speak to you directly. As regards the allegation that I plan to revive the old Benin Empire and make Traditional Rulers pay homage to me. Traditional Rulers can brush that aside as a blatant lie from mischief-makers. Those of you who have been very close to me know that each time I have had occasion to speak on the status of Traditional Rulers I have always had all Traditional Rulers in mind as brothers irrespective of the size of your domains. This is not the place to tell you what I have tried to do on my own with previous Governors for the benefit of all the Traditional Rulers. I will, however, mention that I have recently addressed a letter to our governor setting out the various ways I consider government can enhance our status. When we meet in our council I shall tell you more about this. For now I ask you to disregard their allegation.

On the allegation that I am doing this for the N.P.N., it is a pity that anyone could make such allegation. The Steering Committee as formed is composed of the leaders of the five main political parties in the State—U.P.N., N.P.N., N.P.P., G.N.P.P., and P.R.P. All the parties are represented by their chairmen, except the U.P.N. which is represented by its Deputy Chairman, the Chairman being the Governor himself whom we have not brought into it because of his unique position as the Governor. In addition to these State Chairmen, there are leaders of the main political parties in each of the eight Local Government Council areas nominated by their Traditional Rulers. Also included are two Traditional Rulers, the Speaker of the House of Assembly, the Majority Leader, the Deputy Minority Leader, (the Minority Leader himself being a non-Edo-speaking person), Representatives from among our sons in the National Assembly and two nominees from me.

So you can see that the Steering Committee cannot be said to belong to one political party. From the word go I have stressed that the Committee is not a political party and that all we are out to do is to forestall the champions of the other proposed States from taking our territory along with them. As I have already pointed out, the members of the Steering Committee were chosen by their people at an open meeting in the Conference Hall of the Oredo Local Government Council; so, there was nothing secret about it.

I like to repeat that neither I nor the Steering Committee that I preside over is working for any political party. Its composition makes this impossible for the Committee. It is inevitable in a matter of this nature to completely exclude those who are actively involved in partisan politics. When we began, it was my intention, and it is still my hope, that our action would be seen as one of self-preservation. I did not expect that there would be persons who would like so soon to play partisan politics with a territory not even yet born and whose very existence is threatened by others around us.

The allegation that the Binis are hostile to Etsako people (or any other ethnic group for that matter) is simply ridiculous. I do not wish to embarrass anyone; otherwise I would have mentioned the names of prominent Etsako people who are living well in Benin City and in good business. This allegation is particularly annoying because some of those who are making it are themselves carrying on their good business and living well in Benin City. One wonders why they have not returned home or gone elsewhere. I am sure many of you know there is no truth in this allegation; but, it suits their purpose to come to tell it to those who have not been privileged to travel out! If you doubt it ask your sons living in Benin why they are still there.

The five demands made of me by the U.P.N. only go to confirm that there are some people who are accusing me of having initiated this move in the interest of the N.P.N.; otherwise, how can a political party come to demand from me on the five points I earlier mentioned? It is a pity that some people wish to make partisan politics out of this issue. How can any true son of Ishan, Owan, Etsako, Akoko-Edo or Benin begin by tying our heritage to the apron-string of others when that very heritage is in imminent danger of being destroyed by ethnic groups who are working hard to preserve their own? It is sad that only the Edo-speaking peoples who cannot sink their political differences, as others have done, in order to pursue a common goal.

To me, the issues raised by the U.P.N. are matters that the politicians sell and bargain for if and when the new State comes into being; if and when the territory of the Edo-speaking peoples remains intact. In fact, what I am doing at the moment is to ensure that there would be a State over which politicians can bargain. It would be sheer short-sightedness to be bargaining on these issues before we have saved the area from the clutches of those who want to dismember it. It is worse than counting one's chicken before the eggs hatch! I am in no position to engage in such bargain at this stage and the Steering Committee over which I preside, not being a political party, cannot be involved in it. I would like, in this connection, to remind you that issues similar to the five mentioned by the U.P.N. came up for discussion by politicians only after the conclusion of the Referendum for the creation of the Midwest State in 1963. Before then, all hands were on deck for the common purpose which was to excise the Benin and Delta Provinces from old Western Region. So, I would urge that all of us, party men and non-party men, should let us join hands to save our territory from those who wish to add it to their own states. After that, politicians can then bargain for whatever they want to sell.

I like, however, to say a few words about the activities of some Benin organizations, specifically the one called NEDOGHAMA. It appears a few individuals got their pride injured by a petition the NEDOGHAMA addressed to the Governor in connection with the happening in Auchi Poly-technic last year. Among such persons were some prominent Etsako citizens whom the petition mentioned as having been involved in the disturbances at the Polytechnic. This matter was raised at the meeting of the Steering Committee when I was urged to have the organization. Their reason at the time was that it was wrong for NEDOGHAMA to attack a section of our people when we are trying to come together. I strongly objected to the affected persons trying to make national issue out of it by claiming that it was an attack on the whole of Etsako people. I put it quite strongly to the Steering Committee (and I still maintain) that it would be very wrong for a few individuals who have been offended, this time by NEDOGHAMA, perhaps next time another ethnic organization, to try to escalate it by mak-ing a national issue out of it. No matter how important the individual may be, an attack or offence against him cannot be, an attack or offence against the whole of his ethnic group unless, of course, he is the traditional ruler.

Since then those who felt aggrieved by what NEDOGHAMA did ceased coming to meeting of the Steering Committee. They have been using the incident to destroy what the Steering Committee was set up to do. I have been asked to get the NEDOGHAMA disbanded. To be quite honest with you, I will not do that unless all other ethnic groups who have their own Progressive Unions, Improvement Unions and Youth Associations or Devel-opment Unions will also disband theirs, for NEDOGHAMA does exactly what similar organizations with different names in other places are doing for their own people. Some people are angry now because NEDOGHAMA drew attention to the situation in Auchi Polytechnic, but these people have forgotten so soon that the same NEDOGHAMA, in its Memorandum, defended a very prominent Etsako person who was accused before the House of Assembly Committee on Etete Layout Affair! The person who was so defended knows how NEDOGHAMA defended him! We cannot accept that because this organization highlighted a situation in an institution, therefore it is antagonistic to a whole ethnic group. You know as well as I do that other ethnic societies do the same but perhaps apply a different style to that of NEDOGHAMA!

I like to conclude my comments on NEDOGHAMA by letting you know my ultimate vision for the present Steering Committee. I see it as an organization that can bring together all the Edo-speaking peoples and provide a forum where matters of common interest to Owan, Ishan, Etsako, Akoko-Edo and Benin could be jointly discussed for our mutual advancement. It is, therefore, my hope that whether or not a State is eventually created, we should retain this Committee as a unifying machinery amongst us. We envisage this in the Committee, hence in the Constitution we are drafting, there is a provision to enable us in future to change the name of the Committee or the Movement. It has also been resolved that such matters as were highlighted by NEDOGHAMA petition would in future be brought to the Committee for settlement. One of the problems that beset the Committee was that some of the founders who were thought to be men of standing in their communities had no base whatever at home. It has since been discovered that such members were not coming home to report to you on our deliberations. I therefore call on all Traditional Rulers to consider sending names of new members to me so every one of the eight Local Government Council areas will be adequately and effectively represented. This will enable the Committee to prepare not only for the current issue of State but for the more lofty and important function of unifying our people. You are free to make suggestions for improving the composition of the Committee in order to make it more effective.

I am sorry to have taken so much of your time. I have gone to this length in order to put the whole position regarding the Edo State clearly before you. I hope I have been able to clear your minds of the many misrepresentations that have been made to you and allegations made against me. The sum total of all that I have been saying is this. The Steering Committee was formed for the purpose of setting up a Movement for the Creation of Edo State. It is very essential that we the eight Local Government Council areas should take urgent steps to fulfill the constitutional provisions for creating Edo State so that our neighbors asking for their own states will realize that we do exist as an ethnic group. We have to use the name "Edo State" because at present, as an ethnic group, we are collectively known as "Edo-speaking peoples," and no name can be better than that. No need to argue about another name yet when there is one that can conveniently be used for now. If and when the State becomes a reality, the government that will control it can give it whatever name it chooses. My father proposed "Bendel" for mis State, but the first Government gave it "Midwestern." A subsequent Government dropped Midwestern and gave it "Bendel" which the State now answers. When the time comes perhaps those who do not have Edo origin will propose a new name.

Finally, I am happy to say that we have gone a long way in submitting to the National Assembly our request for the creation of an Edo State. We have secured the signatures of those of the National Assembly men except members from Akoko-Edo and Etsako. We have also secured the required percentage of signatures from members of Local Government Councils. After this round of visits, I and members of the Steering Committee will finalise arrangement to go to the National Assembly. We will also complete arrangements for the formal launching of the Movement. Invitations will be sent to every traditional ruler and public announcement will be made. All Edo-speaking peoples will be invited and it is my conviction you will show up. That will be an opportunity for all Edo-speaking people to demonstrate to other proposed new States that we exist and have no intention to giving away an inch of our fatherland.

In conclusion, I like to say how happy I am to be able to make this visit. Although the visit has been necessitated at this time by this question of Edo State Movement, I wish to seize this opportunity to say a very big thank you to all my brother traditional rulers who attended my Coronation in 1979. This is not the end of it, I still plan to visit as many of you as possible individually to thank you after I shall have performed the final ceremony connected with the Coronation, of which I shall give you due notice.

I thank you all for your patience and attention. If there is any point any one is still not clear about, I will be glad to answer questions.

|||||||||||||||||||||||||||||||||||||||||||

An Address at a Meeting of Representatives of Traditional Rulers and People of the Edo-Speaking Areas of Bendel State, 30 November, 1980.

My Brother Traditional Rulers, Chiefs and Gentlemen, I greet you all, and say welcome to this very important meeting.

On the 19th of July, this year, I summoned and addressed a cross section of Edo-speaking people. On that occasion, as those of you present may recall, I drew attention to the fact that our neighbors to the eastern and southern parts of this State, had embarked on a move to have themselves constituted into Anioma State and Delta State. I sounded a note of warning that while we, the Edo-speaking people, would not be in a position to stop other ethnic groups from their desire to break away from the present Bendel State, their demand had made it obligatory on Edo-speaking people to close their ranks and get more united in order that we would not be taken unawares and be in disarray if the demand of the other ethnic groups were granted.

The topic evoked a lively discussion at that meeting, at the end of which two points of view emerged; there were those who felt that since what would be left after the others had gone would be Edo-speaking areas, it was prudent for us to wait and see; the other view was that a wait-and-see attitude would be alphabetic which the other ethnic groups would take advantage of. In the end it was decided that those present should go home to consult and think about the situation. Three of our sons present were mandated to monitor reactions and to give me a feedback.

I have since received the feedback and today's meeting is intended to further deliberate and take decisions on the subject. Since the last meeting, the demand by the other ethnic groups had gathered more momentum as you no doubt must have read in the news media. Those for Anioma State have sent a number of delegations, including traditional rulers, to Lagos, and the Committee of the National Assembly on the Creation of States had recently visited the area. On the southern side two new States have now been projected, the Delta and the Coast States.

When I addressed the selected group in July my main concern then was that as a people we should be more united. The present indication now calls for a more positive action from the Edo-speaking people than mere appeal for unity because a perusal of the memoranda and pamphlets submitted by the champions of Anioma and Delta States shows that not only do these people want to break away, they also want to share out what would be left of the Edo-speaking area. Specifically, the Anioma want some portion of Orhionmwon Local Government Area and some portion of Okpebho Local Government Area. Those asking for Delta State want what they described as their kith and kin in some parts of Ovia Government. So, it is obvious that their intention is not just to have their own States, but to also dominate and, if possible, even wipe out the present territory of the Edo-speaking people. It ought to be mentioned, in passing, that their move will surely alert the older States that have boundaries with Etsako and Akoko-Edo.

Personally, my stand had been that the present Bendel State ought not to be broken up; if it was possible, one would want to see the State kept, but we cannot stop others from seeking their self-determination. While we would not stop them we cannot let them surreptitiously dismember our own area with a view to subjugating us. In this connection, the feedback I received after our last meeting in July indicated that majority of our people favored a positive action for the eventual creation of Edo State and the immediate establishment of an Edo Movement, one of whose primary objective would be not to oppose the creation of other States but to ensure that no one encroaches on the territory of the Edo-speaking people. It is obviously sheer commonsense that this is a clear case of fighting for survival and, in this regard, it behoves all Edo-speaking people, traditional rulers and all, to stand up firmly to ensure that the Edo-speaking people survive.

We are not to form a political party and I must appeal to all present that if and when the Edo State Movement becomes a reality you should not begin by tying it to the apron-strings of any of the existing political parties. Here in this gathering there are leaders of the various political parties. I appeal to you all to sink your political differences for the time being in the interest of the bigger issue of survival. It is appreciated and inevitable that we have to solicit the support of the existing political parties; this is a responsibility for those of you who are attached to the various national parties. But I must seriously appeal to all of you that we must not dissipate energy at this stage as to which of the existing political parties would control us if we became a State. We must not attempt to cross the bridge until we get there, and let no person be so mean as to sell his rights for Naira!

I like now to mention that in the light of the developments to which I have referred, I convened a small meeting of a cross-section of our people on the 23rd of November to brief them on the events, and to seek the benefit of their advice. Those present decided that immediate steps be taken to summon a larger and more representative meeting to deliberate and take positive decisions in the light of the known development in the other ethnic areas. At that point it was agreed that a panel of eight members, to be approved by me, be selected from among those present to reduce to writing the deliberations and decisions at that and all previous meetings held with me to help you in your deliberation today.

The members of that panel have done so and have submitted their report to me. I have read the report and it is a fair and accurate reflection of our deliberations. It is in two parts; the narrative followed by a set of resolutions. I will ask Mr. Odion Ugbesia, a member of that panel, to read it out to you, but before he does so, I like to mention the three main conclusions arrived at:

(i) that we the Edo-speaking people should demand the creation of Edo State;

(ii) that an Edo State Movement should be established immediately to pursue the demand for the creation of Edo State; and

(iii) that a Steering Committee be set up to work out the machinery for prosecuting the demand and the launching of the Movement.

By virtue of the authority vested in me at the meeting of the 23rd of November, and after due consultation, I have appointed the following to serve on the Steering Committee.

(a) Those I consulted at the meeting on 23 November, 1980;

(b) Speaker of the House of Assembly, Bendel State;

(c) Assembly Majority Leader;

(d) Assembly Deputy Minority Leader;

(e) State Deputy Chairman of UPN;

(f) State Chairman of NPN;

(g) State Chairman of NPP;

(h) State Chairman of GNPP;

(i) State Chairman of PRP;

(j) Nominee of Federal Legislators (to be nominated by themselves);

(k) Representative of Business Community (Mr. A. Anenih);

(l) Representative from Lagos (Mr. Anofi Guobadia);

(m) Representative of the Oba

(n) Traditional Rulers: (i) Onogie of Ewohimi

(ii) Okumagbe of Uleha

It is hoped that this Steering Committee will work speedily and fix a date for the launching of the Movement which all Edo-speaking sons and daughters will be expected to attend.

I hope we will have a successful and not protracted meeting today. I now call on Mr. Ugbesia to read the report. Thank you.

||||||||||||||||||||||||||||||||||||||||||

PROPOSED RESOLUTION

WHEREAS this Assembly of Traditional Rulers, Chiefs, Leaders and Representatives from the Edo areas of Bendel State, are gathered in the Oredo Council Hall, Benin City at the invitation of Omo N'Oba Erediauwa, the Oba of Benin, this 30th day of November 1980, to deliberate on the place and future of the Edo people within the Federation of Nigeria.

WHEREAS the people of the former Delta Province of Nigeria are agitating for a Delta State and a Coastal State, consisting of the Province, to be carved out of the existing boundaries of Bendel State;

WHEREAS the people of the former Asaba Division of the former Benin Province and Ndokwa Local Government Area of the former Delta Province are also agitating for an Anioma State, consisting of the Division and the Area, to be carved out of the existing boundaries of Bendel State;

WHEREAS the people of the Edo areas of Bendel State, consisting of Ovia, Oredo, Orhionmwon, Agbazilo, Okpebho, Etsako, Owan and Akoko-Edo Local Government Areas, will naturally form the remainder of Bendel State after the possible creation of the aforementioned Anioma, Delta and Coastal States;

WHEREAS the creation of new States elsewhere in the Federation would alter the political and ethnic balance in Nigeria to the further disadvantage of the Edos;

WHEREAS the Edo people desire to retain and foster their identity, integrity, history, language and culture within the boundaries of one cohesive State in the Federation of Nigeria.

BE IT RESOLVED, and it is hereby resolved, by this Assembly of Edo people, that a demand be made for an Edo State to be created out of the existing boundaries of Bendel State;

THAT the Edo State shall consist of the existing Local Government Areas of Ovia, Oredo, Orhionmwon, Agbazilo, Okpebho, Etsako, Owan, and Akoko-Edo, the components of which are contained in the Bendel State Legal Notice No. 89 published in Bendel State Gazette No. 24 Vol. 17 of 21 st April 1980, together with such other contiguous areas as may identify themselves with the Edos and express a wish to be included in the Edo State;

THAT an Edo State Movement should be established as an Edo People's enterprise and a non-partisan platform for the purpose of prosecuting the demand for Edo State;

THAT the Edo State Movement should embrace all political parties and community organizations in the Local Government Areas of Ovia, Oredo, Orhionmwon, Agbazilo, Okpebho, Etsako, Owan and Akoko-Edo;

THAT a Steering Committee of 30 Edos be set up immediately to pilot the affairs of the Edo State Movement;

THAT the Steering Committee be mandated, and is hereby mandated, to solicit the active support and assistance of political leaders and community leaders in Bendel State, leaders of other State Movements both in Bendel State and in the rest of Nigeria, and other influential persons, towards the achievement of the goal of the creation of an Edo State;

THAT the Steering Committee should make immediate arrangement for the public launching of the Edo State Movement;

THAT Omo N'Oba Erediauwa, Oba of Benin, as father of the Edos, is hereby reverently appointed Grand Patron of the Edo State Movement, while the Traditional Rulers in Edo-land are hereby respectfully appointed Patrons of the Movement.

THAT the inaugural meeting of the Steering Committee be summoned by Omo N'Oba Erediauwa as soon as may be convenient to His Royal Highness;

THAT this Assembly calls upon all Edos, wherever they may be, to give every support to the Edo State Movement;

AND THAT this Resolution should be given the widest possible publicity and should be formally conveyed to all appropriate quarters.

Chapter 9

On Peace, Religious Intolerance, Students' Unrest and Solutions.

*Our strong plea is that if the rich and powerful man, who happens
already to be at the top of the ladder, will not assist the less fortunate at its
foot to climb up, the poor man should at least be left alone to strive by his
own efforts and should not be pressed down on the head by the man on
top to thwart the poor man's efforts. If the rich and powerful cannot assist
the less fortunate to bear his cross, he should not tie rocks on it to make it
heavier for him to carry. In short, we shall do our best to build a kingdom
of peace where the weak are safe and the strong are just.*
— Omo N'Oba Erediauwa, March 23, 1979

*If I were an undergraduate today, I would inwardly reflect on the
future and pray silently: God, teach me to distinguish between sentiment and sentimentality; teach me to keep my head while others lose
theirs; and teach me to so behave myself as to be not only a pride to my
parents and alma mater but also to deserve the highest honor . . .being
conferred . . .*
— Omo N'Oba Erediauwa, November 17, 1988

IIIIIIIIIIIIIIIIIIIIIIIIIIIIIIIIIIIIIIIIII

Excerpts from Coronation Address, Delivered March 23, 1979

There have been some serious cases of land dispute with our neighbors
and non-Edo people on our soil and borders. Equally the Edo people have

had clashes against themselves for the same reason. We pray there will be no more of these inter and intra-community land disputes, and we will take measures to arrest the situation. We are well aware, of course, that the Federal Government has taken over all land in the community; but in so far as, for us, land tenure and our custom are inseparable, we would like to say that is something still very dear to the heart of our people.

By nature we are peace loving and we will do our utmost to make this land of ours a peaceful place for all. We will, therefore, encourage peaceful settlement of disputes and avoid rancor. This, however, does not mean that our action will be governed by appeasement. We have had occasions in the past to say openly that our ancestors who founded this Edo land intended it to accommodate both the rich and the poor, the powerful and the weak.

Our strong plea is that, if the rich and powerful man, who happens already to be at the top of the ladder, will not assist the less fortunate at its foot to climb up, the poor man should at least be left alone to strive by his own efforts and should not be pressed down on the head by the man on the top to thwart the poor man's efforts. If the rich and powerful cannot assist the less fortunate to bear his cross, he should not tie rocks on it to make it heavier for him to carry. In short, we shall do our best to build a Kingdom of peace where the weak are safe and the strong are just.

||||||||||||||||||||||||||||||||||||||||||||

An Address by the Omo N'Oba as Chancellor, University of Ibadan, on the Occasion of the 40th Foundation Ceremony Tagged "Four Decades of Ibadan (1948–88)" on 17 November, 1988.

It is my great pleasure and privileged to welcome all of you here present to this historic ceremony. Today's ceremony marks the culmination of the fortieth Anniversary Celebrations of the University of Ibadan, which came into existence in 1948 as a College of the University of London and located in this historic City of Ibadan. We thank God Almighty for having led us, especially those who witnessed the beginning 40 years ago, to participate at this year's celebrations.

On behalf of the entire University community, I most heartily welcome the visitor to the University, the President of the Federal Republic of Nigeria and Commander-in-Chief of the Armed Forces, General Ibrahim Badamosi Babangida, GCFR, (or his representative), and all those in his entourage. I also extend our warm welcome to the Military Governor of our host State, Colonel Adedeji Oresanya, who has early in his tenure registered deep interest in the University. I seize this opportunity to congratulate him on his appointment as the Governor of Oyo State and wish him successful tenure. I also seize the opportunity to wish the former Governor, Col. Tunji Olurin every success in his present assignment.

We welcome our respected Traditional Rulers, His Lordship, the Chief Justice of Nigeria, the Judges of State Judiciaries as well as other Judges at the Federal and State levels; other visiting dignitaries; chancellors, Pro-chancellors and Vice-Chancellors of the sister Universities as well as all overseas visitors who have come in their own right or as representatives of friendly organizations. The university welcomes you all for coming to share the joys of this momentous occasion with us.

The University of Ibadan is FORTY years old today. Within the FOUR DECADES of its short but exciting existence, the University has recorded outstanding achievements, endured its share of setbacks, and registered inevitable shortcomings since no human beings or human organization is ever perfect. While celebrating its 40th birthday as a great University, it is only natural for the institution to take stock of itself, counting its blessings, embarking on rigorous self-examination and thereby learning from its past mistakes. I will leave these areas to the other addresses to dwell upon as appropriate.

However, I would crave your indulgence to accommodate a few pertinent remarks. First and foremost, I am sure that I am speaking the minds of all of us here when I say that on an occasion such as this, special tribute should be paid to the FOUNDING FATHERS. Our gratitude goes to the British Government and the University of London for their vision and pioneering contributions towards establishing in 1948 the University College Ibadan, and for nurturing it under the tutelage of the University of London until the attainment of autonomous status in 1962.

We salute the pioneer officers and staff, predominantly expatriate, who translated the British initiative into concrete reality and kept the College and later the University afloat until the Nigerian Government and indigenous personnel took over. We deeply appreciate and publicly acknowledge the assistance in academic, financial, and technical terms by various benefactors, notably the great American Foundations like Rockefeller, Ford, Carnegie and others, towards the growth and development of the University right from its "College' days. This chapter of tribute would be incomplete without formally paying tribute to the dedicated Nigerian officers, staff and students who, from generation to generation, have laboured diligently to make this University a beacon of scholarship in Nigeria and the world of learning at large.

The visitor, distinguished ladies and gentlemen, the ceremony this year has at once an unprecedented and exceptional element. To reflect Ibadan's age of FOUR DECADES, the University is today conferring honors upon SEVEN eminent Nigerians who have distinguished themselves in various spheres of human endeavour and are considered to be deserving of honor by Nigeria's premier University. Taken together, the galaxy of honorary graduands, as you will see, represent a board spectrum of the Nigerian society; viz, a former Head of State, the military echelon, traditional rulers, academics, professionals, business executives, diplomats, industrialists and the clergy. The selection which, incidentally, achieves national spread could not, in our opinion, be better. I keep the "secret" of their identity and merit until all of you will hear their impressive citations. Turning to the Honorary Graduands, our special guest of honor, we say welcome to the University; we thank you for honoring our invitation and we congratulate you on your meritorious achievements.

Let me at this juncture refer briefly to what seems to me an interesting new development in the Nigerian academic field. There was a time in this country when it was fashionable that after a man had "made it"—in money—his next ambition was to become a traditional "chief and he basks under the influence of his traditional chieftaincy title. In recent times, however, one has observed that what is now in vogue is acquisition of doctorate degrees flown from overseas institutions to our business tycoons in this country. I recently had the opportunity to read the kind of letter of offer they write to our countrymen. It was very interesting. I am unable yet to make up my mind what to think of this new development in the world of the academics; I suppose it shows that those businessmen who had been so honored by those overseas institutions were desirous of adding academic laurels to their business acumen. Be that as it may, I like to offer a word of caution and appeal to our Committee of Vice-Chancellors to monitor this new trend. But please I should not be misunderstood. I am sure that those to whom such doctorate degrees have been flown truly merited the honor, and we also congratulate them!

As can be seen in the program, ladies and gentlemen, at today's Ceremony, the fourth in the series for admission to degrees, we have a select team of academic graduands. In the three-tier degree structure, they have won the highest academic laurels, the various doctorate degrees earned through research and by examination. The Vice Chancellor will tell congregation more about them and make us witnesses of his charge to these latest Ibadan output of high level manpower to serve the University system specifically and our beloved nation generally. For my part, I give you all my right hand of fellowship and warmest felicitations in acknowledgement of your remarkable attainment. I also register my appreciation to all those who have contributed in diverse ways towards your success, particularly your parents and guardians as well as your teachers and other University staff.

At Forty, Ibadan has good reason for modest pride derived from the indisputable and varied contributions it has made towards the development and sustenance of modern Nigeria. Apart from its continuing thrust in the spreading of academics leadership light through out the country, the number and quality of its ALUMNI are a source of enviable pride and strength to the University and its friends. Hastening the pace of Nigerianization, Ibadan graduates have come to hold key positions everywhere in the occupational milieu: in staffing, curricula and practices of our Universities; in the Administrative Service of the Federal and State Governments; in the diplomatic Service; in the professions, notably Teaching, Medicine, Law, Engineering; in politics, business and even the Armed Forces. Our thanks are due to all those who have brought this credit to the University and we

fervently pray that the present students follow the footsteps of their prede-
cessors after leaving the University.

Excerpts from an address delivered to congregation university of Ibadan
(UI) on the occasion of the 40th foundation day ceremony, November 17,
1988.

One more word here to our students. Last year this institution honored
the Chief Justice of the Federation with an honorary doctorate. Today seven
eminent Nigerians from different walks of life are to be similarly honored.
If I were an undergraduate today, after witnessing what is to be an inspiring
ceremony, I would inwardly reflect on the future and pray silently: God
teach me to distinguish between sentiment and sentimentality; teach me
to keep my head while others lose theirs, and teach me to so behave myself
as to be not only a pride to my parents and alma mater but also to deserve
the highest honor such as is being conferred on these eminent Nigerians.
What, in effect, I am telling our students is that violent demonstrations
that have now become a permanent feature of our campuses do not pay.

On an auspicious occasion such as this, with a galaxy of such eminent
Nigerians as our Honorary graduands present, I find it irresistible to make
a few comments on some burning current issues. Permit me, therefore, to
seize this opportunity to address our countrymen on the subject of Religion,
an issue which alone, from the current trend, will decide the future of this
our great country particularly in the forth-coming third republic-whether
we shall be a strong, stable, united, and progressive nation . . . by unrest
and instability. I have spoken on this subject in the past at this forum and
elsewhere. I have no apology to make for doing so again today. If those
who are bent on using religion to destabilize the country do not relent in
their efforts, those, like our humble selves, who are striving to avert such
catastrophic situation will also not relent. On this occasion, however, I will
not bore you by repeating what I had said in the past. I will merely quote
sections of the Holy Books—the Bible and the Quran—(which seem to me
to touch on religious tolerance) for the benefit of not only our Christian
and Muslim brothers but also of other Nigerians who do not worship God
according to either belief. I have no doubt that Christians and Muslims are
familiar with the passages I am about to quote. By (my) referring to the

passages I am hoping that all those concerned would reason that if someone who operates in traditional African religion, who does not belong to
either of the two warring religions, can find hope in these passages then
they, the adherents of Islam and Christianity, need to think more seriously
on these things.

Let me then begin by quoting the following passage from the English
Version of the Holy Quran, which, I believe, enjoins religious tolerance. It
is SURAH 109: "In the name of Allah, the Beneficent, the Merciful. Say:
O disbelievers! I worship not that which ye worship; Nor worship ye that
which I worship. And I shall not worship that which ye worship. Nor will
ye worship that which ye worship. Unto you your religion, and unto me
my religion."

From the Holy Bible, I find Romans Chapter 14 equally relevant. Con-
straint of time prevent me from quoting all 23 verses, as I am very tempted
to do. I will therefore pick a few of the verses thus:

Verses 1–4: "Him that is weak in the faith receive ye, but not to doubtful
disputations. For one believeth that he may eat all things; another, who is
weak, eateth herbs. Let not him that eateth despise him that eateth not; and
let not him which eateth not judge him that eateth; for God hath received
him. Who art thou that judgest another man's servant? To his own master
he standeth or falleth. Yea, he shall be holden up: for God is able to make
him stand."

Verses 10–13: "But why dost thou judge thy brother? Or why dost thou
set at nought thy brother? For we shall all stand before the judgment seat
of Christ. For it is written, as I live, saith the lord, every knee shall bow to
me, and every tongue shall confess to God. So then every one of us shall
give account of himself to God. Let us not therefore judge one another
any more: but judge this rather, that no man put a stumbling-block or an
occasion to fall in his brother's way."

And as if to summarize all that, Anobi Yisa, whom the Christians call
Jesus Christ, after preaching to mankind to "love' thy neighbor as thyself
said of "love' that of the three virtues, namely, Faith, Hope and Love, the
greatest of them is Love.

We therefore appeal to the leaders of the two religions to shed their political garb and practice faithfully tolerance as taught by their founders. Of course, I suppose, there is nothing against a religious leader-Muslim or Christian-playing politics, but then such leader should come out to the open as Archbishop Makarios of Cyprus once did; as the Iranian/Iraqi leaders are doing, and as Rev. Desmond Tutu, in a different setting, is doing.

With such clear and unequivocal teaching (and there are many more) in their Holy Books, it is a matter of great disappointment that the debate on the Sharia is almost destroying the Constituent Assembly. After the assembly had managed to scale the hurdle of what to do with traditional rulers and what status to give Abuja, the Sharia appears to have created an insoluble stalemate. I wish to appeal to all concerned, especially those that Mr. President has often described as extremists, to read their Holy Books again and be more tolerant of each other's religion. We pray that the debate on Sharia will not break the Constituent Assembly and the country. Let those concerned work out a compromise or decide what should be done with the three religions (and therefore three legal systems) at present applicable in this country, lest Nigerians resort to the laws of the jungle! The leaders of the two imported religions must exercise more restraint and try to understand and appreciate each other's point of view. The unity and stability of this great country is far more important than the religious inclination of the individual.

Finally, I say once more hearty congratulations to all our students who have graduated these past few days and also to our honorary graduands who will shortly come on the scene. I wish all of you continued success.

The Visitors, the Military Governor of Oyo State, Your Royal Highnesses, Distinguished Ladies and Gentlemen, the stage is now fully set. I take the greatest pleasure to now declare open the congregation commemorating the FOUR DECADES of the University of Ibadan.

Long live the Federal Republic of Nigeria! Long live the University of Ibadan!! And God's blessings on us all!!!.

||||||||||||||||||||||||||||||||||||||||||||

An Address Delivered by the Omo N'Oba as Chancellor, University of Ibadan, to Congregation on the Occasion of the 41st Foundation Ceremony of the University, on 17 November 1989.

It is my pleasure and privilege to welcome you all to yet another Foundation Day Ceremony.

I want to begin by thanking God/Allah for making this occasion possible and for bringing us here safely. A few months back, no one would have thought that this year's Foundation Day Ceremony would hold on schedule or hold at all. This is because, as is well known, this University and five others had to be closed down in May, 1989, by the Federal Military Government to stem the violent riots that erupted in the wake of students anti-SAP demonstrations nation-wide. I also thank the President, General Ibrahim Badamosi Babangida, and his team in the Armed Forces Ruling Council for acceding to the appeal made to them by representatives of Traditional Rulers and prominent citizens which I believe contributed to the reopening of the closed Institutions. I will come back to this later.

Today is remarkable in the history of our University, as we celebrate another Foundation Day, for three special reasons. Since the celebration last year, the University has had a "Second Re-launch" of the Endowment Fund on 17th June, 1989. At that ceremony, donations and pledges amounting to about N15 million were made. Those pledges are already being made good and persons who, for unavoidable reasons, could not attend the Re-launch are still coming in with their donations. We thank all who have contributed and are contributing to the success of the Program. The door is still open for more donors and we are still with "cap in hand." Universities are increasingly being forced to generate funds for their survival, hence we in the Universities will continue to appeal to public-spirited persons through either formal launching ceremonies or private personal contacts for more financial support.

Secondly, the Report of the Visitation Panel to the University is said to have been finally released to the Federal Military Government and decisions taken on the recommendations. It is my hope that the Federal Government will utilize the findings of the various Panels, as applicable, to modernize our Universities and equip them for the challenges of the next decade in galvanizing the resources of our nation for the peaceful, social and economic development which Nigeria so much requires to play its leading role in Africa. It also behooves both the Council and senate of this University in particular to pay attention to those recommendations that touch on the staff and management and ensure that all lapses and loopholes are eliminated and sealed up. I, for my part, am convinced that Government interference with University autonomy will not arise if things are kept on a straight course. A third reason today's celebration is remarkable is that we are privileged to be in a position, once again, to honor five eminent personalities by the award of Honorary Doctorate degrees for meritorious services they have rendered both to the nation and humanity in their own respective fields of endeavour. The Public Orator will, as is the custom, present them; and I feel certain you will agree, from the citation, with the selection. I congratulate them in advance of the presentation. I formally welcome back one of the recipients who was the first Head of a Department in this University. I must keep his name to myself for now until the Public Orator speaks.

Distinguished Ladies and gentlemen, as is now well-known about me, I never miss an august occasion, such as this, to express my mind on some current topical issues. The present Chancellor has become noted (or perhaps notorious) for that! Today, our 41st Foundation Day, will not be an exception, but it will be unusual in that perhaps, for the first time, a Chancellor of a University will use the University congregation platform to purposely high-light some of the activities of the Federal Military Government. But before I come to that let me say a few words about students and demonstrations.

When I assumed office as Chancellor of this University, one of the goals I set myself to achieve was the establishment of a tradition of discipline and exemplary character among all who pass through her, worthy of emulation not only by students in other Institutions in Nigeria but also in Institutions all over the world. In pursuance of this goal, the Vice-Chancellor and I established a practice of holding informal discussions and exchange of correspondence at occasional intervals in the course of which he let me know how things are going in the campus. And also in pursuance of that same goal, I established two Peace Prizes. One prize is in the form of a trophy to be awarded to the most peaceful hall of residence in the course of the academic year; the second is a N500 cash prize to be awarded to the President of the Students body in whose tenure no disturbance occurred. The Vice-Chancellor and his men worked out the modalities for making the award. It is sad and disappointing to note that in the four years, the trophy has been won only once; the cash prize has still not been won even once, because there has been some disturbance every year.

The news of the events of May, 1989, that resulted in the closure of this university, came to me as terrible disappointment. No one is suggesting that students should not express their grievances or opposition to any Government measure. It is their inalienable right which must be respected by the authorities and preserved by all. What is wrong and which no right thinking person will endorse is the resort to street demonstrations which could and often escalate to unintended violence and vandalism as in the May disturbances. The University must be a place for producing men and women with not only academic qualifications but also with good character. When I think of Education my mind goes to what Seneca said: "As the soil, however rich it may be, cannot be productive without cultivation, so the mind without culture can never produce good fruits."

On every occasion during graduation ceremony, we add in the citation the words *"having been found worthy both in character and in learning. . . ."* The point I want to make here is that the students and teachers of all institutions must bear the graduation citation in mind, at all times and strive to ensure that every graduand is in fact really worthy "in character and in learning" to receive the institution's highest honor. Why should it be failure only in "learning" that disqualifies? It should be one of the other, and we have had too many failures in "character."

According to that great philosopher, Daniel Webster, "Knowledge does not comprise all which is contained in the large term of education. The feelings are to be disciplined, the passions are to be restrained, true and worthy motives are to be inspired; a profound religious feeling is to be instilled, and pure morality inculcated under all circumstances. All this is comprised in education." From the events of May, 1989, and indeed as every demonstration has shown, can we rightly say that the feelings of those involved were disciplined; that their passions were restrained; and that they were inspired by true and worthy motives? I leave you to ponder on these questions and judge to what extent the fault is in the educational system or in the students themselves.

Even as I stand here, I am full of anxiety as to what will happen next, judging from reading the print media. I can only hope and pray that now that the Institutions have re-opened all concerned will give peace a chance.

The re-opening of this and the other Institutions is a clear manifestation of the magnanimity of the President and the responsiveness of the Federal Military Government to responsible public opinion. I thank all those who showed concern and worked positively, even behind the scene, for the opening of the Institutions. Some useful suggestions have been made and pray that the Government will find some of them worthy of attention. Some, in fact, have already been adopted. If there is any more benefit to extend to the Institutions, especially by way of improvement of infrastructural facilities and students comfort, Government should act quickly so as to deny mischief makers the opportunity to precipitate a crisis first and come round to beat their chest gleefully that but for them the Government would have done nothing!

Now my final word on the much talked-about Structural Adjustment Program. I have taken the trouble to acquaint myself with the available facts on SAP apart from what is visible and felt around about its effects on the national economy and on the life of the common man in the townships and the rural communities. So much has been said and written about SAP that I will say no more here, except to observe that there are two Federal Ministry of Information and Culture publications in which all that we need to know about the Structural Adjustment Program (SAP) are detailed. They are '20 questions and answers on SAP' and the July, 1989 edition, Vol. 7, No. 2 of the "Town Crier' both of which I commend to all to read.

My father (Omo N'Oba Akenzua II of blessed memory) used to say that the good citizen must support the Government of the day. And I have amplified this by saying that any person or group of persons that does not support the Government is either a critic, an opposition, a confrontationist, a security risk, an outlaw or a saboteur. While a Government will welcome constructive criticism and tolerate constitutional opposition, no responsible Government will accept a confrontationist, a security risk, an outlaw or a saboteur. Hence there is no Government in the world that does not have a law to protect state security. However, there is no Government that is impervious to reason, if constitutionally and constructively approached. And the Babangida Administration has demonstrated admirably that a military regime can be magnanimous, humane, and listen to public opinion.

I did say earlier on that I would use this occasion to highlight some of the activities of the Federal Military Government. When General Ibrahim Babangida took over the Administration of this country in 1985 he took some decisions that endeared him to me as I believe it did to millions of other Nigerians. Let us take a quick look back to that period in 1985. President Babangida immediately released certain persons who were still languishing in prison after they had been cleared by the Courts/Tribunals, and he set up a special tribunal to review the doubtful and border-line cases. I am aware that different persons have different views about that very act of releases and there are some who will tell me that there are detainees today. My answer is that every case must be looked at on its merit and in the circumstance of it. The President next repealed the then controversial "Decree number 4,' to the delight of the Press. He lifted the ban on students unionism on the campuses. And he extended his right hand of fellowship to the Nigerian Labour movement by lifting the ban on them and granting them some benefits. All these acts were early indication of the Babangida Administration humanitarian stance.

We must also recognize what this Administration has done for the common man. The Directorate of Food, Roads and Rural Infrastructures (DFRRI) has been contributing to food and agricultural development. As a result of the program of this body, rural areas in many parts of the country are now enjoying, for the first time since independence as a purposeful Government policy, motorable roads, potable pipe borne water, and electricity, all of which have improved the quality of life for our rural dwellers. To combat unemployment the National Directorate on Employment (NDE) has embarked on many programs to create job opportunities. Thus, there are many avenues for employment (be it as employee to others or self-employed) for graduates and others who are prepared to come down to earth and literally set their hands to the plough.

I must congratulate the Federal Military Government for the bold decisions it had taken in respect of the transition to Civil Rule. It needs a bold, courageous, and patriotic leader to do all that our President, General Babangida, has done. The ban of ex-politicians from participation in politics during this crucial period is laudable. However, it has its merits and demerits. One of the merits is that it gives the nation an opportunity to start the Third Republic on a clean slate with a new breed of persons who, it is hoped, are prepared to render selfless service for the sake of the country. A demerit is that the Third Republic is denied the experience and maturity of the older politicians and would thus be placed in the hands of less experienced persons. This notwithstanding, Nigeria does need a break with the ex-politicians for the time being, a clean slate, and an opportunity to start afresh. In any case there is something like "learning on the job" and partisan politics is not the kind of job the doer cannot learn from within!

We want to use this platform to commend the Armed Forces Ruling Council, for its very wise and bold decision on the "Political Associations." Judged by the report of the National Electoral Commission, coupled with what people like us knew was happening but could do nothing about, I make bold to say that it would have been worse than any past civilian period, had the Federal Government registered any of the thirteen political Associations. (And there are many who believe that "13" is an unlucky number, anyway!) Look at the "New Outlook' of October 22 wherein it was carried in banner headline that political aspirants had sunk N4 billion into the political Associations. The question that has bothered me since all this exercise is whether these people are really motivated by the self-acclaimed desire to serve one's country. Is it not obvious that any one who has pumped in so much money (sometimes borrowed or derived from sale of property) would make it his first consideration, if he succeeded into a political appointment, to first recover his "investment" before directing his attention to the welfare of the country? Is it any wonder then that in the last civilian Government members of the National and State Legislatures devoted the better part of their four years debating personal remunerations? We are all witnesses to what happened during that period. The Armed Forces Ruling Council decision has certainly saved Nigerians from the "moneybags," who, according to Samuel Smiles, are those in society who have made fortunes but do not possess what he termed "qualities of mind, manners, or heart." According to the Japanese businessman, and one time Counselor of the Bank of Japan, Yoshitoki Chino, "those who do not have such qualities are merely rich—nothing more than moneybags."

From the general commentary that one has read in nearly all the newspapers, it is quite certain that the Armed Forces Ruling Council decision was a masterpiece; so much so that the renowned Professor Wole Soyinka with his analytical mind, was credited by the Press with saying that he would now consider participating in partisan politics. I thought that pronouncement by our Nobel Laureate was marvelous, if he was not "misquoted" or "quoted out of context." It only now remains to appeal to the Federal Military Government and the National Electoral Commission as well as all those who have the welfare of this great country at heart to monitor the activities of those seeking to go "a little to the left or a little to the right" (some have said they will remain at the centre!) to ensure that they do so on their own individual personal merit without "fronting" for the "moneybags," especially the banned and the disqualified ones.

When I spoke here in 1987, I made reference to the absence of what I termed the "national ethos" in our nation's polity. Since then the Mass Mobilisation for Economic Recovery, Self-Reliance and Social Justice (MAMSER) which was established by the present Federal Military Government has swung into action. I see the MAMSER as a machinery that can and will evolve that national ethos in view of the many societal ills it is mandated to tackle. And as if to strengthen MAMSER the Federal Government announced only a few weeks ago the establishment of the Centre for Democratic Studies. Although the full program of this body is not yet publicized the content of the President's announcement showed that this new organ is destined to provide a missing link in the evolution of a national ethos.

Ladies and Gentlemen, we would be deceiving the Armed Forces Ruling Council to leave the impression that everything they have done has scored passmark. I would be the last to give such impression. That would be placing them in the position of a king for whom, according to our Benin adage, the oracle always divines good tidings or the Army General whose field officers always told "all correct General" because they knew that is what he always liked hearing even when the "sitrep" showed that things were very bad! The Armed Force Ruling Council, like every organization of human beings, cannot but err sometimes. What is dangerous is the inability to admit a mistake. And I believe the President knows this only too well, hence the practice for which he is now well known of subjecting some of his Government's policies to dialogue, review or public debate. My appeal here is that those who find fault with a policy, particularly if they are persons whose standing in society gives them direct access to the "seat of power' should avail themselves of that rare privilege and go or write in to offer counsel. Unless our men (and women) of "timber and calibre' are forthcoming in this manner, I fear that we may never be able to achieve a stable Government and a peaceful society.

I have gone all this length on the activities of the Federal Military Government because I wish to use this platform to call on all Nigerians to cooperate with this Administration to ensure a smooth transition to Civil Rule in 1992. Nigeria cannot afford another Military Government and no useful purpose will be served by short-circuiting the transition program now. Come what may, Allah/God will help the present administration to hand over in peace to a worthy civilian administration in 1992.

Lastly, on these general remarks, I think it is appropriate that we of this premier University should take cognizance of the achievement recently of our great country in the International arena. We of the University of Ibadan, therefore, join other national and international friends of Nigeria to congratulate the Federal Military Government on its diplomatic success in securing the Presidency of the General Assembly of the United Nations and the Secretary-Generalship of the Commonwealth. We heartily congratulate Major-General Joseph Garba (rtd) as the President of the current General Assembly and Chief Emeka Anyaoku as the Commonwealth Secretary-General. We wish them every success in the onerous task that has fallen on them.

And now back home to our graduands. Let me once more congratulate, in advance of presentation, the five eminent honorary graduands who will soon be honored. I feel a sense of personal pride that during my tenure we have been privileged to honor twelve eminent personalities, seven last year, who have distinguished themselves in various fields. From the warmth of the applause at every citation last year, I had a feeling of satisfaction that the selection was well received. I have no doubt that the performance will be repeated today! I like to commend the brains behind the selection. I also congratulate all students who are graduating. The future is getting brighter as more job opportunities are being created by the Federal/State Governments. In addition, various loan schemes are now available for graduates to go into farming or to establish self-employment. I dare say you can also avail yourself of the facilities of the "Peoples Bank,' for which establishment we are grateful to the Federal Military Government. I appeal to our graduates now going into the employment market to come down to earth and avail yourself of whatever opportunity presents itself. I doff my academic hat for that graduate with the B.Sc. degree on whom the newspapers did a feature write-up not long ago who now earns a good living from making ordinary "akara' for sale and who regrets that he did not start the trade three years earlier when he was going round in search of a job. I also doff my hat for the "graduate drivers" in the employ of the Lagos State Government. The irony of the modern world is that though, job opportunities have increased tremendously, competitiveness has become much keener with the result that a job seeker can hardly now pick and choose. I wish our young graduands every luck.

||||||||||||||||||||||||||||||||||||||||||||

"Students Unrest-Suggested Causes and Solution," a Memorandum Submitted at a Meeting of Traditional Rulers Held in Owerri, 17 July, 1989

I thank the Imo State Council of Chiefs for inviting us to this very important meeting. By what seems a sheer coincidence, it has turned out to be a follow-up of the meeting that some traditional rulers and Chancellors of

Universities held with the President of the Federal Republic of Nigeria on July 7th. We were at Dodan Barracks to appeal to Mr. President to reopen the closed Universities. I believe our meeting here today is to answer the President's charge to traditional rulers/Chancellors to furnish him with suggestions on how to stop the incessant students violence in the country.

On behalf of all of us I like to thank Mr. President for listening to us on July 7th and for giving us the opportunity to help the Armed Forces Ruling Council with suggestions. I believe all will agree that this shows the high esteem in which this Administration holds us traditional rulers.

Before I proceed to comment on the issue on hand which is why we are here I crave indulgence to be allowed to make some preliminary observations.

First and foremost, I like to observe that it is most unfortunate that some see the recent demonstrations and the consequent Federal Government action as a "South" affair. The view has been expressed in many quarters that the decision to close the Institutions is a punitive action against the "South." Those who hold this view have queried why "Northern" Institutions were never closed in like manner.

I like to disagree with such views about the events. It must be remembered that the so-called Southern Universities have students and staff of Northern origin in the same manner that the Northern Universities also have students and staff of Southern origin.

I feel it is important to make this observation so we can be sufficiently broad-minded and objective in our attempt to proffer suggestions to Mr. President. We must see the students' crisis as a well-thought-out plan for a nation-wide disturbance, the execution of which merely began in the o "south' this time around.

I believe that this matter of re-opening the Universities and of students unrest generally, is now at the highest possible citizens level it can be, i.e. a platform of the combined efforts of traditional rulers and Chancellors. No useful purpose, in my view, will be served by the attempts of those who want to score political points by reducing the issue to north/south dichotomy or placing it in religious camps. We must, I urge, call on all such people (and the newspaper are replete with their statements) to refrain from inflammatory utterances which will only encourage the students (and others hiding under their canopy) and will not help the situation anyway since the Federal Government has said emphatically that it will not be deterred from the course it has mapped out for the nation which I think every right-thinking Nigeria ought to endorse. Such inflammatory utterances will, to my mind, undermine our present endorsement.

I now come to the issue on hand, which is why we are here. As I interpreted the President's remarks to us on July 7th, it seems to me we must approach our assignment from three angles:

(i) Causes of students' unrest in the country.

(ii) The recent disturbance and the consequent impasse;

(iii) Possible solution for reducing, if not eradicating, these disturbances.

It is difficult, if not impossible, to list all those factors and situation that have caused or can cause unrest in our Institutions of higher learning. This is not only because they are so many and varied but also because the factors which affect the reaction of students to given situation at different times are also many and varied depending on the state of mind or the attitude towards the authorities of each individual or group of persons that form the student body. What I intend to do in this memorandum is therefore to summarize some of the factors which appear to me to have estranged the students and the authorities in the recent past, hence they vigorously now want to seize every opportunity open to them to express their grievances in violent protests engaging in vandalism and other acts which they expect to cause problems for the authorities or destabilize the Government. The memorandum also offers some suggestions for promoting peace, harmony and a conducive atmosphere for teaching and learning in our tertiary institutions as well as peaceful means of dealing with students' grievances and any misunderstanding that may arise between them and the authorities in the future.

STRUCTURAL ADJUSTMENT PROGRAM (SAP) I believe a good starting point in our discussion is the Structural Adjustment Program and the biting effect on the citizens. At any rate that is what the students claim to be demonstrating against this time.

Everyone is aware of what SAP is about and how it has affected every Nigerian, high and low, without exception. I will therefore not waste any time taking you through the details here. One or two points, however, need to be made. The first is that the Structural Adjustment Program was not meant to be a "magic wand' to bring money into everyone's pocket and produce abundant food, all over night. If SAP is to revamp the nation's economy, produce local self-sufficient, we must first go through the hardship of denying ourselves of some basic amenities. Happily now, the Federal Government is seeing some ray of hope which enabled it to lay on the relief measures recently announced, but it was unfortunate that the demonstration started before the announcement was made. Because of the timing, mischief makers took advantage of the ignorance and gullibility of the lowly persons and come out to claim they were protesting against SAP and hunger. It is, therefore, hoped that because of the good we expect SAP to bring to our economic well-being in the near future and the relief package now introduced by the Federal Government to alleviate its biting effect, students, indeed every well-meaning Nigerian, should be able to exercise some more patience and give the Federal Government a chance to carry through the program. It is feared however, that the students' reaction to SAP is heavily influenced by other factors (some of which this memorandum will highlight) and the activities of mischief makers who are not even within the fold of the student body.

Now to some of the factors that contribute to students unrest:

(1) ON-CAMPUS LIVING CONDITIONS. Poor accommodation, inadequate library, games and catering facilities, poor health-care services, and poor intra-campus transport services are factors which breed discontent among students and engender in them dislike for those in authority both the University and Government. Students blame the authorities for their plight and are willing and ready to move against them at the least opportunity. But I make bold to say that all the "poor' things are not entirely the fault of the Government or the University. Take "poor' accommodation for instance. In Ibadan, where I have been a Chancellor for some years now, it is known that the students population in practically every Hall of Residence has far exceeded the total for which the Hall was meant, and what is even more alarming is the fact that a substantial proportion of the surplus population are no students at all; they are simply friends or relations of students who live in. I am sure

similar situation exists in other Institutions. It is this over-population that is partly responsible for the inadequacy of the other facilities.

(II) INADEQUATE FUNDING. With the opening of more Universities in the country, more Nigerians now have access to University education leading to increase in yearly intake of students. In view of high costs, Government is now unable to cope with the increasing high level of funding per student. Because of the general economic situation, the abolition of bursary and loan scheme, and the measures introduced by SAP, students have become hard hit As a result of the reduction of the number of employees, coupled with the fact that small businesses have been hardest hit by SAP measures, many parents lost their jobs and became unable to provide adequate funds for the maintenance of their children/wards in higher institutions. In this situation many students are subjected to untold financial hardship and thus fall easy prey to mischief makers who may wish to use them to foment trouble to achieve their own ends. Students blame Government for their financial predicament and this breeds dislike for those in authority which in turn incense students to violence when they have the chance to do so. In addition to all these, the situation is further worsened by the mismanagement of fund by some University authorities as is evident in the proliferation of faculties, departments, disciplines, with consequent increase in professional and other staff, increase in students intake, and application of fund for purposes other than that for which it was approved.

(III) HIGH COST OF LIVING. With the introduction of SAP and the consequent fall of the value of the Naira, the increase in prices of essential commodities has led to the high cost of living, and the financial problems of students have been compounded. Whereas in the past, students had their three meals (subsidized by Government) for only N1.50k per day, it is now not possible to have a satisfying meal for that same amount. Consequently, some students cannot afford more than one meal a day. As it is said, "a hungry man is an angry man.' This, no doubt, must be a contributory factor to the violence usually resorted to by students in their protests and demonstrations.

(IV) ACTIVITIES OF DISGRUNTLED ELEMENTS. Because of the factors already enumerated i.e. on-campus living conditions, inadequate funding, high cost of living, students fall easy prey to the activities of disgruntled elements within and outside the University Community who may wish to use students to foment trouble or destabilize Government to further their selfish ends. These disgruntled elements (among whom are also lecturers) could take undue advantage of their position to feed students with wrong information and to incite them against the authorities.

(v) COMMUNICATION GAP. The proscription of the National Association of Nigerian Student (NANS) by the Federal Military Government appears to have worsened the communication gap between the Government and the students. It appears the Association has now gone underground and when students have grievances over national issues there is now no recognized students body to take up the matter with the Federal Government It is realized that NANS was proscribed because of the constant embarrassment it was causing the authorities. But the leaders were accessible and available, when the atmosphere was right, for occasional dialogue. Now nobody seems to know who are directing their affairs. It appears also that most principal officers of the institutions do not sometimes come down from their ivory towers to interact informally with the students. All this seems to have removed the avenue for peaceful dialogue between Government and students. What can result (and has resulted) is what we saw recently when students secretly planned and started to execute their protest actions from institution to institution and from State to State. All the leaders are in hiding and there is no recognized student leader at the national or university level who could be called to question or invited for talks. As at today, students leaders are still very active underground, and the authorities are still trying to discover their hide-out.

(IV) ALLEGED INSENSITIVITY TO AND DISREGARD FOR THE YEARNINGS OF STUDENTS. Students claim that those in authority underestimate their intelligence and so tend to disregard their views, opinions, and protests. They believe (erroneously) that the authorities will not listen to them or act unless they did something dramatic and drastic such as street demonstration and placard carrying. They proceed to destroy properties to show the degree of their concern and the attention they want. It is worthy of mention, however, that many students are more intelligent and reasonable than the elderly administrators generally suppose them to be.

(VII) ALLEGED INTIMIDATION OF STUDENT UNION LEADERS AND OUT-SPOKEN LECTURERS. Students allege that their leaders are often intimidated and victimized by the authorities. This creates an atmosphere of suspicion and distrust which breeds friction and violence.

(VIII) EFFECT OF YOUTHFUL EXUBERANCE. The majority of the body of students in our institutions of high learning are between the ages of 17 and 19 when most people want to assert themselves and exhibit youthful exuberance in what they do. This may account for students excesses and extremism in the manner in which they make demands and express their protests.

(IX) LACK OF MORAL TRAINING. Due to the absence of deliberate effort in primary and secondary schools to give moral instructions for character formation, many students admitted into high institutions do not have the strength of character needed to meet the challenges of university life, and so are prone to social vices.

(X) ACTIVITIES OF SECRET CULT. The most notable in this category is the one that goes by the name "Pirates Confraternity.' One does not know what it stands for or what they do. They are in every Institution and they have been known to beat up other students who refuse to participate in a demonstration. There are other societies with weird names like "Black Axe.' There was a report some months ago from one University where a student who was being initiated collapsed and died in the process! What are these secret cults? Are they the students own idea or they have link with other organizations?

It is my considered view that if the above-stated factors are carefully examined and improvements effected where necessary, and ways and means found to weed out undesirable elements and secret organizations, a situation would have been created in our institutions for peace, harmony, understanding and trust to thrive and where these thrive, there can be no room for violence or, at any rate, the chances will be considerably reduced. Whenever there are disagreements or grievances the issues can always be discussed amicably and settled peacefully.

Accordingly, in respect of the above-mentioned factors, I suggest the following actions for consideration as possible solution:

(I) ON-CAMPUS LIVING CONDITIONS. Government should endeavour to take appropriate steps to improve infrastructural facilities in the campuses for better accommodation, health and library services and for intra-campus transportation. Government should itself do a clean-up exercise in the Institutions for the purpose of:

(a) Sweeping out all non-bona-fide students who, through the connivance of students, merely live in the hall of residence and go to their work from there;

(b) ensuring that each hall of residence keeps within the prescribed population;

(c) checking proliferation of faculties, departments, disciplines;

(d) where Government has to direct an increase in the in-take of students in respect of any particular discipline financial provision for increased facilities, accommodation, etc., should be automatic; and

(e) the University authorities should be encouraged to show more interest in the off-campus accommodation by physically seeing to the accommodation and negotiating for the students the terms of rent with the landlords.

(II) INADEQUATE FUNDING. Government should re-introduce bursary and loan scheme for higher education not only to ease the present financial problems of students but also to serve as a means of curbing violent demonstrations by them; curbing in the sense that the bursary or loan could be withdrawn whenever students engage in violent demonstration. In this regard, it is interesting to note that the appeal to Local Government Councils in Bendel State made by the Vice-Chancellor of the University of Benin, Professor Grace Alele-Williams, is already yielding good dividends in terms of bursary award to indigenes of the respective Councils in the University of Benin. With this successful experiment, we dare to suggest its adoption by other Vice-Chancellors. Many Universities now institute endowment fund with which to supplement what comes from Government. We note with delight that the Federal Government also donates to such fund. All Universities must pursue the endowment fund with vigor. On the other hand, it is important that University authorities should be prudent in the management of scarce resources by avoiding the establishment of unapproved degree programs, departments and faculties. Students themselves should be encouraged to read the University Budget and Auditors' reports to acquaint themselves with how their funds are being managed (or mismanaged).

(III) HIGH COST OF LIVING. The level of bursary and loan to be granted to students under recommendation (ii) should take account of the prevailing cost of living to ensure that the present financial strain on students is minimized now that students feed themselves in many institutions, University authorities must ensure that those who sell food to the students do not fleece them.

(IV) ACTIVITIES OF DISGRUNTLED ELEMENTS. "He who pays the piper dictates the tune." This is an old adage applicable in this case. If the recommendation for the re-introduction of bursary and loan scheme is implemented, this will reduce the temptation for students to be "bought over" by disgruntled elements and detractors of Government. There is no doubt that there are some "heavy weights" behind the students. From what is known of their method of planning and operation, the students sometimes travel by air; they use hired vehicles, they live in hotels; they engage in considerable amount of correspondence and printing work, consuming lots of stationary. It seems obvious that all this is not financed from the union fund or from their individual pocket. It is therefore important that the Federal Government apply all resources at its disposal to unravel the mystery of those behind the students. I believe it behooves those of us here to give every assistance to the Government in this regard.

(V) COMMUNICATION GAP. There is an urgent need for an effective and responsible national student body with which Government should endeavour to maintain constant dialogue on important national issues. I was going to propose in this context the formation of "Parents/Teachers Association' as is found in the post-primary school. But I find, reading the Nigerian Tribune "National Association of Parents of University Students.' I think this is a very good move. When our state Council of Chiefs met with our Governor on 12th June, 1989, over the burning of the State capital, we urged it on parents to do more preaching to their children to develop the attitude of dialogue and following constitutional procedure in venting their grievances. In the hope that the new body, National Association of Parents of University Students, is not an ad hoc formation just for the current situation I would recommend that a chapter of the Association should be established in every Institution of higher learning and it should function like the Parents/Teachers Association of Secondary Schools. Lastly on this, the Principal Officers of the University should cultivate the habit of interacting with the students. A principal officer should not feel too busy to go sit in the students' common room or at sports ground and chat with the students.

(VI) ALLEGED INSENSITIVITY TO AND DISREGARD FOR THE YEARNINGS OF STUDENTS. Authorities should develop the habit of attending promptly to students' grievances. It is dangerous to allow grievances to accumulate and inadvisable to wait until there is a demonstration before taking action. When Government action favors the students after a demonstration the students would feel that but for their pressure Government would not have acted. This is not good for Government image!

(VII) EFFECT OF YOUTH EXUBERANCE. In spite of everything else it must be recognized that the majority of the students are passing through the most delicate age-adolescent age-and the authorities should endeavour to exercise patience and show understanding in dealing with their cases. Students need to be given some recognition and a sense of belonging. There has been indication students resent being looked at as juveniles. It is important the principal officers of Institutions give them some recognition.

(VIII) LACK OF MORAL TRAINING. As a matter of deliberate policy the Federal Government should direct the state Ministries of Education to re-introduce moral and religious instructions in the curricula of primary and post-primary schools. I am aware of Government policy regarding religious matters in schools; but what I have in mind here is what obtained in the colonial days when a given period was set aside for religious instructions in the "Government Schools" and children were grouped and received instructions according to their faith.

On the specific issue of the re-opening of the Universities closed down for the rest of this academic year (1989/90), we must admit that no punishment can be too severe for the gravity of the offence committed by the students. There is no offence in any person or group of persons criticizing any Government measure. What is wrong in the case of the students is their resorting to violence and wanton destruction of not only Government properties but also of properties of innocent citizens for no just cause, and those innocent persons were the persons for whose sake they claimed they were protesting against SAP. This notwithstanding, to err, they say, is human and to forgive is divine. Forgiveness in this case is necessary in the interest of the whole nation and of peace within all the campuses.

By closing the Institutions, innocent persons will be made to suffer unjustifiably. Take the case of thousands of students who have left secondary schools, passed the JAMB examination for admission to these Institutions who must now wait for another year and repeat the JAMB examination to be able to gain admission the following year! We cannot justify the extension of punishment to this group of Nigerians who are completely innocent of the misdeeds of those Government seeks to punish. This also goes for the parents of these students who are also innocent of the misdeeds of those Government seeks to punish. This also goes for the parents of these students who are also innocent but struggling to fund the education of their children and must now be subjected to punishment for offence not committed by them. Furthermore, the additional loss to the nation by the closure is better imagined than quantified. If there must be institutions of higher learning, there must be students and if there must be students we must be prepared to create the environment conducive not only to effective teaching and learning but also to peaceful campus life. Lasting peace can only emerge through peaceful dialogue. It is for these reasons, among others, that we appeal to the Federal Government to temper justice with mercy and re-open the institutions.

Accordingly, it is suggested that simultaneously with the re-opening of the institutions, the Federal Government should:

(i) direct the formation of a new responsible national students body which should go into dialogue with Government over any issues students may consider outstanding;

(ii) call for proposals from Local and State Governments for the re-introduction of a bursary and loan scheme for higher education. In principle, students should be free to express their grievances and protest over any issue but any resort to violence in the process should automatically lead to the withdrawal of bursary in respect of those concerned; and

(iii) ask all institutions to adjust their spending patterns to give attention to the improvement of on-campus living conditions for students within the limits of the funds made available by Government. In this regard, the present level of University funding should be improved as much as practicable having regard to the availability of funds.

I am confident that if these proposals are accepted an era of peace and tranquility will begin in our institutions of higher learning. There may be other specific measures which University authorities may consider necessary to curb violence by students. It is my suggestion that Vice-Chancellors should be given opportunity to advise Government on these, and if they do, Government should consider favorably any financial implication that may be involved.

I cannot close without adding this little bit. I note with satisfaction that the students of the Imo State University of Technology, Owerri and the Bendel State University, Ekpoma have shown signs of remorse according to publications in the newspapers. They should be commended. I wish the others had done likewise rather than taking the Federal Government to court, as was reported in the "Vanguard" of July 11th. In view of what we are doing here today I appeal to those students to withdraw their case from the court so as to create a favorable atmosphere for the Federal Government to receive the recommendations that will be made from this meeting.

I thank you all for your attention.

Chapter 10

On Museums, Treasures of Ancient Nigeria and Matters Miscellaneous

Museums can and do play a vital role in the building of modern na-tions. They recover and bring together the cultural achievements of previous generations and hold them up for the world to see. What was submerged in the crush of colonial domination begins to surface and hold up their bright heads, like so many splendid flowers, to bring glad-ness and pride to the hearts of now independent peoples.

— Omo N'Oba Erediauwa, 26 April 1986

By any criteria we use, "Treasures of Ancient Nigeria" showed that the religious centers and cities of Nigeria's early cultures are civilizations that flourished during the past 5,000 years. The civilizations with their monumental architecture, sculpture, records and complex economic, social, political systems have become the subject of praise and admira-tion the world over as a result of the Exhibition of the "Treasures of Ancient Nigeria."

— Omo N'Oba Erediauwa, July, 1986

|||||||||||||||||||||||||||||||||||||||||||||

An Address on the Occasion of the Launching of a Book and the Opening of an Arts Exhibition by Didi Museum in Lagos on Saturday, 26 April, 1986

I am pleased to have been invited to address you on the occasion of the formal opening of the Didi Museum Exhibition. The Exhibition now appears to be an annual event. This is not only an occasion for the public to see and enjoy the selection of works of art being presented, it is also an opportunity to look more deeply into the nature of this institution, the motivations behind it, and the example that can be drawn from it by others. I shall wish to consider as well the meaning of museums in the larger context of our society, and the importance of museum studies and exhibitions in our nation's culture and development.

Too often the world press and even our own press, at times, focus on the sensational and the negative aspects of Nigerian life. But there are other more enduring values that still prevail in Nigeria, which traditional rulers, by their traditional oath of office, are bound to uphold and to promote. These include service to others, dedication to knowledge, and the preservation of our cultural heritage for generations to come. These values have produced and inspired some of the art works you will see here today-and some of those that are enshrined in the major museums of western nations-and for which the peoples of Nigeria are justly famous. I am happy to say that some of those works now grace our own museums with increasing frequency-a trend that I hope will continue to develop. Towards this development the Didi Museum makes a unique contribution. It encompasses both antiquities and contemporary art. It seeks to preserve the past, and to display the history and arts that contributed to the greatness of Nigeria's many cultures; at the same time the museum aims to discover and promote contemporary Nigerian artists by providing them with the means and space to display their works. The distinctive art of Erhabor Emokpae is to be found in the Didi Museum. This Benin artist is represented in museums and private collections around the world. He is forever associated with FESTAC, and the works he produced for it which have come to symbolize the vitality of contemporary black arts. More than 100 of his works decorate the National Arts Theatre in Lagos, a setting which hosts many art exhibitions for the public. Kenny Adamson, Adamu Ajinam, Chuks Anyanwu, Theorora Ifudu, are among the many talented artists whose works are collected and shown by the Didi Museum. Subject matter varies among them, from a traditional marriage ceremony in *The Weeping Bride* (1985) by Kenny Adamson, to such social commentaries as the dilemmas facing Nigeria, in *Ajegunle 2000* (1983) and *Squares and Circles* (1984), by the same artist, and Professor Aniakor's *One Man One Wife* (1970)

Antiquities in the Didi Museum collection include bronzes from Benin and Ile-Ife, terra cotta heads from the Nok culture, and carved ivories, also from Benin; there are works of art from South America and other parts of Africa. The eclectic nature of the collection is, in part, a reflection of the breadth of personal interests of the founder of the museum. It is, in part, also, a reflection of the stage of development of this museum. It is perhaps necessary to observe that today's major western museums had their beginnings in the "cabinets of curiosities" and art "galleries" of private persons, noblemen and ecclesiastics in the early 17th and 18th centures in Europe. Much earlier, among the Greeks, the "Muselon" at Alexandria, c. 300 B.C., was a center of learning dedicated to the Muses. The combination of educational purpose and pleasure to be found in museums, utilizing a wide assortment of artifacts and specimens, was present at the beginnings of the institution we know today as the museum. It is clear that private persons had a major role to play in those developments and continue to have an important role and function in the museum world today. The basic educational purposes were recognized and pursued from the outset; they are preliminary to the fully staffed, professional, and coordinated efforts of museums in the modern world, and to the complementary relationship that has developed between public and private institutions. The public museum sector in Nigeria has had a longer and more complex history than the private sector, represented here in its seminal stages by the Didi Museum.

The Didi Museum is a private, non-profit making institution; the first of its kind, I think, in Nigeria, apart from private collections in some of the Royal Palaces. It results from the inspiration and initiative of one man, its founder, Chief Newton C. Jibunoh. On his solo trip across the Sahara Desert in 1967, Chief Jibunoh was exposed to a variety of cultures and their arts and crafts. Coming from Bendel State, an ancient center of art and culture in Nigeria, he was able to use his new experiences to formulate the idea of a museum-to think about a place where others could come to enjoy, study, and experience the wonders of art.

Chief Jibuhoh was born and spent his early and happy years in a traditional village, Akwukwu-Igbo, in Bendel State. The memories of village
life and rituals laid the foundation of his interests in art and culture; his
affection for his (late) sister, Edith or "Didi" provided the name for his
museum. It is significant that the origins of this museum are to be found
in deep rooted attachments to village and home and family; they are to be
found, too, in the spirit of hope and adventure that led Chief Jibunoh to
become a professional engineer, and to explore the wider world around him.
Thus, in himself, he weds the old and new, past and future orientations.

Over the past 20 years, the idea of a private museum has grown, as have
the collections. In 1983, on May 11th , His Royal Highness, the Emir of
Kano, Alhaji Ado Bayero, inaugurated the new Didi Museum. Subsequently,
exhibitions have been opened by other traditional rulers and others have
expressed their support for the project. The Ooni of Ife, His Highness Oba
Okunade Sijuwade Olubuse II, the Obi Igwe Ofala Okagbue, the Obi of
Onitsha. As the custodians of the arts and culture, we traditional rulers
have always been willing to support sincere efforts to provide the knowledge
needed to understand and appreciate our past. This is so that we may all
better plan and program for the future, and provide guidance, especially,
for our youths.

This can be accomplished by adopting the criteria employed by museums
the world over; to collect, conserve, and interpret the works of human beings
and of nature for the enlightenment and enjoyment of the public. To these
ends I look forward to the establishments of regular, published hours for
viewing at the Didi Museum so people of all ages, and school children in
particular, may have access to the collections and exhibitions at the Museum.
This will require some additional and trained professional staff to see to visitors, and to the care, research and publication of the museum's collections.

The foregoing concerns bring me, once again, to our youth. It is my
hope that this generation will give serious consideration to the objectives of
museums, and to the worthiness of tasks to be performed therein, as well as
to the arts themselves, and the power they have to transform society. Instead
of a search solely for money and material goods, I commend to the youths the
ideals of service, learning, and communication in making a choice of career.

And I address those responsible for education, funding and compensation in public and private institutions, to make such careers truly professional by attaching decent wages and working conditions to their employment. We are in need of trained art historians, archaeologists, zoologists and others who can take posts in art museums, museums of natural history, and history museums, science and technology centers, and in zoos, arboretums, and in specialized and even corporate collections. There is much to be done.

At this point one might ask what is the role of the private museum, and is there any need for it? It has been, said that Nigeria has the most organized and professionally coordinated museum system in Africa. The National Commission for Museum and Monuments, headed by the Director-General, Dr. Ekpo Eyo, was established by Federal decree in 1979, replacing the earlier Department of Antiquities, set up in 1953, during the colonial period. Its responsibilities include overall supervision of state and local museums, and focus on private and university museums, aside from Federal Museums. While universities have been active in promoting contemporary arts and crafts particularly through various theater arts and applied arts departments, the number of university galleries is small, and exhibitions have often taken place outside the campus. A major art exhibition was mounted in 1985, at the National Arts Theatre, in Lagos, by the University of Benin and another show of antiquities inaugurated the University of Ibadan new gallery at the Centre for African Studies in 1984, under the guidance of Professor Bolanle Awe, with the cooperation of the National Commission for Museums and Monuments. In 1985, the Commission lent support to an exhibition organized on behalf of the Centre for Social, Cultural and Environmental Research of the University of Benin, by Fulbright Professor Flora S. Kaplan, at the Benin National Museum, entitled, Art of the Royal Court of Benin. These exhibitions attracted considerable public attendance and media interest, showing the receptivity of Nigerians to exhibitions of their cultural life.

The existence of large numbers of antiquities in private hands in Nigeria, suggests a growing interest on the part of people in the preservation of their history and art. Private Museums can be more flexible in devising exhibitions and in utilizing these individually owned works for the benefit of the public, and, of course, in returning them to their owners, afterwards. In building provide in culture and art ownership, museum exhibitions help stem the outflow, illegally, of antiquities from Nigeria, abroad.

I like to use this occasion to make a passionate appeal to the Federal Government to increase the financial assistance it has rendered to the National Commission for Museums and Monuments to enable it recover our works of arts now held by museums and in private collections overseas. While thanking the Government for what has so far been done I plead that there is still much more that can be done. We know that many of them, especially the Benin ones, were loots that have either been borrowed or bought by national museums abroad. The National Commission, I feel certain, has judiciously managed the funds at its disposal to recover what can only be described as the smallest and cheapest of them. The more valuable and expensive ones are still out and the managers of our Government finances must not regard the expenditure as non-revenue earning and therefore a wasted effort.

The National Commission for Museums and Monuments is charged with registering and documenting all national antiquities, including those privately held. I understand that between 1974 and 1977 over one million objects were photographed and registered. Discoveries since then have substantially increased the number. Not only can Museums like the Didi Museum help to show and to retain antiquities in the country-they can lead by example to future involvement by other private citizens in the cultural life of our country. I am impressed by the efforts of Chief Newton Jibunoh to preserve our African cultural heritage, and to associate traditional rulers in the process. He has demonstrated, over more than 20 years, a devotion and passion for his chosen avocation that deserves to be emulated. He has been selfless in this, willing to give of his assets-financial, emotional, and physical-to the ideals of service to the community and preservation of the past for the future. Orphaned early in life, Chief Jibunoh had to work long and hard and to seek professional training as an engineer and to begin to reap and enjoy the fruits of his labour and success in life. That he chose to share that success with the public, is a rare and commendable action. In contrast to the rush to acquire and ostentatiously display one's wealth and goods, Chief Jibunoh offers a good alternative model for our youth. He exemplifies the traditional values I spoke of earlier, and which have more recently been lost sight of by many.

There are, however, a small but growing number of successful men and women in the chosen fields of their endeavours-be it business, commerce, the professions, academic and artistic life-who are accepting and even seeking civic responsibility on a personal level for the betterment of their children and country. They are becoming involved in development, and in the encouragement of sports, arts, and the preservation of our environment, natural resources, and beauties of nature for continued enjoyment and learning. This is a heartening direction in our country. I urge you all to take note of it, and to take part in it, as Chief Newton Jibunoh has done in founding and promoting Didi Museum.

Museums can and do play a vital role in the building of modern nations. They recover and bring together the cultural achievements of previous generations and hold them up for the world to see. What was submerged in the crush of colonial domination begins to surface, and hold up their bright heads, like so many splendid flowers, to bring gladness and pride to the hearts of new independent peoples. The 20 national museums of Nigeria each comprise local, regional, and national sections, giving recognition to each ethnic group, taking an active role in the moulding of our nation's unity. Together with private museums, such as Didi, they can cover a broad spectrum of cultural life, including our living artists and artisans.

The Exhibition we open today, therefore, plays a vital role. Such exhibitions contravene mistaken notions of "tribalism" and "primitivism" too long attributed to Africa and to African art and artists. The value of public exhibitions is easily seen in the example of the famed exhibition, Treasures of Ancient Nigeria, which began its world tour in 1981 to finish this year in Lagos. That exhibition, the first to leave Nigeria, commanded the world's respect and attention. By any criteria we use, the religious centers and cities of Nigeria's early cultures, are civilizations that flourished during the past 5000 years. Future generations of researchers will extend these frontiers of our national life even further. These civilizations with their monumental architecture, sculpture, records, and complex economic, social, and political systems have become the subjects of praise and admiration elsewhere, as a result of Treasures of Ancient Nigeria exhibition.

If it were only the past that concerns us, I would not be addressing you here today. The traditions that inspired past achievements are alive and well in Nigeria. They are visible in the efforts of a private individual, Chief Jibunoh, who has given much at his own expense in a labour of love. It is time to give proper recognition to such private efforts as the Didi Museum Exhibition represents, and to dedicate ourselves, our resources and personal energies to our future by associating ourselves with such undertakings. In this way our children and our children's children will come of age in a new Nigeria that shows it does not forget its past.

All that we have been saying, coupled with the whole philosophy, aims and objectives of the Didi Museum seem to be reflected in the title of the book DIDI MUSEUM ARTWAY TO AFRICAN CULTURE by Kayode Shoyinka and Elizabeth Jibunoh, and I am happy, as I am sure you all are, to be associated with the launching of the book. I congratulate the authors. I also congratulate Uti Ndueze and Ray Soko whose works of art the Museum has exhibited for us to view. I trust you will all enjoy the afternoon.

Finally, in declaring the Exhibition open I wish to make a presentation to the Didi Museum and to wish it and its founders continued progress.

I thank you all for your attention.

|||||||||||||||||||||||||||||||||||||||||||||||||

An Address on the Occasion of the Official Opening of the Exhibition, "Treasures of Ancient Nigeria: Legacy of 2000 Years," at the National Museum, Lagos, 5 July, 1986.

On behalf of the traditional rulers and of myself I thank the Honorable Minister of Information and Culture for inviting us to be Special Guests at today's exhibition which has been mounted to welcome back home, so to speak, the new world famous Nigerian works of art that have visited some of the major capital Cities of the world to show to the outside world the Treasures of Ancient Nigeria. It is said that we traditional rulers who have been invited here represent the areas of Nigeria from where these famous works of art were collected. We are glad that our domains have made this contribution to place our great Country, Nigeria, on the world map of art. We are happy to be with this galaxy of eminent persons who have come to honor the Exhibition.

I was glad that from the moment the Exhibition was first opened in the United States of America and throughout its world tour, some European and Nigerian friends who were lucky to have viewed it in some of these countries informed me with joy the great impact that the Exhibition made in those countries. From all accounts, the Exhibition brought great credit to Nigeria. It commanded the world's respect and attention, and above all, its tour round the world demolished the mistaken notions of "tribalism" and "primitivism" too long attributed to African art and artists. By any criteria we use, Treasures of Ancient Nigeria showed that the religious centers and cities of Nigeria's early cultures are civilizations that flourished during the past 5000 years. These civilizations with their monumental architecture, sculpture, records, and complex economic, social, political systems have become the subject of praise and admiration the world over, as a result of the Exhibition of the Treasures of Ancient Nigeria.

It will be recalled that the Treasures of Ancient Nigeria were first exhibited to the public in the American City of Detroit under the auspices of the Detroit Institute of Arts. I was invited to it at the time but I could not go. I, however, sent one of my Chiefs to join my son in the United States to represent me. My Chief, who, of course, was quite familiar with Benin works of art came back with glowing reports of what he saw. Describing the impact of the Exhibition in that American highly industrial city of Detroit, John Coppola, writing in *Topic* magazine, issue No. 128, began his descriptive essay in these words: "In a City famous for forging steel into cars, it was an exhibition of finely sculpted clay and bronze. In a City synonymous with the sounds of black American culture, it was a reminder of its African origins."

Indeed, Museums have and do play a vital role in the building of modern nations. They recover and bring together the cultural achievements of past generations and hold them up for the world to see. In the case of the former colonial countries like ours what was submerged in the crush of colonial domination, or as in the case of the Benin Kingdom, what was looted (during the "Benin Massacre") begins to surface in glory to bring gladness and pride to the hearts of the new independent peoples. And not only that. The 20 or so National Museums of Nigeria each comprise local, regional, and national sections. Giving recognition to each ethnic group and taking an active role in the moulding of our nation's unity.

I sincerely commend the National Commission for Museums and Monuments, its indefatigable Director-General (Dr. Ekpo Eyo) and his staff for the singularly successful role the National Museum has played in projecting the Country's image to the world of art. I like to use this opportunity to make a passionate appeal to the Federal Government to increase the financial assistance it has rendered the Commission to enable it recover more of our works of art still held by museums and in private collections overseas. While thanking the Government for what has so far been done, I plead that there is still much more that the Commission can do. We know that many of the works of art, especially the Benin ones, were sheer loots that have either been borrowed or bought from private owners by national museums abroad. Our National Commission must be commended for the judicious management of the funds at its disposal to recover what can only be described as the smallest and cheapest pieces. The more valuable and expensive ones are still out and the managers of our Government finances must not regard the expenditure with the traditional non-revenue earning criterion and therefore a wasted effort. Only quite recently Gulf Oil Company of Nigeria purchased for a large sum of money and donated to the Federal Government a beautiful piece of carving. I learnt that there were many countries of the world that invited the Exhibition, the Treasures of Ancient Nigeria, but whose invitations could not be answered for logistic reasons. There was a Japanese Professor in Benin City at the time the Exhibition was somewhere in Europe. He told me his country had invited the Exhibition and so had to rush home to meet it. He must have been sadly disappointed. The invitations show the great interest that art lovers and museum experts had in these collections. I am sure all the traditional rulers whose domains are represented in these collections that make up Treasures of Ancient Nigeria join me in appealing to the Federal Government not to allow financial constraints hamper the work of the Commission so it can recover more of these our rare art pieces and have them properly housed and cared for.

We traditional rulers, whose works are involved in these collections, wish to express our appreciation to the National Commission for specially inviting us here. As the custodians of arts and culture and the traditional heads of our communities, traditional rulers the country over have always been willing and ready to support sincere efforts to provide the knowledge needed to understand and appreciate our past, so that we may all better plan and program for the future, and provide guidance especially for our youths. This can be accomplished by adopting the criteria employed by museums the world over i.e. to collect, conserve, and interpret the works of human beings and of nature for the enlightenment and enjoyment of the public. It is, therefore, my hope that the National Commission staff will endeavour at all times to interact with traditional rulers on these matters, bearing in mind that the mere discovery of an artifact through archaeological excavations may not by itself tell the whole history of the people, as interpreted by the museum "expert"!

I have no doubt that the world tour of the Treasures of Ancient Nigeria clearly demonstrated to the outside world the richness of the Nigerian art and artist. Unfortunately, this richness is now being adulterated by the poor production of modern young carvers and bronze casters who simply turn-out anything saleable without any regard for the ancient standards. I wish, therefore, to seize this opportunity to appeal to the National Commission for Museums and Monuments to be more vigilant in checking our works of art to ensure that it is only the best of them that go out of the country. I make this appeal because the artists have now so commercialized their work through the influx of patronage of foreign visitors who buy anything fashioned in wood or brass in the name of art. I dare say such pieces do not necessarily come within the National Commission's legal definition of "antiquities" but outside Nigeria they represent Nigerian works of art. I have on two occasions called our bronze casters in Benin City to warn them on the poor quality of work they sell to foreign visitors. It is my hope that the

National Commission will pay more attention to this aspect of what foreigners buy and carry away. In the olden days our ancestors would use traditional sanctions to make a bad workman sit up; but today one was most likely to face Court action for interfering with somebody's fundamental human right!

I wish to commend the Federal Government for sponsoring the Exhibition of Treasures of Ancient Nigeria to go round the world and to congratulate the National Commission for Museums and Monuments on the great success it made of that sponsorship. There is a note of disappointment though that I wish to make. Our people in Benin have a proverb that runs thus: The masquerade does not move out until it has first performed at home. It is our hope that, in future, if the Commission is ever to embark on such a show again, we at home should first have a preview. It was rather disappointing to learn that the Exhibition had taken off in the United States.

Finally, in the name of all traditional rulers, and more particularly those of us specially invited here, as well as the distinguished guests, I welcome back home the great works of art that represent the Treasures of Ancient Nigeria and commend them to the safekeeping of the Director-General and his staff.

I thank you all for your attention.

||||||||||||||||||||||||||||||||||||||||||||

An Address on the Occasion of the Launching of a Book by Mr. Mbazulike Amechi at Enugu on Saturday, 10th May, 1986

I am pleased to have been invited to participate in the launching of Mr. Mbazulike Amechi's book, *The Forgotten Heroes of Nigerian Independence*. I have read the book and found it quite interesting. I would like however, to say at the onset that my presiding at the launching of the book should not be interpreted as necessarily meaning my agreement with its contents. But this is not to say that there is nothing in it I agree with.

I have two reasons for gladly accepting the invitation to come to launch the book. Firstly, in his letter to me, the author reminded me of his youth and working days in my home, Benin City, where he began his trade union activities before he went into active politics, and of his filial association with my father. Secondly, I, like the author, know that there are "heroes and heroines" who blazed the trail that led to our country's Independence, but who have virtually been forgotten. Only last year, when I addressed the congregation of the University of Ibadan, I made reference to the habit of some of our people condemning those in Government that fell while they sing hallelujah to usher in the new Government which they again proceed to condemn as soon as it was toppled.

A former Head of the Federal Civil Service, whom I regarded as an elder statesman and for whom I had great respect, once described the situation to me in a phrase I love very much. He said, "Nigerians are very good at writing off years" An incident I narrated led him to use the phrase. It concerned a Permanent Secretary who had retired after over 30 years service. About four weeks after he proceeded on pre-retirement leave, there was a very big cocktail party given by the Government. This man was absent. When I met him that evening and observed that he was not at the party, he said he received no invitation. When at a later date I met one of the officials in charge I told him that the officer said he was not invited, the reply was simply that not every body was invited. So he is off the list so soon, I exclaimed! In a party that hosted several hundreds of guests I felt it was too soon for such a man to have been "forgotten." The elder statesman I was speaking to then said that in the nine months since he himself retired he had not been invited to any government party. It was a pity; and there were several like them-forgotten.

Very often one hears of speeches at the commissioning of projects-projects that took 2–3 years to execute. And yet speeches would be made as if the project sprang up overnight. Those who conceived the idea or presided over the initial implementation are never mentioned. As it is in the public sector so it is in the private. This lapse—nay, ingratitude—has, in my view become even more serious in recent years. And I begin to wonder why? Is it the fear of the incumbent; or is it just envy; or the propensity of some Nigerians to bask in praises due to others or reap where they did not sow?

Ingratitude is a bad thing; ingratitude to pioneers is even worse, and in the particular context of the book we are about to launch, it is sad that many of those who struggled for our Independence now appear to have been forgotten simply because they happen not to be in the run of things at the material time. This is not surprising anyway, for most pioneers usually die unsung. And it is written long ago that it is the evil that men do that lives after them, the good is often interred with their bones. Hence, paradoxically, it is the wicked ones that the world often remembers for their wickedness.

This ought not to be so for the Holy Book teaches us not to forget doers of good. Examples abound therein of people remembered and blessed for their good deeds. One such lesson is in the Book of Revelation 3:4, 5 where we are told thus: "Then hast a few names even in Sardis which have not defiled their garments and they shall walk with me in white, for they are worthy. I will not blot his name out of the book of life, but I will confess his name before my Father and before His Angels."

My Muslim friends versed in the Koran tell me that their Holy Book also has something to say on the subject. In other words, it is God's wish that credit must be given to those that went before for any good they might have done. *The Forgotten Heroes* tells us of the many men and women who took up the fight from where the mosquitoes left off and embarked on the struggle to free this our dear country from becoming the "white sellers.' Some were in trade unionism and gradually worked their way into active national politics, like the author. Others remained in trade unionism or in "Movements" of fellowership or simply in the background, all fanning the fire of nationalism, or urging on the older ones to action.

The author is telling us that such people ought not to be forgotten and that he will immortalize them. In this connection, it was a matter of joy to me when I read sometime ago that the Railway Workers' Union decided to build and donate a house to Nigeria's Labour Leader Number One. Pity though that it was only his own Union that was said to be embarking on such a project. There is no reason why it should not be the concern of the entire Nigeria Labour Congress as known today, for although Imoudu was in the Railways, he fought for workers generally irrespective of their Department or Station. I was particularly pleased to see him recently at the Bendel State University which was, I think, the latest Institution of higher learning to recognize his contributions to the country's Independence. Equally heart-warming was the news the other day that the Lagos State Government had immortalized the name of Pa. I. O. Ransome-Kuti of Abeokuta Grammar School fame and the dear husband of the indomitable woman political activist Mrs. Fumilayo Ransome-Kuti. (We shall leave the song about their young offsprings to be sung by those to come later!) In political and educational development of this country the names of those two cannot be forgotten, and the Lagos State Government deserves commendation for it. A third example of expression of remembrance that gladdens the heart is that of Alhaja (now Dr.) Ladi Kwali who received an honorary doctorate from the Ahmadu Bello University sometime in 1970 or 1971 for placing Abuja and Nigeria in world map through her internationally famed Abuja Pottery. It was almost a decade later that she was nationally honored.

There is an interesting bit in the book that I like to comment upon. In describing the trade union and political activities of those days the author made reference to the support given by Obas in different places. I say "interesting' because since the commencement of the Political Debate initiated by President Babangida, some Nigerians who claim to be political analysts have accused some traditional rulers of having given support to politicians in the recent past and have argued that for that reason traditional rulers must be excluded from the new dispensation that may emerge from the on-going debate. I suspect that those who put up this argument will spot what Mr. Amechi has written. I like to observe that the politics of those days was very different from what it is today: in those days it was "black versus white' and all hands were on deck to see that the "white man' left us to manage our affairs. Today it is we against one another. This is not the place to examine whether or not some traditional rulers did engage in partisan politics in the recent past or whether that was a bad thing if, in fact, they did. Suffice it to say for now that the current Political debate takes us back to Mr. Amechi's days gone by, for as they fought then, to rescue this country from the "white man' so today's debate, which is aimed at discovering a new political order, may rescue the country from ourselves because we Nigerians are on the verge of destroying it. Therefore, all traditional rulers must contribute to the debate individually and collectively and more importantly also seek to carve out a place for themselves in the new scheme of things; otherwise traditional rulers would be failing in their duty and forget past traditional rulers who, along with their subjects, first blazed the trail so their children (i.e. we here today) can enjoy a free united and stable Nigeria.

I think at this point I ought to clarify my stand, and issue a little warning or advice. I have thus far advocated, as does the author of *The Forgotten Heroes*, that pioneers in the struggle for Nigerian independence (and indeed pioneers in our national life) should not be forgotten. Yes, they should not be forgotten. But we must be careful that we do not make it a habit of constantly remembering them and singing their praise, otherwise we would be violating one cardinal guiding proverb among my own (Edo) people of Bendel State. There we say "agha s' Odionwere norragbon rae ya gha ye norrerinmwin rre aghi ren w' emwin maghi mafo' (when a people leave the incumbent "diokpa' to be singing the praise of his departed predecessor in office then it is obvious something is wrong). We pray we do not become a nation that is constantly remembering past heroes but we also pray we do not become a nation that remembers only the incumbent in position. And may God help us to know where to draw the line. Let me admit here that I was myself pleasantly surprised to read in the book the names of some of those people whom I had met in official or social circles years ago but whose names I have had no cause in recent years to mention-note that I said "mention.' We thank God some are still with us today and we pray for the continued peaceful rest of those who have departed.

Finally, we must commend the efforts of Mr. Mbazulike Amechi in giving us this book so fittingly dedicated to the heroes and heroines who fought (some of them losing their lives) for the Independence of Nigeria and later to keep Nigeria one. His effort is all the more commendable in that in spite of the loss of much of his collected materials in the civil war he was still able to give a vivid account of what transpired in the pre-independence struggle and assemble so many names of our forgotten heroes and heroines. I congratulate him!

Ladies and gentlemen, it is my pleasure now to launch *The Forgotten Heroes of Nigerian Independence,* and I do so with N1,000.

May it be a true reminder of those heroes and heroines.

I thank you all for your attention.

‖‖‖‖‖‖‖‖‖‖‖‖‖‖‖‖‖‖‖‖‖‖‖‖‖‖‖‖‖‖‖‖‖

An Address on the Occasion of the Launching of the Nigerian Universities Dissertation Abstracts at the University of Port-Harcourt on Wednesday, 20 September, 1989.

Special Guests of Honor: The President, Commander-in-Chief of the Armed Forces of Nigeria, Members of the Armed Forces Ruling Council; Guests of Honor: Honorable Minister of Education, Minister of Science & Technology, Chief Launcher, Pro-Chancellor of University of Port-Harcourt, Professor O. O. Akunkugbe, Pro-Chancellors of Other Universities, Vice-Chancellors, Distinguished Ladies and Gentlemen.

I must confess that when I was first approached to serve as Chairman of this occasion, I was a bit hesitant. I had reasoned that launching of books had become a pastime in Nigeria! But then I realized that the Vice-Chancellor of the University of Port Harcourt, Professor Sylvanus J.S. Cookey, had sent his able Deputy, Professor Andrew Evwaraye to personally bring me the invitation. Furthermore, Professor Evwaraye, brought a copy of the book and explained to me its contents, objectives and value. Any one who has traveled by motor vehicle on the Ughelli-Patani Road in Bendel State to and from Eastern states beginning with Port Harcourt knows the harrowing motoring experience one is subjected to. For Professor Evwaraye to have dared the road twice in a fortnight showed the high esteem the authorities of the University hold me, for which I am immensely grateful. I then reached the conclusion that such a monumental effort to link the "Garden City" with the "Ancient City" was well worth reciprocating. Hence I accepted the invitation, and I am glad to be here.

There is no doubt that there is a crisis in our country's educational system today. This crisis is certainly not peculiar to Nigeria. The deepening crisis of the world economy, global inflation and protectionism by the advanced countries have generated crisis of serious proportions in developing nations like Nigeria. Hence, books, journals, teaching and research materials are not just scarce but where they are available, they cannot be purchased due to high costs. We must commend the Federal Military Government and the Honorable Minister of Education for the multi-pronged responses to the problems of research and teaching facilities in our schools in spite of the dwindling income.

It was with this background in mind that I took time to browse through and evaluate the book we are about to launch today. Three major issues quickly occurred to me. Firstly, I am not aware of any other volume like this one in the country. In other words, this is the very first attempt to put together a compendium of dissertation topics and abstracts written in Nigerian Universities since independence in 1960. Secondly, I realized that with a volume like this, it would be easy for researchers (and also non-academics who may be interested) to identify what has been done; who did what, where such work was done, what the basic issues were and what conclusions were reached. I am sure you will all agree with me that these issues are invaluable to the success of any novel research effort. Thirdly, I took particular interest in what most of our contemporary leaders of thought did in their younger academic days. Today, many of them are journalists, University Professors, top bureaucrats, special advisers, Vice-Chancellors, business magnates and so on. It is refreshing to have an insight into their respective areas of interest in their younger days.

It is in line with this point that I observed with interest, for instance, that Professor Ladipo Ayodeji Banjo, currently Vice-Chancellor, University of Ibadan, wrote his Ph.D thesis on "A Contrastive Study of Aspects of the Syntactic and Lexical Rules of English and Yoruba." This is NUDA 125. Also, Dr. Edwin E. Madunagu, a member of the Editorial Board of the *Guardian*, who originally trained as a Mathematician wrote his M.Sc. thesis on the "The Riccati Differential Equation and its Role in the Calculus of Variations," Nuda 626. Professor B. A. Osifisan, who today teaches at the University of Ibadan and writes for the *Sunday Times* wrote a brilliant work on "The Origin of drama in West Africa" NUDA 115. There is Professor Isa Mohammed, currently Vice-Chancellor, University of Abuja, who wrote his dissertation on "Derivation of Generators and Relations for the Crystallographic and Non-Crystallographic Point Groups" NUDA 627. And Professor Philip Aigbona Igbafe, now of the University of Benin, whose Ph.D thesis in the University of Ibadan was on "Benin under British Administration, 1897–1938: A Study in Institutional Adpatation" NUDA

283. Also Professor Obaro Ikime whose Ph.D. thesis was on "Itsekiri-Urhobo Relations and the Establishment of British Rule, 1884–1936." NUDA 284. There is the Hon. Justice Adolphus Godwin Karibi-White, whose paper was on "Sources of Nigerian Criminal Law." NUDA 305, and the Hon. Justice Joseph Olakunle Orojo who wrote on "Foreign Companies and Part X of the Companies Decree 1968." NUDA 308. Finally, and this delighted me much, is the dissertation of Mr. J. O. Ogbomo, the present Secretary of the Benin Traditional Council, on "Budget Administration in Midwestern State Public Service." NUDA 182. I seriously encourage all of you, here gathered, to go through NUDA and see for yourself the wonderful researches our people have done over the years.

Mr. President, distinguished Ladies and Gentlemen, NUDA is a major attempt at redirecting the method and pattern of research. NUDA confirms the fact that our Universities are responding positively to the challenges of the times; the need for self-reliance, for motivation, for creativity and hard work. The publication of NUDA by one of the second-generation Universities confirms the fact that the future of Nigeria is bright and that our intellectuals are not just idling away on our campuses. I appeal to all of you here gathered to support the University so that the forthcoming volumes of this book will find a dignified and respectable place in our Palace Library in the ancient City of Benin. Professors Igbafe's and Ikime's works have done that. I have no doubt that each and everyone of you here today will secure a copy for your library.

Thanking you for listening.

||||||||||||||||||||||||||||||||||||||||||||

Special Appeal Broadcast to the People on Wednesday, 19 July, 2009.

A CALL TO FAST

We salute all Benin people home and abroad. We also salute all non-Benin people resident in this State Capital Benin City, and all other Bendelites.

We have decided to use the Television to speak this time because, though what we want to say concerns our Benin people primarily, it should also concern all Bendelites who have the peace and progress of our state, and the whole country, at heart.

Our elders say that society's destructive elements do not rest but so also are the repairers-they too do not rest. We call on all you good people who are working ever so hard to save this nation from the destructive elements not to relent in your efforts.

Not long ago we called on Benin people to perform some national sacrifice. That was not the first time we had done a thing like that. We use this medium to thank you all for past performance.

We want to say that the performance of a sacrifice is not a "native" act to laugh at the Benin people about. Offering of sacrifice is not peculiar to us Benin people. The great religions in our society, Christian/Muslim, perform sacrifices; those who are familiar with the Bible and the Koran know that the men of old who communed with God the Father did so through performance of sacrifice-Adam did fervently, Abraham did, Jesus the Christ did, Mohamed did. And their followers still do today. What is different is the mode of performance and materials used. We of Benin Kingdom believe in the efficacy of personal and national sacrifice. So we urge you not to get tired or feel ashamed when asked to come out to do some sacrifice.

Today we have a message to transmit to all Benin people, and to all Bendelites who care to join us. We have all been directed to fast for three days, are Friday, July 21, Saturday, July 22 and Sunday, July 23. Throughout the three days everyone who is undergoing the fasting is required inwardly in his/her mind first to thank God Almighty for all the blessings He has bestowed on us as individuals and as a nation to this day, and then to pray inwardly in his/her mind to God to:

(i) let peace reign in Benin Kingdom in particular, and in Nigeria in general

(ii) bestow His wisdom on the present Federal Military Government so those in authority may see the light to eradicate every form of hardship that now plagues the society;

(iii) help us all succeed in the fight against hunger, public disturbances,

armed robbery, and prevent destructive wind and rainstorm and all undesirable, societal acts;

(iv) send His Spirit into the mind of the evil-doers in the society to
make them change to good;

(v) send His Spirit into the mind of all young persons, whether in educational institutions or not, so they turn away from their evil ways-violent
demonstrations, drug peddling and addiction and other societal ills;

(vi) help job-seekers to find means of livelihood.

Nobody is required to go out to the open place or to stop what you
are doing to offer this prayer. You are to say it in your mind; hence you
can pray even while eating or walking or at place of work or market. We
however, appeal especially to the Muslims to devote their "jumat" prayer
on Friday, 21st July to this special prayer and the Christians to do same
on Sunday, 23rd . The traditional can offer the prayers at any time at their
own traditional places.

We will like to advise you on the method of fasting. There are two ways
of fasting. One is to completely abstain from eating, drinking (and even
smoking) between dawn and dusk, i.e. usually from about 6 a.m. to about
6 p.m. Those who can do this are advised to do it. The other kind of fasting
is to eat one meal during the day but that food must have no pepper, no oil;
no salt in it. This form is good for those who have not previously done any
fasting and the old people and children. Needless to say that there must be
abstention from sexual inter-course during the period of fasting.

This little explanation has become necessary because when last our
people in Benin were called upon to fast some year ago, information came
to us that a lot of questions were asked and some fears entertained after the
event. With the explanation just given we hope every citizen, who is hail
and hearty, will participate. We call on all of you to perform the fasting for
the sake of your own selves and the society in which you live.

We like to use this medium to thank all our people, friends and well-
wishers who have been sending us congratulatory messages on our 10th year
anniversary, and especially for highlighting the peace that has been on the
land these 10 years. The measure of peace and development that you have
all enjoyed these 10 years had been due to the prayers and goodwill of all

of you, and your participating on every occasion we announce the need to perform national sacrifice. We urge you good people not to be tired. We pray God and our ancestors to keep the devil from your side.

We pray God and our ancestors to give all of you the strength to undertake the fasting. Remember it is to last for 6 a.m.-6 p.m. daily on Friday, July 21, Saturday, July 22 and Sunday, July 23. May God and our ancestors also give each and everyone the purity of heart to offer sincere and devoted prayer as already outlined.

We will appreciate it if the Television stations can carry this message daily in any other form as a reminder to the people after this initial announcement.

May God and our ancestors answer our prayers.

|||||||||||||||||||||||||||||||||||||||||||||

Statement to the Meeting of Chiefs, Enigie, Edionwere and Ward Leaders Held in the Palace, on Friday, 19th April, 2009.

I salute all my chiefs, Enigie, edionwere and also representatives of the Local Government Councils of Oredo, Ovia and Orhionmwon. I welcome you all.

In the past when we met like this it has not been the usual practice to address you from a prepared statement. On every occasion I have spoken to you on any matters, you have always listened attentively. This has always impressed me. However, our information, based on the monitoring of action in your areas after I have spoken, always left me with the impression that not much was done to give effect to what I told you here. I attribute this apparent lapse to either because of difficulty in communication in your area or sheer ignorance of the importance of what had been said. I have, therefore, decided to speak to you today from a prepared statement because of the very important subjects I wish to talk to you about. Copies of my statement will be distributed to you. I appeal to all Enigie and edionwere to take this document back to your areas, summon a gathering of your community and read this message again to all your people, men, women and children. Representatives of the Local Government Councils are here and if there is any point you want to ask questions about you can go either to your Local Government Chairman (who I am sure will be willing to answer your questions) or come to the office of the Benin Traditional Council where the Secretary will answer you or bring you to me personally.

Vandalism of NEPA and NITEL properties. The first matter I wish to talk about concerns the current wave of vandalism of the properties of National Electric Power Authority (NEPA) and the Nigerian Telecommunications Ltd. (NITEL). That of NEPA is far more serious. Not long ago top NEPA officials came to address us here in the Palace on the damage certain individuals are causing to NEPA installations. These persons destroy and steal away the cables and the high-tension poles. You must also have heard, not long ago, that in the area of Ekae, Sapele Road, a huge high-tension installation was pulled down to be stolen, but the thieves failed. People are stealing these things all over the country, including Bendel State. NEPA officials believe, and I also believe, that these vandals who are stealing these thing live in houses in our towns and villages: no one is sure where they carry these things to once they have been pulled down but again they must be hidden either in houses or in some bush in and around our towns and villages. I therefore wish to appeal to all of you to be vigilant so that you all can help NEPA to stop this vandalism. The more damage these vandals do the more they keep the country in darkness. And not only that: because NEPA have to spend money to replace what has been damaged, NEPA then become unable to find money to extend electricity to new area. That is one reason why NEPA is unable to meet the demand of communities who are clamoring for extension of NEPA facilities. What I have said about NEPA also applies to NITEL whose cables are also been stolen. Telephones in most parts of the country have been reported to be out of order. So you see that these wicked vandals are enemies of progress and of the people. I hope you will all be on the lookout for them and report any person with suspicious movement to the nearest police or councilor. That is not all. In addition to reporting to the police, I want everyone of your communities to say something about this at your ogua-edion-that God and our ancestors may protect us all from the wicked persons who wish to keep the Nation in darkness.

Census. The second matter I want to speak to you about is the Census or head-count. On 12th March, 1991, those in charge conducted what was called trial census. They have been working out a system which, it is hoped, will give previous occasions people criticized and even rejected census figures. This time around those in charge are determined to produced a figure that will not evoke any controversy. What they did on 12th, 13th and 14th of March was to try out the system. The actual head count which will involve every human being in the country will be conducted later in the year. Government will announce the date. What I want to do today is to appeal to you all to be available where you will be expected to be counted. It is very important for the Government to know the actual number of persons in the country in order to be able to plan effectively for development. As you all know, even the master of the house must know how many children, wives, servants and dependants he has to feed and clothe in order to know how much money he has to bring out for food and clothing. That is why Government wants to know how many persons are in the country. It is not for the purpose of imposing tax on any one.

There is an aspect of it that concerns us Benin people and which I want everybody to take to heart seriously. Since the creation of this state the population of the Benin ethnic group has always been the highest, irrespective of the number of Local Government Councils. But in the recent past, especially since the last civilian regime, our population has been going down-Osa noghe gie evbo ima yeke-and since then we have been trying to find out why. When the last civilian government created several new Local Government Councils, the Benin area recorded low population. Our investigation reveals that this trend has been due to lack of interest of our people to come out to be registered for elections. I am, therefore, appealing to all of you that when the National Population Commission begins the actual head-count later in the year our people must make themselves available to be counted. You are to remain in your homes and those to do the counting will come to you. We have been told that a sick person will be counted on his/her sick-bed as long as he or she is still breathing; a newly born child will be counted as soon as the child touched ground; even disabled persons will also be counted because they are human beings. You must therefore get all those in your houses to make themselves available during the hours of counting. I want us to use the occasion of this head-count to get the correct population of the Benin people in Oredo, Ovia and Orhionmwon Local Government Council areas.

ELECTION. As you all know Local Government Council elections have come and gone and you now elected Chairman and Councillors in the Local Government Councils. According to the Government program the next elections to come are for the Governors, members of House of Assembly and the President and the Federal Legislature. We are told that these will be later this year, and next year. As you know also, there are now two political parties, the National Republican Convention (NRC) and the Social Democratic Party (SDP). By the Grace of God, I am the Oba of Benin and the traditional head of the Benin Kingdom. In that capacity, God and our ancestors have made me the father of all. Therefore, it does not matter to me which of the two parties anybody belongs to. It is however important to me, as I believe it is to all of you, that our Government at the Federal, State and Local Government should be headed and manned by honest, God-fearing and dedicated persons who are prepared to work for the peace, unity, social and economic development of this country. It is also of importance to me as I believe it is to you that whoever will run the next civilian Government (Federal and State) must, God willing, be persons who will sustain and have the highest regard for the traditional institution, that is, the traditional ruler and his chiefs and all that we stand for. These considerations are among the reasons why I myself support the open voting system. Those of you who are going to vote on that day will see and know the person you voting for. And you who will vote will also be seen and known. The person you to vote for must have been going around campaigning; you will see him and know him and because he lives among you, you can decide for yourselves, in your judgment, whether he (or she) has been an honest citizen who has the welfare of the people at heart. In the new open system of voting no one would be put in a small room called the polling booth where some Party Officials would force you to put your ballot paper where you do not want to put it; this time around when some one has "chop" somebody's money in private, that person has to come out into the open to face the shame and the wrath of his fellow party men and the owner of the money. From either side the man will show how mean he is. This time, because the voting is done in the open for all to see, every voter is expected to act according to his or her conscience. You must not allow your conscience to be bought no matter how plentiful the money (what we Benin people term "igho oya, igho osono). Even though your fellow man may not see you taking money the Supreme Being and the gods of the land who watch everybody's action will ensure that whoever want to use money or anything else to buy the conscience of people and give us a Government of bad men will fail. I therefore appeal to all of you to try to follow the guidelines that Government has given and be bold enough to act according to the dictate of your conscience. All voters must do their best to come to the polling station and queue to be counted. We pray and hope that the coming civilian Government will be better than any we have had. May God and our ancestors give voters the strength to act according to their conscience and resist temptation.

TRANSITION TO CIVIL RULE PROGAMME. The last matter I wish to talk to you about is the transition to civil rule program. This is the program designed by the present Military Administration to return the country to civil rule. That is why we are having these elections. As I have just stated the Local Government Council elections have been held; the next ones will be election of Governors and Legislators and finally the President. The President of the Federal Republic of Nigeria, General Ibrahim B. Babangida, has stated repeatedly that this Military Administration will hand over to civilians in 1992, which is only next year. It is therefore important that the citizenry should do everything possible not to disrupt the transition program. The easiest way to disrupt program is to disturb the peace of the country by any form of activity or to do any unwholesome act that would distract the attention of the Government from the implementation of this program. I therefore appeal to all my people to set the example to all other ethnic communities in the country in the maintenance of law and order and in the full support of the program. Any person or group of persons who is aggrieved by or does not understand any Government pronouncement should go to his Local Government Council Office or come to the Palace to seek clarification. Both the Federal and our State

Government have repeated in strong terms that they will not tolerate any act by anybody that will disturb the transition program or distract the attention of the Government from the course it has set for itself to hand over to the civilians. It is my hope that everybody will take this warning to heart. We the Benin people have a record of being law-abiding citizens and I hope we will continue to be so. Now that Party politicians have come to the scene one can only pray and hope that they will help us non-partisan politicians to help them to keep the transition to civil rule program on course; after all it is in their own interest that the military should hand over. I therefore use this opportunity to appeal to the leaders of the two political parties to let good sense prevail so that nothing happens to disturb the transition program.

I have spoken to you at length. I like to repeat what I began with that copies of this paper from which I am speaking will be distributed and I am requesting all the Enigie, Edionwere and ward leaders to convene meetings of the people in your towns and villages and pass this message to them. From time to time as the dates for the census and the elections, draw near, we will find time to talk to you.

I thank you all for your attention and may God bless you all.

||||||||||||||||||||||||||||||||||||||||||

An Address on the Occasion of the Installation of Ohen-Osa Nohuanren, the high Priest of Holy Aruosa, on Sunday, 27 November, 1994.

On behalf of the Ohen-Osa Nohuaren and the Council of Elders of Holy Aruosa, I welcome His Excellency, the Military Administrator of Edo State and members of his entourage, visiting Reverend dignitaries from other religious denominations, all invited dignitaries and distinguished ladies and gentlemen.

We have this morning witnessed a unique ceremony in the installation of Ohen-Osa Nohuaren, the High Priest of Holy Aruosa. The last incumbent installed by my father in 1945 passed to the great beyond in 1984. It is appropriate to take the audience through memory land and, for the benefit of those who may not know, to let them know what all this is about. But before I go further, let me explain the terminologies we have used. Ohen-Osa Nohuaren simply means in English "the Holy Priest of God" and Aruosa simply means the "Altar of God."

What we have done here this morning is only a re-enactment in modern setting of what happened in about 15th century in the reign of my great Ancestor, Oba Esigie. Those who are familiar with the history of the Benin Empire and Christianity in Nigeria will know that it is this City that Christianity, through Roman Catholicism, first touched ground in what is now Nigeria. Since the so-called modern people, especially those in the academics, do not very much like evidence of traditional history, where there is no book whose author can be cited, I will rely on contemporary historians whose volumes on Benin history are available. But I am happy that these modern historians confirmed what we know through our traditional history.

In the reign of Oba Esigie, Portuguese traders had extended their influence to this part of West Africa and into the hinterland of the King of Benin. Oba Esigie, whose primary objective was the advancement of commerce for the benefit of his people, welcomed them with warm hospitality. From this first visit, close friendship evolved between Oba Esigie of Benin Empire and King Dom Manuel of Portugal. Visits and gifts were exchanged between the two Monarchs culminating in Oba Esigie sending an Ambassador to the Court of the king of Portugal, and later personally visiting Portugal at the King's invitation. In the course of the activities of the Portuguese traders, they noticed that the local people, from the manner they worshipped God, would be receptive to evangelism or teachings of Jesus Christ, and they decided to introduce the process of evangelisation in order to take the people off their kind of worship that was regarded as idolatry. As a result of their reports back home the King of Portugal decided that a Christian missionary group would accompany the trading mission on their next visit to Benin Kingdom. And so they came; they were satisfied with the information given them regarding the hospitality of the King and people of Benin and also their mode of worshipping God.

The next stage in the development was that on a subsequent visit of the trading company, the Christian missionary that accompanied them had the specific duty to establish the Church, the Roman Catholic Church. When the Christian missionary arrived, Oba Esigie directed that they be shown round the City to select any location of their choice. The missionaries were lead to a spot in Ogbelaka (area where the High Court now stands). For reasons that were apparently never disclosed, the missionary did not find that location suitable; it was good but not suitable, whatever they meant by that. As they proceeded in their search they stopped at a location in Idunmwun-erie, at the junction of present Aruosa Street with Igbesanmwan Street. Again they found the place good but not suitable. They then proceeded from there until they finally got to the present site where we are now. They found this location good and suitable; they erected the Church here and introduced Christian form of worship, and that was the first Church on the land or country that is present-day Nigeria. We have not been able to discover the reason (or reasons) that disqualified the first two locations or what the missionaries meant by good but not suitable. Our conjecture is that they must have found the first two locations were not on any major road unlike this Akpakpava Road where the building now stands which had been one of the seven major highways that led into the Ancient City. And the Church of God (Aruosa) has been here ever since. But our people did not write off the other two locations; since they believed that the visitors from overseas brought the Message of God, the Supreme Being, our people decided to build a house of worship or altar of God at Ogbelaka and Idunmwun-erie where they still are to this day.

Before I proceed further from here, I like to express deep appreciation to the Head of the Anglican Communion in Nigeria, the Most Reverend J.T. Adetiloye, for deeming it fit to correct some modern historians who wanted to twist history recently. In the course of writing the history of Christianity in Nigeria the Historian published (ignorantly or deliberately) in widely circulated newspapers that Christianity first touched ground in Nigeria in Badagry. But His Grace Archbishop Adetiloye came out publicly to correct that claim and explained, without mincing words, that Christianity in modern-day Nigeria first touched ground in Benin City. We are very grateful to His Grace for that bold statement and may God give him the strength to lead the Anglican Communion for many years.

Back again to Aruosa for which reason we are here gathered. With the establishment of the Roman Catholic Church, many Benin people got converted to Christianity including, it is believed, Oba Esigie himself. Thus, the Christian Church became one of the many different shrines (or altars) where Benin people worshipped, and it continued in this altar here for quite some time until it became moribund. The practice died away after the Portuguese traders had been displaced by the Dutch. This was a rather unfortunate development both for the Portuguese and the local people. After the Christian work had ceased, our people and, in particular the Oba himself, did not let their work die there. As far as our people were doing, and still do, praying to Father in Heaven. However, there was the innovation, the Benin people, in that the altar of God could be "housed." Until then the altar of God was never in any building probably because of the belief that no building could contain the altar of the Almighty God! So, our people continued to use this altar before which we are all gathered. Since there was no more Pastor, the Oba then appointed an Ohen (a High Priest) for the altar, and since our people did not know the intricacies of the Christian procedure, we decided to be worshipping God in this altar in the way we had always done. Hence in the reign of subsequent Obas, we reverted to the practice of offering the blood of those animals that we believed were (and are) associated with the worship of the Supreme Being. I need not mention the names of those creature here. I daresay there was nothing strange in the practice because of the evidence in the Bible and the Koran of the offering of blood to the Supreme Being. Of course it is known that adherents of all known Religions in the world worship God Almighty, the Almighty Creator, the Great Architect of the Universe. The only difference is the intermediary through whom they reach Him: while Christians pass through Jesus Christ, the Muslims and adherents of traditional religion, like the Benin people, pray direct to God or Allah. So in the case of the Benin people, after the disappearance of the Christian practice, our people continued to use this altar to pray to and worship the Supreme Being (God) and making the sacrificial offerings when necessary.

The land mark and turning point in the development occurred in the reign of my father, Oba Akenzua II of blessed memory. Being the enlightened Oba that he was, he decided that the worship in this Aruosa should be modernized to enable all those who believe in direct supplication to God to participate. He felt that the continued practice of the offering in Benin manner would be seen as fetish. Thus about 1944/45, he started reorganizing the method of worship to modernize it. First of all the native objects of worship removed and stopped the offering of blood. He directed the design and preparation of the altar that you now see. Then in 1945, he appointed a substantive Chief Priest with the traditional title of Ohen-Osa Nohuaren. I will not bore you with the innovations and changes that my father introduced; all have been reduced to print, as you will be able to observe when the Ohen-Osa conducts the service. I will however draw attention to one aspect of the practice for which our father was severely criticized by the Christians of 1945, and that is in the use of ema, egogo, ukuse, (drum, gong and maracas). There was a particular Bishop in Lagos who engineered all other Christians leaders against this practice, describing it as idol worship, and he did it with so much ferocity that our father, Oba Akenzua II, in answering that Bishop on the pages of the newspapers of those days, nick-named him "the fighting Parson." I refrain from mentioning the Bishop's name here. Even though we were in school then, the antagonism of that "fighting parson" surprised us because from what we read in the Bible, even as students, we knew that the Bible was full of praises to God with songs and different kinds of musical instruments known to those days. Of course our father drew the Bishop's attention to this and we believed that was what finally silenced the "fighting parson." Today there is no Christian denomination in which musical instruments are not used with songs of praise to God. The other aspect of the practice here that may raise the eye-brow of the Christians in our midst is the method by which the Chief Priest will sanctify the congregation. We believe that any person entering the altar of God must "honmwegbe," i.e. cleanse himself or herself of unholy things. I only want to assure you that when he sprinkles it on you, it is no juju or native medicine. So, please, do not get scared or have a feeling of remorse if it touches you. We are doing it in this form today being a special day, for even this method of purification has also been modified by my father as subsequent worshippers to this place will find.

I like to make reference briefly to the "National Church of God." Just about the time my father was re-establishing the Holy Aruosa here in Benin, the political party known as the NCNC, claiming to be a Nationalist Party, took a leaf from what we were doing in Benin and, under the championship of Mr. K.O.K. Onyioha, were establishing a Nigerian type of worship with the name "National Church of God." Mr. K.O.K. Onyioha became the head of that organization and was very inspired by what our father had done in Benin. This led to our own Aruosa being sometimes called the Edo National Church of God . When K.O.K. Onyioha built the first Chapel of the National Church of God in Port Harcourt, he invited my father in 1956 who traveled all the way to Port Harcourt to open it. That was a great boost not only for the philosophy of Aruosa but also Mr. Onyioha's newly established National Church of God. The "National Church of God" has since been re-christened the "Godian Religion" with Chief K.O.K. Onyioha as its Spiritual Head. He is also one of the leaders of African Traditional Religion and has continued to show interest in the progress of the Holy Aruosa.

Let me make a special appeal to all, particular to Edo people, we do not worship Ogun, Oronmila, Olokun or any other African deity here. The only Entity that is worshipped here is the Supreme Being known to some people as God or Allah and to us Edo people as Osanobuwa, the Creator of all things. As I earlier pointed out, there is no religion whose adherents do not offer prayers or supplications direct to that Supreme Being. Even those who the modern people term native doctors or idol worshippers never start anything without first of all invoking the Name of the Supreme God. What I am leading to therefore is that this house we call Aruosa, being the place for the worship of the Supreme God, is open to all persons who believe in saying his or her prayer direct to God. Since there is no intermediary of any kind and if you believe you can commune with your God direct, you are free to come and worship here, and there will be nothing said or done that will be at variance with your belief. The songs that are rendered, if translated into English, will be found to be in praise of or supplication of the Almighty God (Osanobuwa). We also believe that one can pray to the

Almighty God in any language and He will answer. Just one more point, and it concerns the day of worship, which is Sunday. I like to explain that we have fixed the day of worship here on Sundays not because we want to make it in line with the Churches. Our father explained at the inception in 1945 that it was best to make it Sunday which is a non-working day for the convenience of people who have other things to do on working days, Sunday being generally a free day for all. Otherwise on strict customary practice, worship here should be conducted on either Ekioba (Oba Market) day or Agbado Market day which are our recognized days for worshipping God. But that may not always fall on a free day.

Before I hand over to the Ohen-Osa, I wish to use this occasion to appeal to all Nigerians in both high and low places that the time has come, in fact long over due, for us all to return to God. The Country moves from one problem or the confused situation to another almost daily; perpetration of anti-societal acts by both the old and young is on the increase. Even the well-knit togetherness of individual families is no longer there. All this, to my mind, is the result of human beings having turned away from God to face materialism. But in our traditional religion, as it is in other religions, "Osa orodion" (God is first). Why will people not turn to material wealth rather than seek the path to God's Kingdom when many evangelists these days amass wealth and tell their congregation from their pulpit that their own God is not a poor God. Adherents of traditional religion now do ugly things that were forbidden to their forebears, all to make money! And yet the age-old adage keeps on ringing in their ears that "the love of money is the root of all evil." I therefore plead with all Nigerians, and in particular Edo State people, to let us return to God. I do not know how that can be done but I believe that if we keep praying to Him individually, not only in congregation on Sunday, He will show us how. I also believe that if people give less importance to adoration of affluence; if the affluent realizes that the good he thinks he did with his money could have been done with one of two motives, one to boost his personal ego (which is unacceptable to God), the other to genuinely show pity for God's sake; if the Governments in the Federation cease to give pride of place to "money men" (and women!) whose personal character or source of wealth is never questioned or how much tax, if any, they pay, then we will probably be on the road back to God, for as that singer advises "seek ye first the Kingdom of God and His Righteousness, and the rest na jara." And one of the songs you may be hearing during this service is one in which we implore God that we have devoted time to serve Him, may it please Him to give us a little time for ourselves. Let all Nigerians look inward, mediate, and remember that Osa orodion (God is first), not wealth.

Having said all that, I like to thank you for your attention and I hope that I have been able to explain that there is no idol worship here. I will now leave the rest of the proceedings to the Ohen-Osa Nohuaren. I thank you all for coming and may God bless you all.

Chapter 11

Giving and Receiving Honors . . .
Like Father, Like Son.

"The good leader must follow his people!"
— Winston Churchill, cited per Omo N'Oba Erediauwa,
March 23, 1979.

ııııııııııııııııııııııııııııııııııııı

Excerpts from the Address Delivered by the Omo N'Oba Erediauwa on the Occasion of His Coronation as the 38th Oba of Benin on March 23rd, 1979

In the name of God Almighty, and of our Ancestors, we wholeheartedly welcome the Head of the Federal Military Government and all of you distinguished persons to this momentous gathering. Today, the day of our Coronation, marks a turning point in our life. When one at such a point stands up to speak, one is either so heavy at heart that one is short of words or one goes all out to unburden one's soul to one's audience. We must, therefore, ask you to bear with us while we reflect on the past, touch on the present and look at the future.

Our Coronation today makes us the 38th Oba of Benin in Oba Eweka I Dynasty that began at about 12th Century A.D. and it ends forty-five years of reign of our father, Oba Akenzua II of blessed memory. His was a reign in the services of the people as it should be.

Let us remember a few things about our father that must be told. Shortly after Oba Akenzua II ascended the Throne in 1933 he saw the need for the expansion of the Oredo pipe-borne water system that was commissioned in 1910 and the necessity for financial contribution by his people. Consequently, he accepted the introduction by the Native Administration 1936/37 of the levy of water rate. A move which would have inculcated the spirit of self reliance and social responsibility in the people, however, generated dissention which came to be popularly known as the "water-rate agitation"; agitation he had to contend with for a couple of years.

There followed a long period of peace and quiet during which he served as a nominated member in the Nigerian Legislative Council (1945–57). Subsequently, he became a member of the Western House of Chiefs; and it is on course of a debate that as a source of increasing its Revenue, the Government (in 1952) should introduce the Lottery, on the lines of the then popular Irish Sweep-Stake.

Majority members opposed the idea, which they derisively termed gambling, and immoral means of earning money. Yet, barely five or six years later, Government Lottery became (and today is) a major source of internal revenue.

He took active part in the politics of the day, but only as a means to an end, that end being the creation of what came to be known as the Mid-Western Region of Nigeria. In the old Western Region he was one of the First Class Obas, a member of the House of Chiefs, and a member of Government. In the fifties he had seen the vision of, and sowed the seed for, the creation of a new Region in the country through which to secure the rapid development of the area comprising the Edo-speaking peoples, the Itsekiri, the Urhobo, the Ijaw, and Western Ibo. He began to advocate the amalgamation of what were then the Benin and the Delta Provinces. He christened this union "Bendel." He personally led campaign tours to whip up enthusiasm for the creation of the proposed State, and so in 1963, after nearly six years of vigorous campaigns, the Mid-Western Region was born, and Oba Akenzua II saw his vision come true. Although the new Region was christened "Mid-Western," but today, almost two decades later, the name "Bendel" which Oba Akenzua II has proposed for the new Region, re-echoed, and happily we now live in "Bendel" State.

The British Government in 1937, in appreciation of his services to his people, saw it fit to return to Oba Akenzua II some of the royal regalia removed during the reign of his grandfather (Oba Ovonramwen) in 1897. Some years later, in 1943, the British Government awarded him the CMG, again for his services to his people.

In 1950 he had his first and only holiday in 45 years when he visited Britain at the invitation of the British Council, a holiday that he more than merited.

In 1966 he got introduced to academic circles when he was appointed the Chancellor of Ahmadu Bello University; and in 1972 he was awarded honorary Doctor of Laws of the University of Benin.

These honors, no doubt, were the crowning glory for a man whose interest in promoting education dated back to the 1930s, for in 1934, shortly after his Coronation, he was invited by the then Colonial Government to participated in the formal opening of the first Institution of Higher Learning in the Country-the Higher College, Yaba. Three years later, in 1937, as a result of his active encouragement, Edo College was opened in this City; and throughout his reign he never hesitated to give money, and land freely in support of education. All this is not surprising for a man who was himself highly educated by the standards of the time; Oba Akenza II, as Okoro (Prince) attended Government School, Benin City, Kings College, Lagos, and had professional training in Administration in Egba Native Administration, the most advanced in its day.

But the greatest service he rendered to his people was the golden opportunity he gave to everyone of his subjects to become affluent. It is within memory that early in his reign he realized— again seeing farther ahead than most—to finds ways to engage in gainful pursuits. So Chiefs, Palace attendants, and all, went to town in search of gainful means. As if that was not enough, he liberalized the ownership of land to such an extent that the generality of the people benefited; many became affluent thereby. He had the satisfaction of seeing the standard of living of his subjects improve.

Such was the period that has just ended. It is sad though to have to cramp into a few sentences a full active reign of forty-five years. But enough has been said for one to be able to draw a lesson for the present, and that lesson may be summed up in the words of the great Sir Winston Churchill when addressing his party men, "I am your leader and that is why I must follow you." Yes, ironically, the good leader must follow his people!

We will end as we began repeating that today is a great day, and a turning point in our life. We would like, therefore, to mark this day, the 23rd day of March, 1979, with something concrete in the form of Prizes. First and foremost we will honor the memory of our illustrious father for his services to the nation by establishing a N10,000 Fund in the University of Benin to be known as Oba Akenzua II Fund. This amount should be invested and the interest yield should be used by the University to award a Prize to be known as Oba Akenzua II Memorial Prize, to the student in the Department of History and Creative Arts that produces a published price of work that is relevant to Edo culture or History. Secondly, in order to promote education, we will donate two trophies, one each to be awarded annually to the Boys' Secondary School and Girls Secondary School in the Benin Local Government areas that obtain the highest percentage pass in the West African School Certificate Examination. Along with this we will donate audio-visual aid equipping to each Secondary School on Benin land. As a means of encouraging more interest in farming in the Local Government Councils in Edo area we will donate audio-visual aid equipment to each Secondary School on Benin land. As a means of encouraging more interest in farming in the Local Government Councils in Edo are we will donate a trophy to be awarded to the village community that produces the widest variety of food stuff determined in a joint agricultural Show. Lastly, but by no means the least, in view of our position in the entire state, we will donate a trophy to be awarded to the Local Government in the state that makes the greatest contribution to rural development.

‖‖‖‖‖‖‖‖‖‖‖‖‖‖‖‖‖‖‖‖‖‖‖‖‖‖‖‖‖‖‖‖‖

"Honor to Whom Honor Is Due ," a Speech at a Send-Off Party in Honor of Brigadier Abubakar Waziri, then Military Administrator, Bendel State, at the Palace on September 21, 1979

Brigadier Waziri, the Military Administrator, Bendel State, Service Chiefs,

Civil Commissioners, Traditional Rulers, My Lords Spiritual and Temporal, Traditional Chiefs, Distinguished Ladies and Gentlemen.

I have invited you here today to join me to do honor to whom honor is due in the person of our Military Administrator, Brigadier Abubakar Waziri, who will leave the State in a few days for new posting.

If I may begin with a bit of history, in 1933, shortly after my father had ascended the Throne, he had occasion to use an Edo adage which says "emwinogbomwan gha de nosinmwinomwan gha de" which may be translated to English to mean "when danger lurks on one's way Providence usually sends a saviour or protector." Such a situation usually occurs when a person overcomes a dangerous or unpleasant situation through the humane intervention of a third party. The biblical Good Samaritan. My father used this adage to the then expatriate Resident in charge of Benin Province who stood by him like a brother during the period my father was performing the Royal Funeral Rites of his father, my grandfather, and throughout the period of Coronation. The situation in which I find myself here today is very similar to the experience of my father with the expatriate Resident of Benin Province!

Uzama, Eghaevbo n'ore, Eghaevbo n'ogbe, Enigie, my brother Traditional Rulers, Brigadier Waziri assumed duty in this State last year at a time when the situation here in the Palace was causing us great anxiety. A few days after he arrived I was most pleasantly surprised when he took the initiative to call on me and to ask how things were in the Palace. We exchanged views and I was delighted to find how much he readily appreciated Benin custom and my own position. From that moment on, sensing my personal anxiety, he never kept away from me; rather he let me know that he was available any time if I wanted to consult him. I seized the opportunity and I cannot count how many times I called on him, even when he should be having a quiet rest at home, to brief him and obtain his advice on the preparation for the ceremony connected with my title as Edaiken.

Then came the announcement last December and the contact became even closer. I was constantly on him by telephone or notes scribbled on pieces of paper. I kept him informed at every stage of what our custom required me to do and I asked him questions and sought his advice. If he did not answer me immediately I was sure to hear from him by noon of the following day. There was a time he was away to Lagos and I needed his advice badly on a matter. I had to write to him in Lagos and my joy knew no bounds when, in spite of his time-consuming official duties in Lagos, he was able to attend to my request, and he got his reply to reach me the following day, all the way from Lagos! As you all know the period covering the ceremonies connected with title as the Edaiken, followed by the Royal Funeral Rites and then my Coronation were difficult times that were marked by elaborate ceremonies and rituals of secret and public nature that cut across the social fabric of this cosmopolitan State Capital.

I am happy to say that Brigadier Waziri's understanding of our custom and tradition, the opportunity he created for him and me to be in constant consultation, his advice and suggestions at various times, were of immense help to me in planning and organizing all that we had to do. Above all he was able to make due allowance for what our custom and tradition demanded on those occasions. This was amply demonstrated in that memorable broadcast he made during the Funeral Rites. I like my people in particular to know that were it not for Brigadier Waziri's interest and cooperation and the constant touch he maintained with me who knows we might have done some things to earn the displeasure of the Government. His personal advice and suggestions were not all. His Government was most generous with its financial assistance. I therefore call on all my relations, all Edo people and all you invited guests to join me to say a very big thank you to Brigadier Abubakar Waziri. Alas, the phrase "thank you" is so inadequate, but I am sure Brigadier, you know how I feel.

I have spoken thus far of his personal relationship with men. I know that his kindly disposition, his understanding of people and sense of fair play extended to other parts of the state and to other people as well. I know that he has had to remedy the misfortune that certain individuals inside and outside the Civil Service had suffered. And, generally speaking, I believe you all can testify to the comparative peace that has reigned in this State in the period he has been here.

Such, Ladies and Gentlemen, has been the role of Brigadier Abubakar Waziri since he arrived in this State. To me he has been both a friend in need and the Good Samaritan. And I hope, nay, I believe, I am speaking the mind of the population of this State when I say he has been a true friend of our State. Brigadier, you are leaving us now for a new assignment. It is the prayer of us all that you go in peace, and that success will be yours wherever you may be.

I like now, at this juncture, to explain briefly the significance of the reference to my father's experience that I began my speech with. The atmosphere that surrounded the passing away of my grandfather and the consequent Funeral Rites that my father had on hand was very charged in 1933: here was the grandson of the Oba whose remains lay low in far away Calabar; the son of the Oba whose road to his ancestral throne was made difficult by human machination. The Establishment, the powers that be, was therefore full of suspicion that the new Oba would do like his ancestors in the name of custom! So the authorities tightened up security and literally planned armed police and soldiers on every inch of these very Palace grounds. My father was not to be permitted to perform any secret or night ceremonies.

Had the plan of the authorities been executed, the Funeral Rites in particular might have been drastically curtailed, if not disrupted. But good old Captain William, the then Resident, the highest Government functionary in Benin Province and a good friend of my grandfather, had infinite confidence in my father's integrity. Captain William, therefore, staked his reputation in vouching for my father and defending the ceremonies by explaining to the authorities whatever there was to explain, as Brigadier Waziri did on my behalf, and offering suggestions and advice to my father as Brigadier Waziri did to me. In the end Captain William's stand by my father was vindicated; the fears on Government side were unfounded and the authorities found that the reinforcement of Army and police contingent in Benin was unnecessary after all, as was also found last December.

At last the day came for Resident William to leave Benin, as Brigadier Waziri is now about to leave us. There was no other way my father could fittingly demonstrate his gratitude to the whiteman than to quote the Edo adage I earlier referred to and to present the good man with the highest symbol of authority of the Oba himself. My father gave him ADA ERONMWON. Like my father who found in Resident William an understanding and sympathetic man I too have the greatest pleasure, Brigadier, to present you with this ADA ERONMWON, together with this carved elephant tusk in sincere appreciation of all that you did to make my ceremonies go through smoothly. We have three grades of ADA. This one of eronmwon is the highest and it is rarely given out. May this Ada bring blessing to your home. I know it is in good hands for you are a Prince in your own right being a full blooded son of the Royal family of your home. I also present this necklace coral bead to Mrs. Waziri. And with these gifts go the gratitude and best wishes of myself, my family and the Edo people. I thank you all for your attention and for coming.

|||||||||||||||||||||||||||||||||||||||||||||

Excerpts from an Address Delivered at the Official Opening of Agip Gas Bottling Plant Area Office and Warehouse on March 27, 1982

I am pleased to be here, and I thank Agip Nigeria Limited for inviting me to participate at this formal commissioning of their Gas Bottling Plant, Area Office and Warehouse. I am particularly delighted that the Bottling Plant is sited here in Benin City. We in Benin City do not wish to grudge any other area, but I am sure I am correct when I say that this State headquarter, Benin City, is the only State headquarter that has been provided with the least amount of industries. It is difficult to understand why this has been so.

Benin does not lack the land or natural resources or is our labour more expensive than elsewhere. So while commending the Agip Nigeria Limited for deciding to site their Gas Bottling Plant here, I wish to call on Bendel State Authorities to do all in their power to attract more industries to this State headquarters. I am talking now about Benin City as Bendel State Headquarters and not so much as the Authorities to strive harder to attract more Federal Projects to Bendel State in general. What have been commissioned in the recent past were things planned long before the present Administration was born. A Federal project, if sited in Bendel State, will not cry out that it was owned by the Federal Government. On the contrary, people would happily associate the establishment of a particular project or amenity with the tenure of office of a particular Governor as if he initiated it.

I must seize this opportunity given me by Agip Nigeria Limited to appeal once more to the Federal and State Authorities, National and State Assemblymen, to take steps without further delay to abrogate the Land Use Decree. It has become an ill-wind that blows no-one any good. There are many instances where the application of this Decree has brought Federal and State Governments into head-on collision. Private enterprises are not finding things easy either, as the procedure to follow is now more protracted and the cost of going through it now is higher. There is no doubt that this cost element adds to place the price of locally produced goods at the higher level that investors complain about. Thus the Decree itself is having a negative effect on the concerted efforts of all the Governments to fight inflation in the country. The Decree was ostensibly aimed at helping the so-called common-man. One would like to know how this common-man has benefited when he cannot now, with any degree of confidence, lay claim to full ownership of the small piece of land he builds or farms on; and worse still he cannot bequeath it to a child. The so-called common-man in our society would normally not have any lump sum of money or mansion to be inherited by his children when he is gone, but before the Land Use Decree, there would at least be perhaps one small house and certainly a farm land for the children to look forward to. It is not so now, because on-one can pass the ownership of what he does not own. What is even worse, is that it is now possible for an influential person in society, if he likes your own piece of land, to get the provisions of this Decree interpreted to give him the Certificate of Occupancy over somebody else's land!

In the name of the so-called common-man, I appeal to the Heads of the Federal and State Governments, the National and State Assemblymen to abrogate this law so as to relieve the hardship on the ordinary man in the street and investors.

I will conclude this part of my address by thanking all those investors from both Public and Private Sector who have approached me personally for land for development projects. If finding suitable land will bring the industry to Benin, then I hereby assure investors that I and my people are ready at any time to make land available. I do not consider that such action by us would usurp the function of the State Land Allocation Committee or violate the provisions of the Decree, for I expect the recipient of such land to then take necessary steps to fulfil the requirements of the Decree.

In conclusion, I heartily, once more, congratulate the Agip Nigeria Limited for this achievement. Please do not let this be the last you will do here. Your industry is on Edo land and like all good things on this land it will be blessed to great success so that you recover your investment within a minimum period and be able to expand or bring in yet another industry soon. May I appeal to the State Government and the entire Bendel State Community to encourage the Company, at least by way of patronage and all other means, to make their venture a success so that other Companies or Institutions may emulate Agip Nigeria Limited. I call on the workers to give of their best, as all Agip works are used to, so you may all be blessed on our land.

I wish the directors, management and entire staff more successes both at work and in your private homes.

I have great please in declaring this factory open and wish it every success. Thank you.

||||||||||||||||||||||||||||||||||||||

An Address at the Reception for his Excellency Alhaji Shehu Shagari, President of the Federal Republic and Commander-in-Chief of the Armed Forces of Nigeria and the Ceremony of the Award of National Honor of Commander of the Order of the Federal Republic (CFR) to Omo N'oba Erediauwa at the Oba's Palace, Benin City on 19th February, 1980.

Your Excellency Alhaji Shehu Shagari, President of the Federal Republic and Commander-in-chief of the Armed Forces of Nigeria, Your Excellency

Professor Ambrose Folorunso Alli, Governor of Bendel State, Traditional Rulers, Distinguished Guests.

In the name of the entire Edo people, I heartily welcome you, Mr. President, to our Palace. Today is a great day for us. We Bendelites in general and the Edo people in particular must consider ourselves blessed to be the third State that you have officially visited and the first in which you have spend two nights since assuming office. We like to regard this as a demonstration of the President's personal interest in the Federal Government's development program within Bendel State. I hope that this visit will usher in more developments for us, for nature has blessed this State with all the resources and facilities that make development possible. I pray and hope that it will not be long before the President will visit again-on that occasion, to lay the foundation-stone or turn the first sod of a major Federal Government project on Benin soil!

To us Edo people the President's visit today is particularly significant and is, indeed, a red-letter day. A few months ago, the last Administration, headed by General Olusegun Obasanjo, was gracious enough to include me among deserving Nigerians who were awarded the country's National Honors. I was among those made the Commander of the Order of the Federal Republic (CFR). All the recipients of the award were invited to Lagos at the end of last September to be presented with their Award. But, owing to the ceremony I was engaged in at that time, I was unable to go to Lagos to receive mine. I am thankful to God Almighty and to our ancestors who have made it possible for me to receive mine in our home and in the midst of my people. I am immensely grateful to the President who thought it fit to include the performance of this ceremony in what must be his very tight program in Bendel State.

I must publicly let our people know of the President's keen interest in us and how anxious he has been to personally make this presentation, for when we visited Lagos last November, out of his own volition, he had thought of doing the presentation there, but for one reason or the other, it unfortunately did not materialize. I like to believe that it was ordained that the presentation must be witnessed by all my people: Chiefs, brothers and sisters, and our citizens. I like to recall, with some feeling of pride, that some 35 years ago our father was similarly decorated on his same palace ground with the British insignia of the C.M.G., the ceremony having been performed by the British Monarch's Representative. Today, I am the proud recipient of the Nigerian National Honor presented by our own President! I very much appreciate it that the president and his host, the Bendel State Governor, have made it possible for the ceremony to take place not just in Benin but here in the palace.

I am immensely grateful to the president for the many nice things he has said about me. Such compliments, coming from a person of his standing, make one feel humbled and they also instill in one a feeling of great responsibility. I like to assure you, Mr. president, that I will do everything that lies in my power to maintain the dignity of this Award and to make myself worthy of it

At this juncture, I must address a few words to our people, the Edo people. This Award must not be taken as personal to me, the recipient. Rather the honor conveyed by it is on all Edo people. I must, therefore, appeal to you to assist me, by your own actions in domestic and national affairs, to fulfil the promise I have just made to the President to uphold the high dignity of this National Honor.

I cannot end this address without saying a few words about the position of Traditional Rulers. I have been privileged to discuss with you, Mr. President, and I know the high hopes you have for Traditional Rulers.

Traditional Rulers are part and parcel of the Government machinery and the writers of our Constitution wisely found a place for us in it. All Traditional Rulers acclaim as a singular act, the inclusion of Traditional Rulers in the membership of the National Council of State. It is to be hoped that this is the beginning of reviving what was becoming the dwindling status of Traditional Rulers, and that your thinking on these lines will be in accord with that of the State Governors. You have today presented me with this National Award. I must let you know, Mr. President, that in my capacity as the President of the Bendel State Council of Traditional Rulers, the honor that has been conferred on me has in fact been conferred on all Traditional Rulers in this State and on their behalf I pledge our unflinching support to you as we do to our Governor.

Finally, in commemoration of your visit, I have great pleasure in presenting to you this gift and with it go our very best wishes for a successful tenure of office. I pray and hope you leave this State with happy memoirs. I wish you well.

llllllllllllllllllllllllllllllllllllllll

A Speech Delivered on the Occasion of the Presentation of a Prize Gift to Ahmadu Bello University, Zaria, 18–19th December, 1982.

I was in Ilorin some weeks ago when I first read in the "Nigerian Herald" that your famous University had decided to honor me with a Doctorate Degree. My immediate reaction was to exclaim: "What, me?" The surprise was not that I did not consider myself qualified-I am myself a product of Cambridge University, England! The surprise was that I never had any inkling that this was coming until I read the newspaper. It was when I returned home from that tour that I found the official letter waiting for me.

I am most grateful to the University Authorities for the Award of the Honorary Degree. Personally, I do not know what I have contributed to deserve the honor from this premier University of the North and the third oldest in the country. Hence I listened with humility as the Public Orator read out the Citation.

My father, as you know, was a past Chancellor of this University, appointed a few months before the civil war broke out. He had attended only one Convocation before the war escalated and the Mid-Western State (as it was then known) was over-run by the rebel forces. In view of the prevailing situation in that year and subsequent years my father decided to keep an eye on the events at home. And anyone familiar with the role of the Oba (or Traditional Ruler) when it comes to watching events at home, knows how time and resources consuming it can be! By honoring me with the award, for which I am grateful, I assure the University Authorities, that I am very happy at the opportunity to continue with this University the association that my father began and, as alumnus hereafter, I hope I will be able to make my own little contribution to the development of this Institution.

As an earnest of that hope, I am donating a Prize to the University to be known as OMO N'OBA EREDIAUWA Prize. It consists of a cash gift of N5,000 which I ask you to invest in such a way that the annual yield will be utilized to give a Prize annually to the best student in any discipline of your choice. I leave it to the University Authorities to choose what Department and what discipline.

Once more, I thank the University for the award of the Honorary Doctor of Laws Degree to me and I wish the Institution continued good progress.

Ogisos of the 1st Benin Dynasty (about 1000 BC–1190 AD

7. Ogiso Igodo or Obagodo
8. Ogiso Ere
9. Ogiso Orire
10. Ogiso Odia
11. Ogiso Ighido
12. Ogiso Evbobo
13. Ogiso Ogbeide
14. Ogiso Emehe
15. Ogiso Akhuankhuan
16. Ogiso Ekpigho
17. Ogiso Efeske
18. Ogiso Irudia
19. Ogiso Etebowe
20. Ogiso Odion
21. Ogiso Imarhan
22. Ogiso Oria
23. Ogiso Emosa
24. Ogiso Ororo
25. Ogiso Ogbomo
26. Ogiso Erebo
27. Ogiso Agbonzeke
28. Ogiso Edia
29. Ogiso Oriagba
30. Ogiso Odoligie
31. Ogiso Uwa

32.   Ogiso Eheneden
33.   Ogiso Ohuede
34.   Ogiso Oduwa
35.   Ogiso Obioye
36.   Ogiso Origho
37.   Ogiso Owodo
Source: The Palace, Benin City.

Names and Period of Reign of Past Obas (The 2nd Benin Dynasty) About 1200 A.D. to the present day

	MONARCH	PERIOD OF REIGN
1.	Oba Eweka 1	1200–1235
2.	Oba Uwakhuahen	1235–1243
3.	Oba Ehenmihen	1243–1255
4.	Oba Ewedo	1255–1280
5.	Oba Oguola	1280–1295
6.	Oba Edoni	1295–1299
7.	Oba Udagbedo	1299–1334
8.	Oba Ohen	1334–1370
9.	Oba Ogbeka	1370–1400
10.	Oba Orobiru	1400–1430
11.	Oba Uwaifiokun	1430–1440
12.	Oba Ewuare the Great	1440–1473
13.	Oba Ezoti	1473–1473
	(Reigned for 14 days)	
14.	Oba Olua	1473–1480
15.	Oba Ozolua	1481–1504
16.	Oba Esigie	1504–1550
17.	Oba Orhogbua	1550–1578
18.	Oba Ehenguda	1578–1606
19.	Oba Ohuan	1606–1641
20.	Oba Ahenzae	1641–1661
21.	Oba Akenzae	1661–1669

22.   Oba Akengboi 1669–1675
23.   Oba Ahenkpaye 1675–1684
24.   Oba Akengbedo 1684–1689
25.   Oba Oreoghene 1689–1700
26.   Oba Ewuakpe 1700–1712
27.   Oba Ozuere* 1712–1713
      (Reigned for 9 months)
28.   Oba Akenzua 1 1713–1735
29.   Oba Eresoyen 1735–1750
30.   Oba Akengbuda 1750–1804
31.   Oba Obanosa 1804–1816
32.   Oba Ogbebo* 1816–1816
      (Reigned for 8 months)
33.   Oba Osemwede 1816–1848
34.   Oba Adolo 1848–1888
35.   Oba Ovonranwen 1888–1914
36.   Oba Eweka II 1914–1933
37.   Oba Akenzua II 1933–1978
38.   Oba Erediauwa . . . . .1979–Present day

*Ambitious princes who usurped the throne.
Source: The Palace, Benin City.

Various Morning Salutations (UKHU) in Benin

FAMILY . . . . SALUTATION
1. King Ogiso . . . . Delaiso/Laiso
2. Eweka 1* . . . . Lamogun
   (up to the present-day Royal Family)
3. Oliha . . . . Laogele
4. Edohen . . . . Latose
5. Ero . . . . Lamosun
6. Ezomo . . . . Lagiesan
7. Eholo Nire . . . . Laire
8. Oloton . . . . Lamehi
9. Iyase of Benin . . . . Lavbieze
10. Ogieamie . . . . Laiso
11. Elema . . . . Lagba
12. Ogiefa . . . . Larendo
13. Ine N'Igun . . . . Delani/Lani
14. Osa . . . . Delaiki/Laiki
15. Iyase of Udo . . . . Lagiewan
16. Enogie of Ugo Neki . . . . Delakun/Lakun
17. Enogie of Ugo N'Iyokorhionmwon . . . . Labo
18. Elawure of Usen . . . . Delauhe
19. Iyase of Uselu . . . . Layede
20. Ezima of Okeluhe . . . . Layeru
21. Enogie of Uvbe . . . . Lauvbe
22. Enogie of Ehor . . . . Delaiho
23. Enogie of Igieduwa . . . . Delaihon
24. Ohen Ukoni of Ikhuen . . . . Delagun
25. Olokhunmwun of Okhunmwun . . . . . Delagun

26. Enogie of Irhue . . . . Delalu/Lalu
27. Enogie of Ute . . . . Lagite
28. Ise of Utekon . . . . Delaru/Laru
29. Enogie of Evboekabua . . . . Lavbiuwa
30. Enogie of Umoru . . . . Lamoru
31. Aide . . . . Laide
32. Emeri . . . . Lameri
33. Agia . . . . Lagia
34. Egie . . . . Laigie
35. Oloke . . . . Laloke
36. Era . . . . Lamere
37. Emezi . . . . Lamezi
38. Old Emehe . . . . Lamehe
39. Umekon . . . . Lamekon
40. Umako . . . . Lamako
41. Ughe . . . . Laughe
42. Igina . . . . Lagiena
43. Eni of Uzea . . . . Lamore
44. Akpan . . . . Delakpan
45. Umodu . . . . Lamodu
46. Umolu . . . . Lamolu
47. Ize . . . . Laize
48. Ugha . . . . Laugha
49. Ureni . . . . Laremi
50. Idu . . . . Laidu
51. Iren . . . . Lairen
52. Igie . . . . Laigie

9 781588 383679